FAMILY
TRADITION

FAMILY TRADITION

*Three Generations of
Hank Williams*

SUSAN MASINO

An Imprint of Hal Leonard Corporation

Published in 2011 by Backbeat Books

An Imprint of Hal Leonard Corporation
7777 West Bluemound Road
Milwaukee, WI 53213
Trade Book Division Editorial Offices
33 Plymouth St., Montclair, NJ 07042

Book design by Publishers' Design and Production Services, Inc.

Printed in the United States of America

Library of Congress Cataloging-in-Publication Data
Masino, Susan, 1955-
   Family tradition : three generations of Hank Williams / by Susan Masino.
     p. cm.
   Includes bibliographical references and index.
   ISBN 978-1-61713-006-9
   1. Williams, Hank, 1923–1953. 2. Williams, Hank, 1949– 3. Williams, Hank, 1972– 4. Country musicians—United States—Biography. I. Title.
   ML420.W55M27 2011
   782.421642092'2—dc22
   [B]

                                            2010047585

www.backbeatbooks.com

This book is dedicated to the late Mary Wallace, a founding member and acting president of the Hank Williams International Society and Fan Club. She organized the annual Hank Williams Festival held in Georgiana and served on the board of directors for the Hank Williams Museum and Boyhood Home. Mary loved Hank dearly and devoted her life to preserving and celebrating the legacy of Hank Williams Sr.

CONTENTS

CONTENTS

INTRODUCTION

I COULDN'T HAVE BEEN MORE THAN FIVE OR SIX years old when I fell in love with the music of Hank Williams. My parents owned bars, hotels, and restaurants, including the Riverview Ballroom in Sauk City, Wisconsin, and several times a day his voice would call to me from a neon jukebox. Though I was just a young child, the emotion Hank Williams poured into a song engulfed me with feelings I didn't even understand at the time.

Hank Williams's *Greatest Hits* album was one of my grandmother's favorites. When she opened the record-player cabinet and slid the turntable out, that platter was always one of the first she would play. If we were lucky, she'd play the whole album more than once, and that's how I learned the words to "Your Cheatin' Heart," "Hey, Good Lookin'," and "Jambalaya." The man who sang those songs had a way of grabbing your attention while touching your heart. Surely only a tortured soul could sing like that. Someone who knew real suffering but found a way of transcending it through music.

When *Your Cheatin' Heart: The Hank Williams Story* came out in the mid-1960s, my father took us to the movie theater to see Hank's life up on the silver screen. Starring George Hamilton and Susan Oliver, the movie portrayed a poor young boy from Alabama who grew up to create some of the most influential country songs of all time.

Although loosely based on Hank's rise to fame, the movie covered his struggle to write and perform while battling a drug and alcohol addiction; his troubled marriage to his first wife, Audrey; and her driving obsession to see him become a star. While watching the movie, I was overcome by the sadness and heartache he felt during his life. I challenge anyone to find a song more melancholy than "I'm So Lonesome, I Could Cry."

What the movie didn't show was that Hank was born with spina bifida, which caused him constant back pain. Using alcohol and drugs to cover his misery, he often showed up at his performances too wasted to play, and many times, he didn't show up at all. For someone who became known as "the Hillbilly Shakespeare," his reputation was constantly in jeopardy, getting him permanently kicked out of the Grand Ole Opry. After three years of being one of their biggest stars, Hank was fired and to this day is still not a member, a travesty that has resonated through the generations and inspired his grandson, Hank III—also not exactly the picture of a well-behaved Nashville cat—to launch a grassroots campaign to get his grandfather reinstated.

The end of the movie depicted Hank, who had been on his way to a performance, found dead in the back seat of a car on New Year's Day, 1953. The film's final scene showed a theater full of people waiting on Hank's arrival, and his longtime manager (played by the actor Red Buttons) coming out onstage to tell the audience that Hank had passed away. All of a sudden, someone in the crowd stood up and started singing "I Saw the Light," one of Hank's most spiritual compositions. One by one, the audience joined in and sang along while tears streamed down their faces. Even though I was a kid at the time, that movie left me sobbing. It also changed my life.

When I walked out of the theater that night, I wanted to grow up and work in the music business. I wanted to befriend those tortured souls who released their demons through music. How did angels like Hank Williams go through hell and still leave us with songs like that? Where did his inspiration come from? How could he write such incredible music—and then leave us so soon?

The amazing legacy of Hank Williams didn't die with him on that New Year's Day back in 1953. His only son, Hank Jr., was groomed to follow in his father's footsteps. In reality, his domineering mother insisted that Hank Jr. *become* his late father. Hank Jr., whom his father affectionately nicknamed Bocephus, was never given the chance to develop a style of his own. He was pushed into his father's spotlight and almost died when he fell 442 feet while climbing Ajax Mountain in Montana, shattering every bone in his face. After nine surgeries and an extensive recovery, Hank Jr. continued to write and began to perform his own brand of country music laced with southern rock. Eventually stepping out from beneath his father's shadow, Hank Williams Jr. has rebuilt his career, becoming an icon in his own right.

Carrying on the family tradition, Hank Jr.'s eldest son, Hank III, was born with his grandfather's voice, along with his penchant for raising hell. "Full Throttle," as he is known, refuses to perform what is expected of him and chooses to mix traditional country with grindcore, punk, and metal, or what some call "honky-tonkin' punk rock." A prolific songwriter and high-octane performer, his path has caused him more than enough trouble, resulting in an estrangement from his famous father. Only three when his parents divorced, Hank III never had the privilege of growing up with his family's money or fame.

When I originally heard Hank III's voice, I got tears in my eyes. The first thing that came to mind was, "Thank God, he inherited Hank Sr.'s voice." When I thought of writing a book about him, it was natural for me to want to write about all three men. I had so many questions about the Hank Williams legacy. What makes his DNA so special, and did he pass on a blessing, or a curse?

Within these pages you will find the real story of the legacy of Hank Williams Sr., Hank Jr., and Hank III, three generations of outlaws, whose songs have shaped—and battled—country music for over sixty years.

FAMILY TRADITION

1

CRAZED COUNTRY REBEL

"Hank III has that high and lonesome voice with a crack in it. He has the righteous fury of the deeply wounded, and there's blood in his eyes." —TOM WAITS

DRIVING THROUGH THE SMOKY MOUNTAINS on my way to Knoxville, Tennessee, on a hazy summer evening in July, I wondered just how many times Hank Williams Sr. had made this journey. He had spent most of his career traveling from one city to another, always finding his way back to Nashville on Saturday nights to appear at the Grand Ole Opry.

This time I was on an assignment to see Hank's grandson, Hank III, perform live at the Valarium, a cavernous warehouse-type building with a stage along the back wall, facing a bar at the front of the room, just below a balcony. The rowdy crowd consisted of country/metal music fans who really weren't all that different from the folks that used to show up for Hank Sr.'s shows. That is, if you looked past their tattoos, piercings, rock T-shirts, and long hair. These were Hank III fans, and Hank III has put a whole new twist on the Williams family tradition. Actually, instead of a twist, I'd prefer to call it a headlock.

Refusing to obediently follow in his father and grandfather's footsteps, Hank III has forged a career that fuses traditional country music with heavy metal. His live shows consists of a country set and a "hellbilly" set with his Damn Band, finishing up with a set from his metal band, Assjack.

While waiting for the band to appear that night, the impatient crowd started chanting, "Hank! Hank! Hank!" which brought to mind what his grandfather used to hear just by walking out onstage. From the time they started, Hank III and his band never let up, playing for almost four solid hours. Seemingly sporting a superhuman energy level, he covered everything from his own originals, like "Country Heroes," "Shades of Black," and "Crazed Country Rebel," to covers of Johnny Cash and David Allan Coe. His show also included a version of his father's anthem "Family Tradition" and a nod to his grandfather with "I'll Never Get Out of This World Alive," one of the last songs Hank Sr. ever recorded.

Hank III also brought up his mission to get his grandfather reinstated into the Grand Ole Opry. Many of Hank Sr.'s fans don't realize that he was fired from the Opry, due to his alcoholism. During the three short years that he was a member, Hank Williams was one of the Grand Ole Opry's biggest stars. After showing up drunk or missing some of his performances altogether, he was fired, and to this day he is not a member, although the name Hank Williams and the Grand Ole Opry are practically synonymous.

"The Grand Ole Opry Ain't So Grand" is the song Hank III wrote about the Opry's refusal to reinstate Hank Sr. and is included on his fourth album, *Damn Right—Rebel Proud*. When the Family Tradition exhibit opened at the Country Music Hall of Fame and Museum in March 2008, Hank III spearheaded a grassroots movement to pressure the Opry into reconsidering. By setting up a table at various events, including the opening of the Family Tradition exhibit, Hank III has collected thousands of signatures requesting Hank Sr.'s reinstatement.

Passion is one thing Hank III definitely doesn't lack. After hammering the crowd for four hours into total submission, he stood outside of his tour bus at 3:00 a.m. to sign autographs for fans who didn't mind standing in the pouring rain. It had been a stressful night for the band, just finishing up the first leg of the tour to promote Hank III's new album. There had been a shooting in the club parking lot the night before, and the security personnel were being overly vigilant. While the band was onstage, their tour manager happened to notice a fan being roughed up by the police at the front door, so he stepped in to help out. That stunt landed him in a Knoxville jail for the evening for obstructing justice.

Regardless of the confusion going on around him earlier in the evening, Hank III never stopped playing. As a matter of fact, he didn't even take a break! At one point, his band did walk offstage, leaving Hank III alone, still singing and playing his guitar. According to Hank III, he didn't like the way his fans were being treated and he was determined not to give the security guards a break. As he said, "I was trying to prove a point." So he never left the stage, demonstrating that attitude goes a long way in the Williams family.

His relentlessness brought to mind the concert Hank Williams Sr. played in Austin, Texas, on December 19, 1952. That night they say Hank Sr. performed for four hours straight, playing every song he knew, some more than once. It would be his last concert performance.

At one point at the Knoxville performance, Hank III, obviously angered by what had happened to his tour manager, declared that they would come back to play for two nights and really "show this city how it's done!" He went on to say that for those of us that knew the true story, "This is where my granddaddy really died." He was referring to the two shots of morphine Hank Sr. received from a doctor in Knoxville back on New Year's Eve day in 1952, on his way to perform in Canton, Ohio. He never made it to Ohio.

When the Country Music Hall of Fame and Museum opened in Nashville in 1961, the first three people inducted were Jimmie Rodgers, Fred Rose, and Hank Williams. Williams's plaque reads: "Hank Williams September 1923—January 1, 1953. Performing artist, songwriter ... Hank Williams will live on in the memories of millions of Americans. The simple, beautiful melodies and straightforward plaintive stories in his lyrics, of life as he knew it, will never die. His songs appealed not only to the country music field but brought him great acclaim in the pop music world as well."

Since his death, Hank was added to the Country Music Hall of Fame Walkway of Stars, received the Pioneer Award by the Academy of Country Music, was awarded a Grammy in 1983 for "Your Cheatin' Heart," and in 1987 was inducted into the Rock and Roll Hall of Fame. Also in 1987, Hank was given a Lifetime Achievement Award from the National Academy of Recording Arts and Sciences, and *Life* magazine ranked Hank Williams number one on its list of the Most Important People in Country Music.

If there is any doubt about the impact that Hank Williams has had on country music, just take a stroll down Broadway in Nashville on a Saturday night. That stretch of honky-tonks, which lies between Second and Fourth avenues, includes Tootsie's Orchid Lounge, one of the oldest establishments on the strip. Right across the street is the Ernest Tubb Record Shop, which opened in 1947. Except for the few places that dabble in karaoke, most of the bars feature live music.

As you walk by, at almost any given moment you will hear a band covering a Hank Williams song. Inside the various establishments, Hank Williams himself stares down at you somewhere from a picture, a poster, or a painting. There is even a life-size cardboard cut-out of Hank standing at the back of the stage in Ernest Tubb's shop, where Tubb used to broadcast live concerts on WSM 650 AM at midnight every Saturday.

Just around the corner on Fifth Avenue is the Ryman Auditorium, which was built as a church in 1892. The Ryman, also known as "the Mother Church of Country Music," hosted the original Grand Ole Opry from 1943 to 1974. The Ryman was completely renovated in 1994 and received the Pollstar Concert Industry Award in 2003 and 2004 for "Theater of the Year." From 1949 to 1952, Hank Williams performed there regularly. Even today, walking into the Ryman on a Saturday night, you can feel his presence in the building, which still features the wooden church pews where hundreds of fans enjoyed Hank Williams live. Many believe the Ryman to be haunted.

2

HILLBILLY SHAKESPEARE

"I chose his name from the Scripture, 1 Kings, 7th Chapter, 13th verse." —LON WILLIAMS

THE MAN WHO WOULD BECOME KNOWN as "the Hillbilly Shakespeare" was born Hiram Williams in a log cabin in Mount Olive, Alabama, on September 17, 1923. He was the third and last child of Elonzo Huble "Lon" Williams and Jessie Lillybelle "Lillie" (Skipper) Williams. The couple's first child died shortly after birth, and Hiram's older sister Irene was born just thirteen months before him on August 8, 1922.

Lon claimed to have named his son after Hiram I of Tyre, from the Bible scripture. When the Williamses finally registered him with the Bureau of Vital Statistics, his name was misspelled as Hiriam. During his childhood, his family called him "Harm," or "Skeets." Some sources state that Hiram's middle name was King, but that name does not appear on his actual birth certificate.

Lon Williams had been born in Macedonia, Alabama, on December 23, 1891. His family, originally from North Carolina, settled in McWilliams, Alabama. From the time Lon was twelve years old, he drifted around the area, taking work where he could get it. He was seventeen when his father died. Lillie, a formidable woman of almost two hundred pounds, was born on August 12, 1898, in Butler County. She was eighteen when she married Lon on November 12, 1916.

A year after their marriage, Lon was drafted into the army toward the end of World War I and served in France with the 113th Regiment of Engineers, 42nd Division. According to Harry Rockwell, in *Beneath the Applause*, Lon got into a fight with another soldier over a French girl. The GI struck Lon across the face with a wine bottle, knocking him out. Lon spent a week at an army hospital and was honorably discharged in 1919, although his injury would come back to haunt him. When he returned from the war, he found work driving the logging trains for the Ray Lumber Company in Atmore, Alabama, and W. T. Smith in Chapman, Alabama.

Right before Hiram was born, his family moved to Mt. Olive, leasing a farmhouse which consisted of two conjoined buildings. One side was converted into a country store, while they lived in the other. Lon and Lillie had started a strawberry farm, which was wiped out in a late frost in the spring of 1924, forcing Lon to go back to work in the lumber business. By 1927, Lon was doing well enough to buy them a house in McWilliams, where Hiram attended the first and second grades.

"Harm" was known as a frail child who "went his own way." In *Sing a Sad Song*, Roger Williams quoted Hank's cousin J. C. McNeil as saying, "Hank was a real loner. He never was a happy boy, in a way. He didn't laugh and carry on like other children. It seemed like somethin' was always on his mind."

His natural musical ability came from his parents, who were both musicians. Lon played the Jew's harp, and Lillie played the organ at the Mt. Olive Baptist Church and at other churches they attended over the years. Hiram learned to sing hymns sitting alongside his mother. He once told journalist Ralph J. Gleason, "My earliest memory is sittin' on the organ stool by her and hollerin'. I must have been five, six years old, and louder than anybody else." This experience would serve him well, and his devotion to gospel would never leave him.

Hiram's love of music might have been fueled by his lack of farming and athletic abilities, due to his back problems. He had been born with a raised spot on his spine, which is a condition called spina bifida occulta, where the spinal vertebrae don't come together. This affliction would cause Hiram back pain throughout his life, leading to an addiction to alcohol and painkillers. His suffering found its way into his songwriting, with one of his earliest compositions being a song called "Back Ache Blues."

Around 1928 or 1929, Hiram's father started to experience facial paralysis caused by the wartime blow to his head, making him unable to blink or move his facial muscles and eventually rendering him speechless. As his condition worsened, Lon was forced to quit working for W. T. Smith and took a lighter job with the Ralph Lumber Company in Bolling. By September of 1929, he was unable to work at all and was admitted into the Veterans Affairs Clinic in Pensacola, Florida, where he was diagnosed with a brain aneurysm. In January of 1930, Lon was transferred to the VA Medical Center in Alexandria, Louisiana, where he remained for the next eight years. Poor Hiram spent most of his childhood without a father and expressed his loss in one of his first songs, "I Wish I Had a Dad."

Right after Lon was hospitalized, Lillie's brother-in-law, Walter Mc-Neil, moved them to Garland, Alabama, to live with them and Lillie's mother. When she saved enough money to move out, Lillie relocated her family to Georgiana, Alabama. The first house they lived in was a rundown shack on old Highway 31 that eventually burned down, forcing her to move back in with her relatives. When Thaddeus B. Rose, a local gentleman, heard about their plight, he offered Lillie a house rent-free.

After moving into the Roses' house, Lillie was able to find work at the WPA cannery and as a night-shift nurse at the Tippins Hospital. She worked nights and slept during the day, and she would stomp her feet on the floor to quiet Hiram, who would be playing music under the porch.

According to Mary Wallace, a founding member of the Hank Williams International Society and Fan Club, "Hank used to sit on the front steps and make music blowing a piece of wax paper and comb.

The boardinghouse across the street would open their windows to hear him play."

Lillie also started taking in boarders, keeping everyone fed with the help of a large garden. Thanks to the assistance of U.S. Representative J. Lister Hill, she also started collecting Lon's full military disability pension.

Hank III would say, "I always heard that she ran a brothel. I also heard that she was really a tough woman, a fighting woman and a controlling one. Trying to take care of a lot of less fortunate [people], just giving some outsiders a home. She was a real ballbuster, no doubt about it."

To encourage Hiram to develop his musical talents, Lillie paid for singing lessons at a school in Avant, Georgia. In Colin Escott's book *Hank Williams: The Biography*, Lillie's neighbor Harold Sims remembered how they used to sit outside and listen to the music coming from the "Negro church." He recalled, "It was about a mile away. It was prayer meetin' night. The most beautiful music in the world. The breeze came from the south and it would undulate the sound. One minute soft, the next minute loud, like it was orchestrated. One night, Hiram looked up at me and said, 'One day, I'm gonna write songs like that.'" The music that would stay with him included everything from gospel songs like "The Blind Child's Lament" and "I'll Fly Away" to old folk standards like "When the Saints Come Marching In," and "On Top of Old Smoky."

To help make ends meet, Lillie sent both Hiram and his sister Irene out to sell parched peanuts, deliver newspapers, and shine shoes. Even at an early age, Hiram was an enterprising soul. He sold the bags of peanuts for a nickel, and he figured out a way to pilfer a couple of peanuts out of each bag, making up a whole one on his own to sell, earning him an extra nickel. According to Lillie, one day he spent his own money on fixings for his favorite gumbo, and the next day his profits went to caps and firecrackers. When Lillie found out what he had spent his money on, she claimed she whipped him so hard she caused the caps to explode. Being a domineering woman who had to wear the pants in the family, Lillie didn't have any trouble disciplining Hiram when she felt he needed it.

While living in Georgiana, Hiram encountered a black street musician by the name of Rufus Payne, also known as "Tee-Tot," who lived up the tracks in Greenville. Rufus had acquired the nickname "Tee-Tot" from a mixture of home-brewed alcohol and tea that he always kept close at hand. Hiram's cousins remembered Tee-Tot as a street musician who played the guitar with cymbals tied between his legs. He also played the Jew's harp and the jazz horn, collecting money in a cigar box that sat on the ground at his feet.

Tee-Tot was a charismatic character who enchanted passersby. He had to be, to eke out a living that way during the Depression. Hiram was taken in the moment he met Tee-Tot and followed him around every chance he could. According to the Alabama Department of Archives and History, Lillie used to pay Tee-Tot with food. Tee-Tot would go over to the Williamses' home, where he and Hiram would sit underneath the high front porch, out of sight. In those days, it wasn't usual for whites to follow blacks around, so the two of them had to hide out. Hiram also spent as much time as he could at Jim Warren's Jewelry and Instrument Store and Cade Durham's shoe shop, which were local musicians' hangouts.

When he was ten years old, Hiram moved to Fountain, Alabama, to live with his uncle and aunt, Walter and Alice McNeil, in effect trading places with their daughter, Opal, who went to live with Lillie and Irene so she could attend high school in Georgiana. Walter worked for the Pool Company, where his family lived at the logging camp in three boxcars. There the preferred entertainment was a weekly dance, which exposed Hank to back-country music.

Not only did Hank enjoy a father figure in his uncle, but the Mc-Neils' son, J. C., gave him the brotherly companionship he never had. His aunt taught him songs, and his uncle and cousin taught him how to hunt and fish, two passions that someday Hank Jr. and Hank III would inherit. This was also where Hank and J. C. learned how to steal a nip here and there of moonshine or beer from the loggers, getting so drunk they would end up lying on the ground in the woods to keep from falling down.

Within a year, Lillie once again moved her family, to Greenville, a city fifteen miles from Georgiana and four times larger. There she opened another boardinghouse, next door to the Butler County Courthouse. Hiram moved back from Fountain, rejoining his mother and sister and rekindling his relationship with Tee-Tot.

Tee-Tot taught Hiram gospel, black spirituals, and traditional country songs like "My Bucket's Got a Hole in It," while showing him how to hold an audience. Hiram also talked some of the local musicians into teaching him how to play the fiddle along with the guitar Lillie had bought for him for $3.50 out of the Sears and Roebuck catalog. Hiram loved listening to the radio, and he used to tell his classmates that his ambition was to play and sing, constantly repeating the lyrics, "I had an old goat, she ate tin cans, when the little goats came out, they were Ford sedans."

Clearly, Tee-Tot had a profound influence in fueling Hank's desire to become a performer. As Fred Dellar recounted in his article "The King of America," for *Mojo* magazine, Hiram had claimed many times that "all the musical training I ever had was from him. I learned to play gittar from an old colored man. He played in a colored street band. I was shinin' shoes, sellin' newspapers, and following this ole nigrah around to get him to teach me to play the guitar. I'd give him fifteen cents or whatever I could get hold of for a lesson."

Rusty Russell (in *Guitar Player*, November 1996) quoted performer Marty Stuart, who said, "A lot of people don't understand how much of a blues guy he was—a blues guitar player … He truly comes from that E-chord blues thing, and I'm sure he got it from Tee-Tot."

Tee-Tot's influence definitely added the streak of blues that would run throughout Hank's future compositions. Years later, Hiram would search for Tee-Tot, who died in a charity hospital in Montgomery, Alabama, on March 17, 1939. It was the same city where Hiram became Hank and his musical career took off.

3

DRIFTING
COWBOY

*"There ain't nobody I'd rather have alongside me in a
fight than my mama with a broken bottle in her hand."*
—HANK SR.

W HILE IN SCHOOL IN GREENVILLE, Hiram had gotten into a fight with
his physical-education teacher, infuriating Lillie, who demanded
that the teacher be fired. When the school board refused to comply
with her, she decided to move her family to Montgomery, which at the
time was the capital of and third-largest city in Alabama. On July 10,
1937, Lillie, Irene, Hiram, and his two cousins Bernice and Marie Mc-
Neil settled into 114 South Perry Street. Lillie converted it into another
boardinghouse, and Hiram was once again sent out to sell peanuts and
shine shoes. When business was slow, Hiram would put away his shoe-
shine rags and sing and play guitar.

That fall he was enrolled in the Abraham Baldwin Junior High School
and also worked weekends as a painter for the Heath Decorating Company. By now Hiram had changed his name to Hank, believing it more
suitable for pursuing a career in music. Schoolmate Bob Barnes remembered meeting Hank in the eighth grade, recalling him as "a happy-go-
lucky young man who didn't seem too crazy about going to school."

After school Hank and Bob would meet up on Barnes's front porch
to play guitars. Barnes was amazed by how strongly Hank could sing for

his age. Hank was a huge fan of Roy Acuff and enjoyed covering "Wabash Cannonball," "(Beneath That) Lonely Mound of Clay," and "The Great Speckled Bird." Hank was still playing his mail-order guitar, but Barnes had a Gibson with a sunburst finish. Soon Lillie took Hank down to Art Freeling's Music Store in Montgomery to buy him a similar model.

Lillie eventually relocated her boardinghouse to 236 Catoma Street, which was downtown and within walking distance of the WSFA radio station. WSFA had been started by Howard Pill and by Gordon Persons, who later became the governor of Alabama. They went on the air in March 1930, broadcasting with one thousand watts from the Jefferson Davis Hotel. Hank would hang around the radio station every chance he got, trying to capture the attention of anyone who worked there. Bill Hunt, advertising manager of WSFA at the time, remembered Hank would pester anyone who came in and out of the building. Leaborne Eads, a performer on WSFA, later claimed he discovered Hank outside the building and would run a remote down to him so he could broadcast live from the sidewalk.

For the next four years, Hank appeared on WSFA, and Lillie encouraged everyone to call in and ask for "the Singing Kid." He eventually became so popular that the producers offered him his own fifteen-minute show, twice weekly, for a salary of fifteen dollars.

Allen Dunkin, one of Hank's future bandmates, said, "Hank had a way of singing that won over new friends and listeners on the radio show. I guess one reason people liked him so well was that he talked and acted just like an old-country boy, and that is what we all were." Needless to say, singing on the radio had become much more lucrative than selling peanuts and shining shoes.

For his first public appearance at the age of fourteen, Hank entered the amateur-night contest at the Empire Theater in Montgomery, singing "WPA Blues," a parody of "Dissatisfied" by Riley Puckett; Hank had begun composing songs by writing his own lyrics to popular melodies. He won the contest and was awarded fifteen dollars. With his new victory and weekly radio appearances, and since regular jobs were scarce, Hank and Lillie decided it was time for him to put together a band.

Hank had been a faithful listener of guitarist Braxton Schuffert, who had his own early-morning show on WSFA. Lillie claimed that she couldn't drag Hank away from the radio to put him on the school bus when Schuffert was on the air. Schuffert was also a delivery man for Hormel Meats and made a regular stop at Lillie's boardinghouse. One day he noticed Hank's guitar, and the two musicians sat down and played together. Schuffert was a star in Hank's eyes, and Schuffert once said about him, "Hank got what he got from the Lord, not a college. Whatever he got, God gave to him." They became fast friends, and Schuffert started taking Hank along with him to help with deliveries.

Schuffert also introduced Hank to the harmonica player Smith Adair, who went by the name "Hezzy." Adair had been part of the group the Hoosier Hotshots, who appeared on the *National Barn Dance* in Chicago. He became known as Hezzy for always introducing his songs with, "Are you ready, Hezzy?" making it a popular catchphrase. After moving to Montgomery at the age of sixteen, Schuffert discovered Adair playing harmonica on the street. Together they teamed up with Hank, his sister Irene, and fiddle player Freddy Beach, to become Hank and Hezzy's Drifting Cowboys. Hank named the band after his love of western movies. As a matter of fact, he loved the westerns so much when he lived in Georgiana, his neighbors nicknamed Hank "Two-Gun Pete."

Hank's regular radio appearances helped to get the band dates at school dances, church socials, and honky-tonks. Their first official gig was at a Georgiana high school. Lillie became one of the original stage mothers by acting as their manager, booking the shows, driving them to the venues, and collecting money at the door. Like everything she did, Lillie handled Hank's business with an iron fist, and she even made their relatives pay when they came to see the band.

Hezzy and the Drifting Cowboys played bluegrass, folk songs, and country tunes, including songs by Hank's hero Roy Acuff. Acuff had started out in the band the Crazy Tennesseans, becoming one the original stars of the Grand Ole Opry. He was also one of the first country performers to prove that hillbilly music could be commercial. Acuff sang with a "sob" in his voice that Hank learned to emulate, although Hank once said, "I was a pretty good imitator of Roy Acuff, but then I found out they already had a Roy Acuff, so I started singin' like myself."

Some of the roadhouses they played in were known as "blood buckets," referring to how much blood would be spilled during the night. For protection, Hank took his band members to a pawn shop to buy them each a blackjack. Apparently he had lost a few guitars by using them to smash people over the head, and that form of defense was getting too expensive. Hank's real secret weapon was his mother, Lillie. He once said, "There ain't nobody I'd rather have alongside me in a fight than my mama with a broken bottle in her hand."

Fights broke out on a regular basis, and Hank's son Hank Jr. later recalled, "Those clubs along the Alabama–Tennessee border were mean. Once Daddy had to club a guy with the stainless steel fret-bar from a steel guitar, which Daddy had observed worked very well as an argument settler. And it would have worked well if the other fellow had followed the rules instead of raising up and taking a huge bite out of Hank Williams' eyebrow, hair and all."

That summer, Hank's father briefly came back into his life. During his hospital stay, Lon had survived the bursting of a brain aneurysm, with blood coming out of his ears, eyes, nose, and mouth. Lon told biographer Roger Williams "that it sounded like a .22 gun going off in his head." Instead of considering him cured, his doctors diagnosed him with dementia praecox and kept him in the hospital against his will. After being moved to the VA hospital in Biloxi, Mississippi, Lon was released in August 1938, with the help of his relatives. When he showed up on Lillie's doorstep, she rejected him, having told everyone that he was dead. Lon left Montgomery just after Hank's birthday on September 17, checking himself back into the hospital.

Along with occasionally appearing on WSFA, Hank launched with Hezzy a new radio program that aired five days a week on WCOV. Hank also performed a Saturday-morning show at the Empire Theater and a Saturday-night dance at the Fort Dixie Graves Armory, so that keeping up with his schooling had become next to impossible. He graduated from Abraham Baldwin Junior High, then went on to Sidney Lanier High School, but dropped out at the age of sixteen.

In 1939 the band added accordion player Pee Wee Moultrie, who worked with Hank on WCOV. Moultrie remembered how well Hank could handle a live radio show, even though he was so young. In Steve A. Maze's book *Hank Williams and His Drifting Cowboys* Moultrie said, "Those Opry stars would shake their heads in amazement at Hank's ability to fire up the crowd. He would sometimes get the Opry stars backstage and pitch songs to them, but they ignored him. They all started singing his songs, however, after Hank became famous."

Hank's band went on a movie-theater tour of Georgia, Florida, and Alabama, playing before the films started. The promoter for the theater tour requested that they add a girl singer, so Pee Wee and Hank hired Sue Williams (no relation to Hank), who was known as "Sweet Sue." Around the same time, the band added another female singer, by the name of Carolyn Parker, who was billed as "Little Caroline, the Little Girl with the Golden Voice." Parker remembered Hank as being protective toward her, even though he was only fifteen years old at the time.

Carolyn Parker told author Steve A. Maze, "We were all just kids, but Hank was all business when it came to the band. He was just like a big brother and watched out for me. One time his mother put a lot of makeup on me before a show, but Hank came by and wiped it off with his handkerchief. He thought I was too young to be wearing that much makeup. Another time we were booked at a place that had a swimming pool. I had met some twin girls there and we decided to go swimming. Later, Hank came by and told me to get out of the water because it was getting too cool. He always treated me like a sister."

When Hank's original band broke up in 1940, he decided to follow some of his band members who were relocating to Texas. Hank traveled around the state playing with various musicians, and he wrote his mother from a suburb of Fort Worth in November, apologizing for not being able to send her any money. While in Texas, the most exciting thing that happened to Hank was meeting Ernest Tubb, who had moved to Fort Worth to broadcast on KGKO. Tubb eventually became known as the "Godfather of Country Music," after breaking through with his 1941 hit "Walking the Floor over You."

After he fell off a horse, which made his back problems much worse, Hank left Texas and returned to Montgomery, where he put together another version of the Drifting Cowboys. The new band secured a regular appearance at Thigpen's Log Cabin, where they played from 8:00 p.m. until 1:00 a.m. and the cover charge was twenty-five cents. Between the years 1940 and 1942, Hank became their main act, mixing square dancing into their set. Hank's fiddle playing had become really handy for getting people out on the dance floor—he was becoming even more accomplished at entertaining the crowd.

Jimmy Porter started playing with Hank when he was just thirteen years old. Porter, often billed as "the steel-guitar wizard," once said, "Hank was one of the finest people to work with I've ever known, he never got mad at you, he was just a cool fella, easy going, friendly, and would give you the shirt off his back. The second job I played with him was Thigpen's Log Cabin. The front part was the service station. The honky-tonk part was on the side. It was a rough place, but it wasn't rough on the inside. All the rough stuff went on outside. He wasn't doing all that much writing then. He had written two or three songs and we played them, but we played a lot of Ernest Tubb and Roy Acuff."

Pee Wee Moultrie commented in Maze's book, "I could tell Hank was special due to the way an audience would react to him. His ability to influence a crowd was like none I have ever seen—either then or since."

Allen Dunkin, who was a Drifting Cowboy from 1941 until he got drafted in 1942, told Maze, "Hank was a nice guy to work with. I have always been grateful to Hank for giving me the opportunity to play country music. I never worked with anyone who could put a song together as quickly as Hank. There was a deep personal meaning in each of his songs. They were a strange combination of misery, worry and blues, yet they are also full of happiness. I believe he lived the things he wrote about in his songs."

Hank also had a great sense of humor, always giving everyone he knew a nickname. When Daniel Jack Boling filled in on rhythm guitar for the Drifting Cowboys, Hank started calling him "Beanpole," because of his slender build. When he would introduce him to the audience, Hank would say, "Here's a fellow that I have to tie a rope around his neck every time he gets in the bathtub to keep him from going down the drain."

Hank's first recording was an acetate he cut for the owner of Griffin's Radio Shop in Montgomery in the spring of 1942. He recorded Bob Miller's "Rockin' Alone in an Old Rockin' Chair"; Red Foley's "Old Shep"; "Happy Roving Cowboy"; Roy Acuff's "(Beneath That) Lonely Mound of Clay"; Ernest Tubb's "I Aint' Gonna Love You Any More"; a black spiritual song, "Jesus Walked That Lonesome Valley"; and Rex Griffin's "The Last Letter."

That summer, Hank's father, Lon, was permanently released from the hospital, and he and Lillie were divorced. Lon moved to McWilliams and married Ola Till on September 12, 1942. One week after her divorce, Lillie married Hank's guitarist at the time, Joe Hatcher, who performed in the band as Joe "Indian" Hatcher, or, as Hank called him, Indian Joe "Hatchet." He soon died of appendicitis, and Lillie quickly married a Cajun serviceman by the name of James C. Bozard.

After World War II broke out, most of Hank's band members were drafted—Hank himself tried to join the army but was rejected due to his bad back. It was difficult to find replacements because of his already established drinking problem, and in August of 1942, WSFA finally fired him due to "habitual drunkenness." Even his idol, Roy Acuff, advised him to lay off the alcohol, saying, "You've got a million-dollar voice, son, but a ten-cent brain." After earning a living exclusively by hosting a radio show and performing onstage for five years, Hank was forced to find a day job.

When Kaiser Shipbuilding in Portland offered free accommodations, good wages, and training, Hank took off for the shipyards of Oregon, but within a couple of months he wired Lillie to send him the money to come home. When he returned to Alabama, he moved in with his uncle Bob Skipper and went to work at the Alabama Drydock and Shipbuilding Company in Mobile as a welder, although this detour from show business didn't last for long.

Lillie later wrote in *Life Story of Our Hank Williams*, "I believed in Hank. I knew he had what it took, so I rented a car and went to every schoolhouse and nightclub in the Montgomery area. I booked Hank solid for sixty days. When Hank saw the datebook for those shows, he gave me the sweetest smile I've ever seen."

Hank's career had barely been put back on track when he encountered a striking blue-eyed blonde one night while playing a medicine show in Banks, Alabama. She would change his life forever, becoming the inspiration for some of his greatest songs—and the cause of some of his deepest heartache.

4

HEY, SWEET BABY

"Audrey Sheppard was beautiful—long blond hair and a figure that could melt the wax off a Dixie cup at fifty feet."—HANK JR.

AUDREY MAE SHEPPARD, the shapely blue-eyed blonde who swept Hank Williams off of his feet, was born on February 28, 1923, near Banks, Alabama, in Pike County. The oldest daughter of Shelton and Artie Mae Sheppard, Audrey grew up on a cotton and peanut farm, dreaming of someday becoming an actress or a singer. She fell in love with a boy named James Erskine Guy, and the two eloped while she was still in her senior year of high school.

To escape the fury of her father, she and her new husband settled 150 miles away from her family in Gadsden, Alabama, and by the summer of 1941 Audrey was pregnant. When she was only six months along, Guy went off to work one day and never came back. Audrey gave birth to a daughter, Lycrecia, on August 13, 1941, and returned home to live with her parents. They were so happy to have her back that her father bought her a car. Audrey found work as a drugstore clerk in nearby Brundidge and began rebuilding her life.

Two years later, while on their way to a club in Troy, Alabama, Audrey and her aunt Ethel were driving through Banks when they noticed a group of people standing around a makeshift stage built onto the back of a flatbed truck. They decided to pull over and check out the show, although they stayed within the safety of their own car. One of the performers was Hank Williams, whom Audrey had never heard of. During the intermission, the performers, including Hank, were sent out into the crowd to sell a fifty-cent cure-all bottle of herbs guaranteed to take away your aches and pains.

As Audrey recalled in her unfinished memoirs, which appear in Lycrecia Williams's book *Still in Love with You: The Story of Hank and Audrey Williams*, Hank walked up to Audrey's car and started to say, "'Ma'am, don't you think you need … 'He kind of glanced and looked back, did a double-take, and said, 'No, ma'am, I don't believe you do.'" Right then her aunt mentioned that she and Audrey were on their way to a club in Troy and asked Hank if he wanted to come along. He replied, "Yes, ma'am, I would if you'll just wait until I do the next show." They waited until he finished his performance, and after they all had a fun night out together, the women dropped Hank off back at his trailer. When he said good-bye, he asked Audrey to return the next day to see him, since she had a car and he didn't.

The next afternoon she picked him up, clearly unimpressed with his appearance. He was barefoot, shirtless, unshaven, and slightly intoxicated. At first Audrey wanted to drive off, but he asked her to wait for him to get cleaned up. She did, and they spent the afternoon driving around and talking about their lives. While she fed him tomato juice and black coffee, he told her all about his band and his radio show on WSFA. As Audrey remembered in Lyrcrecia Williams's book, "Then, with a faraway look in his eyes, he said, 'To tell you the truth, I drank too much and the radio station let me go. So here I am working on a medicine show. There's something else I want to tell you,' he added, 'but I can't now.'"

The next night after his show, on what was only their second date, Hank proposed marriage to Audrey by saying, "I know you're gonna think I'm crazy, but will you meet me in Troy tomorrow and marry me?" Audrey, concerned about his drinking, managed to hold off on accepting his proposal for over a year. She also was not yet officially divorced from Guy. Meanwhile, Hank left the medicine show, moved back in with Lillie, and spent some of his time recording more acetates in a booth at the local Sears and Roebuck store. Taking any gigs he could find, for a while he toured through Alabama with Pee Wee King and his Golden West Cowboys. While working with King, he managed to sell him a patriotic song, "(I'm Praying for the Day That) Peace Will Come," for a quick fifty dollars.

Times were tough, and for a while Hank and Audrey were forced to work side by side as welders on the Liberty ships in the shipyards of Mobile. After a couple of months of hard labor, and living in a tiny motel room where the two washed their clothes in the sink, Audrey told Hank that he needed to go back to playing music steadily. He agreed, and they returned to Montgomery. Hank put together another new version of the Drifting Cowboys.

Once pedal steel guitar player Don Helms joined the band, the band secured dates in the small towns across southern Alabama, including Andalusia, where they played one of the biggest dance halls in the state, the Riverside Club, quickly becoming the star attraction. On the weekends, the Drifting Cowboys packed as many as six hundred people into the Riverside. Helms eventually became one of Nashville's most accomplished pedal steel guitarists, appearing on Patsy Cline's "Walking After Midnight."

Enjoying the regular work, Hank rented a trailer near the club, and Audrey moved in with him. Divorcing a soldier who was serving active duty in the war was extremely difficult, but Audrey finally managed to end her marriage to Guy, citing "voluntary abandonment." Ten days later, Hank and Audrey were married on December 15, 1944, in an Andalusia gas station, which was owned by a local justice of the peace. Don Helms, along with a few of the other Drifting Cowboys, served as witnesses.

As soon as their dates in Andalusia ran out, Hank handled the situation by getting blind drunk. Audrey responded by going off on him, and the fight ended when Hank threw Audrey's clothes out into a mud puddle. Audrey called the police, and Hank was hauled off to jail. The next day, Helms went and bailed him out.

Everyone knew Hank's drinking was out of control, and whether he was a mean drunk or a happy drunk depended on his mood when he started drinking. When Hank drank, Audrey would raise hell, and he would fight with her even more for putting up a fuss. When he didn't drink, the two of them got along very well. When things got bad between them, Audrey would run off to her parents' house, where her father would side with her if she got to him first, but if Hank beat her to it, he would side with Hank; Audrey's dad was the nearest Hank had come to having a father, and the two of them became really close. Other times, Hank would run off to Pensacola, Florida, where he would hide out with "Pappy" Neal McCormick at the San Carlos Hotel.

Hank loved to hang out with "Pappy," a Native American who passed himself off as a Hawaiian to avoid segregation in the 1930s. Known as "the Hawaiian Troubador," Pappy predated Les Paul's early version of the electric guitar in 1940 by developing an electric guitar pickup from parts taken off a Model T in 1929 or 1930. McCormick later went on to build three recording studios in Nashville.

Making things more complicated between himself and Audrey, Hank decided it was time for him to take her home to meet his mother. Audrey's daughter, Lycrecia, stayed with Audrey's parents, and she and Hank moved into Lillie's boardinghouse in Montgomery. As soon as Audrey became involved with Hank, she had taken over Lillie's role as the band's manager. Lillie wasn't very excited about turning Hank over to another woman, and Audrey wasn't prepared to sit quietly in the background. Hank's solution to this conflict was to get drunk, giving the two women the only point they actually did agree upon, which was that something had to be done about Hank's drinking.

In Lycrecia Williams's book, Hank's cousin Marie recalled, "Aunt Lillie and Audrey didn't get along. I walked in the door one day and I heard this awful noise and I went in the bedroom. Aunt Lillie and Irene had Audrey down on the bed and they were fighting. I went to pull them off her, and my hand got tangled in Audrey's hair. They ganged up on her quite often if I was there. But Audrey wasn't afraid of nobody. Hank knew how they did her, but what could he do about it? They had to stay because he wasn't making enough money to get out."

By early 1945, Hank was able to get another radio show on WSFA. As the fan mail poured in and more people showed up in the lobby of the Jefferson Davis Hotel to see the Cowboys, the management had to ask them to use the back entrance when they came to work. Hank became so popular that he was able to demand an exclusive deal stipulating that WSFA couldn't feature any other country acts.

Hank was writing his own songs now, and he paid to have a collection of them printed in a pamphlet called *Original Songs of Hank Williams, "The Drifting Cowboy."* He sold out the first printing within a year, at thirty-five cents a copy. He followed that print run with another edition, called *Hank Williams and His Drifting Cowboys, Stars of WSFA: Deluxe Song Book*, which included photos and thirty songs. Most of the compositions were angry love songs like "Never Again (Will I Knock on Your Door)" and "My Love for You (Has Turned to Hate)." His gospel upbringing came through in "Wealth Won't Save Your Soul," with the only real keeper in the bunch being a version of "Honky Tonkin'." The books contained only the lyrics—Hank couldn't read or write music. He once told the *Montgomery Advertiser*, "I have never read a note or written one. I can't, I don't know one note from another."

Audrey's musical aspirations were as strong as Hank's, and she learned how to play guitar and stand-up bass well enough to perform in his band. She also liked to sing but was known to not be very good at it, although that small detail didn't stop her from pursuing a career right alongside him. Without telling her, Hank would often make sure that Audrey's microphone was turned off, once saying, "It's bad enough to have a wife who wants to sing, but it's hell to have one who wants to sing and can't."

Toward the end of the war, Don Helms was drafted into the army and was replaced by Bernice and Doyle Turner. Bernice was a rhythm guitar player, and her husband Doyle played pedal steel guitar. They moved into Lillie's boardinghouse and managed to stay in the band for almost a year. Bernice was the only female to be hired as a full-time Drifting Cowboy. One of her favorite memories is of working with Hank on the radio, where he always closed his show with a hymn. She and Doyle would hum in the background while Hank did the narration. Coming back to the boardinghouse, they would often find the boarders crying after listening to Hank's powerful renditions.

Along with Hank, Audrey, Doyle, and Bernice, the band now included bassist/comedian William "Lum" York. Lum stayed the longest with the Drifting Cowboys, playing with Hank for almost five years. York, who became close friends with Hank, remembered how he never liked being by himself. "Hank didn't like to be alone. He'd come get me and we would go over to his house, but all he did was read funny books. He even got ideas for some of his songs from the comics. I don't know why he would want me over there with him, because most of the time I'd be sitting there with no one to talk to."

Audrey's sister Lynette told Lycrecia, "Hank was a very smart man. I've come across so many people that thought he was illiterate. Well, he was not. He constantly had a book in his hand. He read poetry, he read comic books—the floorboard of his car was always full of comic books. If he was stretched out on the sofa, he would either be reading the paper or a book or something."

The Drifting Cowboys started working seven nights a week throughout Alabama and Georgia, including a weekly gig at the Cavalier Club in Gant Beach, Alabama. That's where Bernice Turner remembered having the most fun, fishing and enjoying the lakeside resort. Their enthusiastic audiences were really reacting to some of Hank's stronger songs, like "Wedding Bells" and "Lovesick Blues."

Unfortunately, Hank handled his growing popularity by continuing to drink too much and showing up too drunk to perform, or not at all. Even though this time he was too popular for WSFA to fire, he was gaining a reputation for being unreliable. For the first time he was hospitalized for his alcoholism when they admitted him to a sanitarium in Prattville, Alabama.

Treating alcoholism as a disease was fairly new with the formation of Alcoholics Anonymous just ten years earlier. At the time a hospital stay merely gave Hank a few days to "dry out."

Hank was able to go weeks without drinking, but once he started, he couldn't stop. Watching Hank's battle with the bottle, Bernice Turner recalled in Steve A. Maze's book, "Hank was a great singer who I thought would go to the top if he would stay sober. He was shy and humble and laughed a lot. Most country music fans do not know what a loving and caring person Hank Williams was. He was always for the underdog. I know for a fact that he treated his band members well."

Once Audrey tried to drink as much as Hank just to see what he would do, and he was so drunk, he didn't even notice. Audrey ended up in the hospital, sick for several days. Even though they fought a lot, Audrey kept pushing Hank to succeed in the music business. By the summer of 1946, they were able to put enough money together to rent a house at 409 Washington Avenue, just a few blocks away from Lillie's boardinghouse. Audrey went to her parents' house to pick up Lycrecia, and for the first time since their marriage, they settled in together as a family.

Hank had already made one trip to Nashville, with the intention of auditioning for the Grand Ole Opry. He only got as far as talking to Jud Collins, who worked at WSM, the Opry's home radio station. Collins told him he had to go see Jack Stapp and audition like everybody else. When Collins wouldn't personally take Hank to meet Stapp, Hank turned around and went back to Montgomery.

Audrey kept insisting Hank return to Nashville, and by September of 1946 she had secured a meeting with Fred Rose, who was the co-owner of Acuff-Rose, Nashville's first publishing companies designed to feature hillbilly music. Rose himself was an accomplished composer who wrote the songs, "'Deed I Do," "Red Hot Mama," "Blue Eyes Crying in the Rain," "Honest and Truly," and "Tears on My Pillow."

Rose and Hank had a lot in common. Rose had started as a radio performer in Chicago on WBBM, hosting "Fred Rose's Song Shop," where he would compose songs for listeners who called in with ideas. His drinking problem cost him his job, and he went to New York before landing back on the radio on WSM in Nashville. Over the next few years, Rose bounced around between New York and Hollywood, where he wrote songs for Gene Autry, while continuing to commute back and forth to Nashville.

After converting to Christian Science, Rose successfully beat his drinking problem and settled permanently in Nashville, where he approached Roy Acuff with the idea of starting a publishing company. Acuff came up with the finances, and Acuff-Rose was launched in October 1942.

Hank once told journalist Ralph Gleason, "Fred Rose came to Nashville to laugh, and he heard Roy Acuff and said, 'By God he means it.'" Acuff-Rose would become one of Nashville's most prestigious publishing companies. And when Fred Rose agreed to set up a meeting with Hank Williams, it would be one of the best decisions of his life.

5

MANSION ON
THE HILL

*"I got a lot of other boys on record, Hank hit and the
others didn't. Nobody made Hank but himself. He was
quite a boy!"* —FRED ROSE

O N SEPTEMBER 14, 1946, Hank and Audrey Williams boarded a train
bound for Nashville, to meet with Fred Rose. That afternoon they
went to the fifth floor of the National Life and Accident Company, where
Fred and his son Wesley were playing a lunchtime game of Ping-Pong
in the recreation room of WSM. Rose was looking for songs for one of
his clients, Molly O'Day, and was originally interested in Hank only for
his songwriting abilities.

The popular legend surrounding Hank and Fred's first meeting was
that Fred allegedly challenged Hank to write a song on the spot, giving
him the storyline of a girl who marries a rich boy, instead of the poor
boy who truly loves her. Supposedly Hank took a half hour and came
up with "Mansion on the Hill," which would become one of his first
hits. What really happened was that Hank sang Rose a couple of his
songs, including "Six More Miles to the Graveyard" and "When God
Comes and Gathers His Jewels." He wrote "Mansion on the Hill" after
he returned home; where, as Audrey pointed out, it took him a while
to write the song because it wasn't his original idea.

Rose signed Hank to a publishing contract on the spot at their initial meeting, taking the first six songs Hank offered him, giving him three cents for each copy of sheet music sold and 50 percent of future record royalties. Hank and Audrey proudly returned to Montgomery with a publishing contract, although they didn't realize that this was the turning point of Hank's career. When Rose heard that Sterling Records was looking for a country singer, he brought Hank back to Nashville on December 10, 1946, to record in the WSM Studios.

Taking their call letters from the slogan "We Shield Millions," WSM was Nashville's first professional recording studio, opening in 1944 and recording Eddy Arnold's debut session on December 4 of that year. In 1947, a self-contained studio was built in a remodeled dining room at the Tulane Hotel and was called Castle Studios, because WSM was known as "the Air Castle of the South." Here, Hank would record most of his songs.

His first recording session, on December 11, included "When God Comes and Gathers His Jewels," "Never Again," "Wealth Won't Save Your Soul," and "Calling You." During this session, Hank was backed by the Willis Brothers, who also went by the name the Oklahoma Wranglers. In Colin Escott's book *Hank Williams: The Biography*, Vic Willis remembered going out to lunch with Hank: "Hank was a quiet guy and kinda negative. But he had a hell of a dry sense of humor. Someone asked Hank if he wanted a beer with his meal, and he shook his head [and said], 'You don't know ol' Hank. Hank don't just have *one* beer.'" When they got back to the studio, Rose asked Willis if Hank had been drinking. Willis told him no and wondered why he would ask.

The only problem Hank did have with recording the songs was the way he pronounced some of the words. His southern accent was so thick—he sang "purr" instead of "poor" in "Wealth Won't Save Your Soul," for example—that Rose finally gave up changing the way Hank was singing it and exclaimed, "Dammit, Wranglers, sing it the way Hank does!" As soon as they were finished, Rose pressed acetates of all four songs and sent them over to Sterling Records.

In January of 1947, Sterling released "Calling You" and "Never Again." *Billboard* magazine reviewed the record favorably: "With real spiritual qualities in his pipes, singing with the spirit of a camp meeting, Hank Williams makes his bow an auspicious one."

For his second session in the studio, Hank recorded "I Don't Care If Tomorrow Never Comes," "Pan American," "My Love for You Has Turned to Hate," and "Honky Tonkin'." This time Hank's sound featured the "crack" rhythm, which became a familiar Williams trademark—an electric guitar keeping time on the deadened bass strings. That is, Hank's music used the guitar instead of drums to keep the beat. It was a quality that Johnny Cash would later add to his own music by making a "boom-chicka-boom" sound.

Molly O'Day eventually recorded four of Hank's songs between 1946 and 1947, including "Singing Waterfall," "Six More Miles to the Graveyard," "I Don't Care If Tomorrow Never Comes," and "When God Comes and Gathers His Jewels." The only song written especially for O'Day, and the only one credited to both Hank and Audrey, was "On the Evening Train," which O'Day recorded in April 1949.

Rose was not satisfied with Sterling Records, because it was a small company, and when he heard that the Loews Corporation, which owned MGM Pictures, was starting its own record label, he promptly negotiated a new recording contract for Hank. Their agreement was to record all of his records in Nashville, and Rose became Hank's manager. Hank's first sessions for MGM were held on April 21, 1947.

Rose knew that Hank had to score a hit for MGM; otherwise he would be dropped from the label. In those days, session men weren't the norm in Nashville, but Rose hired some of the sharpest musicians he could find, who happened to be the core of Red Foley's band. They included Zeb and Zeke Turner on guitars, Tommy Jackson on fiddle, Brownie Reynolds on bass, and Smokey Lohman on steel guitar. Foley, a singer and radio and television personality, would go on to release in 1951 the first million-selling gospel song, "Peace in the Valley."

The first song Hank and the band recorded for MGM was "Move It on Over," which was a variation of the melody for "Your Red Wagon." "Move It on Over" really rocked, and some historians considered it the first rock-and-roll song recorded, predating Ike Turner's "Rocket 88" by four years. The second song of the session was "I Saw the Light," followed by "(Last Night) I Heard You Crying in Your Sleep" and "Six More Miles (To the Graveyard)."

MGM released "Move It on Over," with "(Last Night) I Heard You Crying in Your Sleep," on June 6, 1947, and within two months it became Hank's first *Billboard* hit. The *Montgomery Examiner* called Hank "the spur-jangling Sinatra of the western ballad." This song would finally bring Hank some real money, selling approximately 22,000 copies to garner $439.55 from MGM and $1,709.11 from Acuff-Rose. In today's dollars, that would be $3,616.30 and $14,061, respectively.

With his newfound riches, Hank helped Lillie buy a bigger boardinghouse, at 318 North McDonough Street. Lillie had since divorced J. C. Bozard and married her fourth husband, one of her boarders, William Wallace "Bill" Stone. Hank also bought Audrey a fur coat, and she talked him into putting a down payment on a house at 10 Stuart Avenue in Montgomery. It wasn't a mansion on the hill, but it was a start.

"I Saw the Light," which was the flip side to "Six More Miles (To the Graveyard)," became one of Hank's most well-known hymns and closely followed the melody to the traditional hymn "He Set Me Free." This song was also recorded by Clyde Grubbs for RCA Records, and in November of 1947, Roy Acuff covered it. Both versions came out before MGM released Hank's recording. Audrey tried talking Hank into letting her add background vocals to "I Saw the Light" prior to its release, but luckily, Fred Rose choose not to replace it with what they already had.

Many people have claimed they inspired this song, but the most believable version came from R. D. Norred, who told Steve A. Maze his story in *Hank Williams and His Drifting Cowboys*. Norred, who briefly played pedal steel guitar for Hank, remembered how the band would watch a beacon light near the Montgomery airport while they were on the road to gauge how close they were to getting home. One night Hank and the band were packed into a 1942 Chevy, and it was about 2:00 or 3:00 in the morning, so most of them were trying to get some sleep. Norred said, "It was hard to get any rest since we were so cramped in the car. Lum [York] raised up to change sleeping positions and looked out the window. As he laid back down, he said, 'We're getting into Montgomery now, I saw the light.' Hank started mumbling something about that being a good title to a song. When we met Hank at WSFA the next day, he started picking out the tune on his guitar."

Anticipating a strike by the American Federation of Musicians set to begin December 31, 1947, Fred brought Hank back into the studio on August 4 to record as many songs as they could. This way Rose would have product to distribute during the strike. Rose refused to let Hank bring any of his Drifting Cowboys along with him, so Hank was backed by guitarist Zeke Turner, rhythm guitarist Louis Innis, fiddle player Chubby Wise, and pedal steel guitarist Jerry Byrd. Together they recorded "I'm Satisfied With You," "Fly Trouble," "On the Banks of the Old Pontchartrain," and "Honky-Tonk Blues."

Before the end of the year, Hank went back into the studio for two days on November 6 and 7. On the first day he recorded one of Rose's songs, "Rootie Tootie," and three of his own, "I'm a Long Gone Daddy," "I Can't Get You Off of My Mind," and a new version of "Honky Tonkin.'" "Rootie Tootie" was also covered by Paul Howard, and Pee Wee King used it for the flip side to his biggest hit, "Tennessee Waltz."

The second day Hank recorded three more originals, "I'll Be a Bachelor 'til I Die," "My Sweet Love Ain't Around," and "The Blues Come Around." He also laid down tracks for "Mansion on the Hill," which gave writing credit to both Hank and Fred Rose.

Hank collaborated with Fred on many of his tunes, and one of Hank's strongest qualities was to write songs that grabbed your imagination using simple lyrics that everyone could relate to. Hank's future fiddle player Jerry Rivers once said, "Hank's novelty songs weren't novelty—they were serious, not silly, and that's why they were much better accepted and better selling. 'Move It on Over' hits right home, 'cause half of the people he was singing to were in the doghouse with the ol' lady"—subject matter Hank would become all too familiar with.

After these recording sessions were finished, Hank went back to Montgomery and continued to play with his Drifting Cowboys. This version of the band consisted of Hank, Lum York, Little Joe Pennington, R. D. Norred, and Winston "Red" Todd. To enhance their image, Fred convinced the men that they should dress alike onstage. Hank and Audrey took out a loan at the Montgomery Loan and Finance Company to buy them all matching outfits, which included khaki pants, pea green shirts, and cowboy boots. The suits cost thirty dollars each, and both Lum and Red had to sign loan papers to guarantee that they would pay Hank back.

With all of his personal troubles, Hank never forgot what it was like to be down on your luck. Often, as the band traveled from town to town, Hank would stop the car and hand money to hitchhikers, apologizing for not being able to give them a lift due to all the equipment they were carrying. When the band played their 1947 Christmas show on WSFA, R. D. Norred left his wallet on the studio piano. It contained his weekly fifty-dollar salary and an extra ten dollars, which was a lot of money back in those days. Hank assured him that someone would keep it for him, but it was never found. When Norred got ready to go home for the holidays, without his Christmas cash, Audrey walked up and handed him fifty dollars to help replace his losses.

Norred had fond memories of Hank working on songs on a piano in his back room with Fred Rose for two or three days at a time and remembered how he liked to entertain the audience with little jokes in between songs. Hank nicknamed Norred "Sonny," and one joke he used to tell was about looking over Norred's shoulder when he was writing a letter to his wife. Hank would say that Sonny sent a check in the letter for one thousand hugs and kisses. Then he would say, "He sure was downhearted three or four days later when I caught him reading a letter his wife had sent back. She said thank you for the check. The milkman cashed it this morning."

Hank's career was going so well that he boasted to the *Montgomery Advertiser* that he had fans coming to the WFSA studios who drove from as far away as fifty miles to see him. Hank told them, "A lady from Opelika wrote me just this mornin'. She says, 'Say, Hank, how much do it cost to come up and hear you sing? If it don't cost too much, we may come up there.' If anybody in my business knew as much about their business as the public did, they'd be all right. Just lately, somebody got the idea nobody didn't listen to my kinda music. I told them ever'body on the radio, this was my last program. If anybody's enjoyed it, I'd like to hear from 'em. I got four hundred cards and letters that afternoon and the next mornin'. They decided they wanted to keep my kinda music."

"Move It on Over" peaked on the *Billboard* charts at number four, and Hank's music was finally starting to take off. At the same time, his personal life was falling apart. By February 1948, Audrey and Lycrecia left the house on Stuart and moved back in with her parents in Banks. Being in the country music limelight meant keeping an impeccable image, which was a tough thing for Hank to maintain. He could go weeks without drinking, but once he started, he would binge-drink for days. His chronic back pain exacerbated the situation, and when the band would notice him eating aspirin by the handful, they knew a drinking binge wouldn't be far behind.

To deal with his pain, Hank took off for Pensacola for a few days, always finding refuge with his pal "Pappy" Neal McCormick. There he could drink and party as much as he wanted away from the watchful eyes of the women in his life. Broadcasting a radio program from the Carlos Hotel, McCormick once recorded Hank promoting him for sheriff. Hank sincerely expressed his admiration of McCormick, calling him "a man that I had the pleasure of working with when I first started pickin' and singin' years ago and … one of the finest guys in the world."

In despair, Hank turned to Fred Rose. Rose's frustration was expressed in a letter to Hank, which appears in Colin's Escott's book *Hank Williams: The Biography*. Rose wrote, "Wesley [Rose] tells me you called this morning for more money after me wiring you four hundred dollars just the day before yesterday. We have gone as far as we can go at this time and cannot send you any more. Hank, I have tried to be a friend of yours but you refuse to let me be one. I feel you are just using me for a good thing, and this is where I quit. You have been very unfair, calling the house in the middle of the night and I hope you will not let it happen again. When you get ready to straighten out let me know and maybe we can pick up where we left off, but for the present I am fed-up with your foolishness."

When Hank returned to Montgomery, he sold his house and moved back into his mother's boardinghouse. After getting his $2,200 down payment back, he went on a spending spree. Hank had become trapped in a downward spiral that would follow him to the end of his life. He was once again showing up for his performances drunk, if at all, and even his best friends didn't want to be around him.

When he opened for Cowboy Copas and Johnny Bond at the 31 Club, Bond told the audience, "You people don't know 'bout this boy here. He won't be 'round here very long. His records are going like wildfire all over the West Coast." But after Hank went on a three-day bender, the owner of the 31 Club offered the performance spot to his band, without Hank. When the band caught up with him to tell him about their plans, he flatly replied, "Well, do what you want to."

After moving out of their house, Audrey filed for divorce in April 1948, stating, "Hank Williams my husband is twenty-four years of age. He has a violent and ungovernable temper. He drinks a great deal, and during the last month, he has been drunk most of the time. My nervous system has been upset and I am afraid to live with him any longer." Hank and Audrey's marriage lasted a little over three years, and there was never any doubt that they loved each other. They just had, as Don Helms remembered, "some funny ways of showing it." Their divorce was granted on May 26, 1948.

Concerned that Hank would end up signing a new deal with someone else, Rose offered Hank a three-year contract guaranteeing him a fifty-dollar-per-month retainer against royalties and promising to publish at least six of his songs per year. After holding off for several weeks, Hank finally signed the papers. By now, his band had also given up on him. His old band members would see Hank sitting on the swing in front of his mother's boardinghouse all by himself, wearing his hat and suit. All dressed up with no place to play.

Hank's reputation for drunkenness had ruined his chances of finding work in Montgomery, and the only hope he had now was to leave the area. Lillie was reluctant to see him go, but both Audrey and Rose knew he could do better in a bigger market.

Right after their divorce was finalized, Hank and Audrey reconciled. In June, Hank sent Rose a postcard from Norfolk, Virginia, with a cartoon drawing of a lady riding a mule. The caption said, "I'm not the first jackass to support a woman." He wrote on the back, "Having Big Time," and signed it "Hank and Audrey." It was Hank's way of letting Rose know he was putting his life back together. A year later, the couple's divorce would be declared null and void.

Earlier that year, Rose had heard that KWKH in Shreveport, Louisiana, was starting a new program in the style of the Grand Ole Opry, to be called the *Louisiana Hayride*. It would be a live show broadcast to several cities throughout the South. As Hank was unable to gain a spot on the Grand Ole Opry, this type of radio show was his saving grace.

Saturday-night jamborees, including the *National Barn Dance* on WLS in Chicago, and the *Boone County Jamboree* (also known as the *Midwestern Hayride*), on WLW in Cincinnati, were becoming popular across the United States. Rose knew Hank had a long way to go before the Opry would give him a chance, so he approached the *Louisiana Hayride*. Convincing them to work with Hank was no easy feat.

Calling in favors from anyone he knew, Rose went to work on Dean Upson, the commercial manager of KWKH, which led him to the man in charge of the *Hayride*, Horace Logan. Logan told Rose that he would give Hank a shot if he could stay sober for six months. Hank started to call Logan every week, from his morning show on WSFA. He finally made a trip to Shreveport with Audrey to meet the bosses of KWKH and hang out with some of the *Hayride* performers. Showing that Hank was clean and sober and ready to work, Rose was finally able to sign a deal with the *Hayride*, and Hank broadcast his last WSFA show on July 29, 1948.

Hank's new contract promised him fifty dollars per week, and it included hosting his own show every morning at 5:15 on KWKH, playing the live show over the weekend, and performing in cities all over the South. The big difference would be the venues. Where he had been limited to roadhouses and local clubs, now Hank would appear in auditoriums in Birmingham, Baton Rouge, and New Orleans. Lum York was the only Drifting Cowboy able to follow him to Shreveport.

KWKH, which began broadcasting in 1932 with fifty thousand watts, was a major station, considering Hank's previous show on WSFA was broadcast at only one thousand watts. This radio exposure would prove to be critical for Hank's career. The *Louisiana Hayride* was a minor jamboree when it signed Hank, but between 1948 and 1954 it became known as "the Cradle of the Stars," helping break acts like Kitty Wells, Slim Whitman, Webb Pierce, Johnny Horton, Faron Young, Tommy Sands, Jim Reeves, Johnny Cash, Elvis Presley, and Hank himself. Hank Williams stayed in Shreveport for only ten months, but that was just enough time to turn him into a major star.

6

MOVE IT ON OVER

"I'll tell you one damn thing. You might not like the song, but when I walk offstage and throw my hat back on the stage and the hat encores, that's pretty hot."
—HANK SR.

Hank and Audrey piled whatever they could into an old Chrysler and took off for Shreveport, stopping in Houston on July 31 so Hank could appear at Pappy Daily's Record Ranch and Daily's jukebox distributorship, Southern Amusements. After renting a garage apartment at 4802 Mansfield Road, Hank settled in and made his debut on the *Louisiana Hayride* on August 7, 1948. That night he followed Johnnie and Jack, a well-liked act who were also booked by Fred Rose. When someone backstage apologized to Hank for having to go on after such a popular act, he replied, "I'll eat 'em alive." The crowd wasn't that responsive until he lit into "Move It on Over," and by the end of the song, they were on their feet. Later in the show, Hank came back out with Audrey, and together they sang "I Want to Live and Love."

In the audience that night was a starstruck teenager by the name of Merle Kilgore. Years later he would open for Hank's son, Hank Jr., and eventually become vice president of Hank Williams Jr. Enterprises. Kilgore also wrote "Wolverton Mountain," and co-wrote "Ring of Fire" with June Carter Cash. He claims that Hank had the same look in his eyes that night that Elvis had when he performed there, describing it as, "That 'I know something you don't' look."

Three days before, Hank had launched his morning radio show on KWKH, with Drifting Cowboy Lum York, fiddle player George Brown, and guitarist Chris Criswell, who had all followed him to Shreveport. Hank tried in vain to get Don Helms to join them, but Helms had a solid job making more money playing for Boots Harris. Harris had been a Drifting Cowboy back in 1941 and was the first guitarist allowed to play electric steel guitar on the Opry stage. Hank understood why he couldn't make the move, but they made an agreement that when Hank finally did make it to the Opry, Helms would come along.

With Hank not as well known in Shreveport as in Montgomery, regular gigs were very hard to come by. One by one his band members left to make more money elsewhere, so Hank had to resort to using musicians from the *Hayride* as a backup band. Before long he was picking up dates in northern Louisiana and eastern Texas.

His radio show went so well that he signed a sponsorship with Johnnie Fair Syrup, a product made by the Shreveport Syrup Company. Every morning he would play whatever he wanted, pitching syrup as "The Ol' Syrup Sopper" and promoting his live appearances. Along with his own songs, he filled his show with some of his favorite tunes, like "Someday You'll Call My Name" and "I Wish I Had a Nickel," by Jimmy Wakely. He also loved to cover "Cool Water" by the Sons of the Pioneers and Bill Carlisle's "Rocking Chair Money."

By January of 1949, Hank was on the air every morning for fifteen minutes at 5:45 a.m., again at 6:30 a.m., and later at 8:15 a.m. At the close of every show, he pretended he was talking to his maid by saying, "Get the biscuits ready; I'm coming home and I need something to put my Johnnie Fair Syrup on." The show became so popular that the station had Hank prerecord his segments to be broadcast when he was out playing on the road.

Before sunrise, waiting to go on the air, Hank would often sit drinking coffee in the Bantam Grill, a regular hang-out for the Hayride performers, located across the street from the KWKH studios. Murrell Stansell, the owner of the Bantam, recalled in Lycrecia Williams's book

Still in Love with You that Hank would ask for a roll of nickels to play the pinball or marble machine, and how much he loved ketchup. He even poured it on his waffles. Stansell joked, "I wanted to stop selling him the waffles. I was only gettin' twenty cents for them, and he would use up a whole bottle of catsup that cost me eight or ten cents!"

Hank's home life was also much calmer, considering Lillie and Audrey were now hundreds of miles apart. Right after arriving in Shreveport, Audrey became pregnant. Hank was thrilled with the thought of becoming a father, and he thoroughly enjoyed being a stepfather to Lyrcrecia, who fondly remembers how kind and attentive he was to her. Supposedly Hank never legally adopted Lycrecia, because Audrey was afraid she would lose custody of her in case they divorced.

As Audrey's pregnancy progressed, she naturally couldn't fit into her stage costumes anymore and spent more time staying at home with Lycrecia. She and Hank had become good friends with Zeke and Helen Clements; Kitty Wells and her husband, Johnnie Wright; and Curley and Georgia Williams. Johnnie and Hank loved to go fishing on Sundays and then host a fish fry that night. Curley played fiddle in Hank's band, and they became so close that they used to introduce each other onstage as brothers. A few years later, Hank would record one of Curley's songs, "Half as Much," adding that to his growing collection of hits.

Things were finally coming together for Hank after all his years of struggling in Montgomery, and for the first time in a long time, he was happy. He bought a Packard limousine to travel in and always kept fishing poles in his car, pulling off the road whenever he came upon a lake or a stream. Hank was even becoming popular with the teenage girls, who reacted to him like he was the Frank Sinatra of the country set. Once, after a show in Corpus Christi, Texas, a gang of girls went after him with razor blades, attempting to cut off a bit of clothing or his necktie for a souvenir. They went as far as slashing the tires on his car to keep him from leaving.

The only problem with Hank being happy was that he wasn't writing much, and MGM was running out of songs to release. To check up on him, Rose sent Mel Foree, his promotions man, down to Shreveport. Together Foree and Hank went out on the road together, to Jacksonville, Texas, stopping along the way to fish. This respite prompted Hank to write four songs, which he quickly cut onto acetates in the KWKH studios as soon as he got back to Shreveport.

Foree reported that each song was written to one of Hank's existing melodies, and the set included only one that Rose didn't care for. The disliked song, called "'Neath a Cold Gray Tomb of Stone," was eventually recorded by Charlie Monroe in 1950. Hank also came up with a couple of novelty songs with Curley Williams, including "Honey, Do You Love Me, Huh?" and "No, Not Now."

During the recording ban of 1948, MGM utilized what Hank had already recorded by issuing a new Hank Williams single every two months. Just before he got to Shreveport, MGM released the new version of "Honky Tonkin'." *Billboard* praised the song for its "deft ork beat." To avoid confusion with the original release of "Honky Tonkin'," Rose bought up all the remaining masters from Sterling Records for two thousand dollars and sold them to MGM.

"Long Gone Daddy" had peaked at number six on the *Billboard* charts, but nothing much happened with "Pan American" or "I Saw the Light."

Now that the recording ban was being lifted and MGM's stockpile was running out, Hank was pushing to record a song he had been performing in Montgomery called "Lovesick Blues." This song contained minor chords on the bridge, making it an unusual number for him.

Originally Rose didn't like the song and wanted no part of it. The first time Hank performed it on the *Hayride*, he didn't have his own band. This time he was backed by Buddy Attaway on guitar, Felton Pruett on steel guitar, Dobber Johnson on fiddle, and Tillman Franks on bass.

In Colin Escott's book *Hank Williams: The Biography*, Franks remembered, "We were rehearsing up there and Hank was singing it in F. Then there was this part where it went from F to B-minor or something, and I said, 'Hank, that one chord you got in there, I can't figure it out.' He says, 'Don't worry 'bout it, hoss, just stomp your foot and grin.'"

On December 22, 1948, Rose booked a session for Hank in Cincinnati. Rose wanted to use Red Foley's band again, and that was the city they were based in. A few days before, Hank and Audrey took Lycrecia to her grandparents' house in Alabama, dropped Johnnie and Jack and Kitty Wells in Nashville, and continued on to Cincinnati with Johnnie and Jack's mandolin player, Clyde Baum.

Hank met Fred Rose at E. T. Herzog studios, and the two went at it over recording "Lovesick Blues." Rose felt it was a disaster of a song, stating that the opening verse should have been the chorus, and the chorus should have been the opening verse. Hank didn't understand what he was talking about and defended the song, citing how well it went over every time he played it in front of an audience. Screaming at Rose, Hank said, "I'll tell you one damn thing. You might not like the song, but when I walk off stage and throw my hat back on the stage and the *hat* encores, that's pretty hot."

Hank had told Rose that he paid Rex Griffin for the arrangement, but what really happened was that Hank and Griffin got drunk together one night, and Hank paid him a few dollars to use his arrangement. Even though Griffin had recorded it for Decca Records in 1939, the song actually dated back to the 1920s. Irving Mills had written the words, and Cliff Friend, a vaudevillian, wrote the melody.

Mills later wrote "Time Waits for No One," and "When My Dreamboat Comes Home." "Lovesick Blues" had first been recorded by Elsie Clark in 1922, and again by Emmett Miller in 1925 and 1928. Miller also wrote "Everybody's Trying to Be My Baby," which was eventually covered by Carl Perkins and the Beatles.

Backed by Jerry Byrd on steel guitar, Zeke Turner on electric, Louis Innis on rhythm, Tommy Jackson on fiddle, and Willie Thawl on bass, Hank recorded his version of "Lovesick Blues," along with "There'll Be No Teardrops Tonight"; a hymn he had written, called "Lost on the River"; and one Audrey had written, "I Heard My Mother Praying for Me."

Clyde Baum played mandolin on the hymns, but the recordings were unusable, due to Audrey singing out of tune, sometimes drowning out Hank's voice altogether. Those in the studio that day saw the competition between Audrey and Hank. Horace Logan, the *Hayride*'s producer, once said, "Audrey was a pure unmitigated, hard-boiled, blue-eyed bitch. She wanted to be a singer and she was horrible, unbelievably horrible. She not only tried to sing, she *insisted* on it, and she forced herself on stage when Hank was out there. I'd never let her go out, but Hank would say, 'Logan, I've got to let her sing. I've got to live with the woman.'"

"Lovesick Blues" was the last song to be recorded that day, with Rose leaving the studio to get a cup of coffee. He was so disgusted over the song's inclusion that he didn't even want to hear them record it. On his way out, he offered the musicians time and a half if they finished the song before the three hours of studio time ran out. Knowing that studio costs came out of his royalties, Hank shouted to Rose as he walked out the door, "You're mighty damn free with my money!" When Rose returned and listened to the final product, he said, "My God, Hank, I still say that's the worst thing I've ever heard." Regardless of how Rose felt, the band was relieved that they navigated the difficult rhythms and chord changes, and Hank was pleased that they had gotten it recorded at all.

As soon as the session was finished, Hank and Audrey drove Baum back to Nashville and continued on to Montgomery to celebrate Christmas. After returning to Shreveport, Hank met Johnny Bond backstage on the *Hayride* and revealed to him how worried he was about his career. Hank confided to Bond, "I'm tired of tryin' to get on the Opry. It's just too rough. I've recorded one song that's in the can now, a thing called 'Lovesick Blues'; if that don't make it, I'm thinkin' seriously of gittin' out of the business."

Judging from the audience's reaction to "Lovesick Blues," Hank had nothing to worry about. The *Shreveport Times* ran an article on January 9, 1949, titled "'Lovesick Blues' About to Be Released," reporting, "Capacity crowds at the 'Louisiana Hayride' nearly 'tear the house down' for encores of 'Lovesick Blues.' This, among other reasons, necessitated the advance sale of tickets to the Saturday night KWKH songfest."

When MGM released the song on February 11, 1949, the credits read, "Composer: Rex Griffin; Arrangements by Hank Williams; Publisher: Acuff-Rose." According to MGM's royalty accounting, "Lovesick Blues" sold over forty-eight thousand copies in the first seventeen days of its release. Hank joined the local American Federation of Musicians on February 4 and signed a mortgage to buy a house on Charles Street for $9,500.

Audrey had been sick most of her pregnancy, so Hank went out and bought her a chair and a record player so she could sit and listen to music. As the weather heated up, so did Hank and Audrey's fighting. Horace Logan recalled seeing Audrey throw a set of crystal Hank had bought her out onto the carport, smashing a piece at a time. One night he came home and tripped over a vase in the hallway. Thinking he was drunk, Audrey threw some tea glasses at him, sending him to the hospital.

In Hank Snow's autobiography, he recalled a night when he was a guest on the *Hayride*. Hank invited him home afterward, and on their way, they stopped downtown to pick up a ring for Audrey. When he gave it to her, she threw it back at him, saying, "If you can't do any better than that, forget it." Before long, Hank was back to drinking as soon as he walked out of the house.

For a performance in Lake Charles, Louisiana, Hank was so drunk when they got there, the band had to help him out of the car. Once on-stage, he continued to play the fiddle even after the band begged him to stop. Hank just continued, saying, "Naw, naw, them people jus' eatin' it up." That night the band sold ninety-seven dollars worth of pictures at ten cents a piece. Steel guitarist Felton Pruett said, "They loved him down there. Drunk or sober, it didn't matter. Funny thing was, his time was right on. If you could get him out there and prop him up, he'd do the show." Unfortunately, this would become a pattern that Hank would repeat until the end of his life.

Still intent on being part of Hank's career, Audrey pressured him into recording more songs with her. Rose booked a double session in Nashville on March 1, 1949, and she, Hank, and Clyde Baum drove there together. Zeke and Zeb Turner returned with a new lineup of musicians. Hank and Audrey recorded two duets, "Dear Brother" and "Jesus Remembered Me." Afterward Hank cut "Lost Highway" and "May You Never Be Alone." The latter featured the only mandolin solo ever included on a Hank Williams song. After a short break, Hank recorded "Mind Your Own Business" and "You're Gonna Change (Or I'm Gonna Leave)," both songs clearly inspired by his problems with Audrey.

Since Rose felt none of the songs recorded were strong enough to follow "Lovesick Blues," Hank was sent on his first-ever flight to Nashville to record with Red Sovine. Hank had helped Sovine get signed to a contract with MGM Records, and Sovine took Hank's place on the *Hayride* when Hank finally made it to the Opry. Although he told the *Shreveport Times* that flying was "the only way to travel," Hank sent a telegram to Rose just before takeoff that read, "Flight 58 will arrive 5:45. I hope." Once in Nashville, he recorded "Sunshine," "I've Just Told Mama Goodbye," and "Wedding Bells."

"Wedding Bells" and "I've Just Told Mama Goodbye" were released at the beginning of May 1949, and just a week later, on May 7, "Lovesick Blues" knocked "Candy Kisses" by George Morgan out of the number-one spot. It stayed in that position for the next sixteen weeks, remaining on the charts until the following January. "Wedding Bells" peaked at number two and also spent the rest of the year on the *Billboard* charts.

Hank found out that "Lovesick Blues" made it to number one while sitting in the Bantam Grill. Bassist Tillman Franks had bought a copy of *Billboard* at a newsstand and walked in and showed it to Hank. Franks stated in *Hank Williams: The Biography*, "It shook him up pretty good. He just sat there silent the longest time. He realized what that meant."

To make full use of Hank's newfound stardom, the Shreveport Chamber of Commerce organized a whistle-stop tour of Louisiana and

Texas, stopping at crossroads and depots, where Hank would close the show with two songs and sign as many autographs as he could before the train pulled away. Hank was getting so popular that no other performers would follow him in Shreveport or on the road.

When he performed at the Municipal Auditorium, at the end of his set he would announce that he was going to sing a gospel song, prompting the lights to go down, leaving him standing alone in the spotlight. Backing away from the audience as they screamed for more, Hank would tip his hat and quietly say, "Ain't it a shame, ain't it a shame, ain't it a shame."

Once Hank was receiving decent royalty checks, plus cash from sales of his photographs and songbooks, he hired a full-time band, bought a trailer for his equipment, and signed with a manager by the name of Oscar Davis. Davis was a promoter who booked Pee Wee King, Roy Acuff, and other members of the Grand Ole Opry. He was known as "the Baron" and had fallen into country music after working in vaudeville and motion-picture promotion. Davis became famous for promoting the 1947 Carnegie Hall concerts that took country music to New York City. He had a reputation of being a relentless promoter, and some in Nashville used to joke that he still promoted a concert two weeks after it happened.

Even before he recorded "Lovesick Blues," Hank called Davis and told him, "Now I'm ready for you. Now you'll want me." Davis shared the same opinion of the song as Rose did, saying, "This is the most horrible goddamn thing I heard in my life." Neither man could have predicted that the song would hit number one. Davis later claimed that Hank had promised him 25 percent of his bookings if he could get him into the Opry.

When Hank played two shows in Many, Louisiana, on April 12, 1949, dozens of people had to be turned away at the door. A couple of days later, Davis signed him to a personal-management contract and booked him on an Opry tour with Red Foley, Cowboy Copas, Ernest Tubb, Rod Brasfield, and Minnie Pearl. They started out in Houston and played in Amarillo, Texas; Oklahoma City, Dallas, and New Orleans, grossing forty-one thousand dollars in six days.

On this tour, Hank renewed friendships with Ernest Tubb and Minnie Pearl. Pearl first met Hank with Pee Wee King in 1943, and Hank had come a long way since then. She recalled, "I'd never been to the *Louisiana Hayride*, so I'd never seen him perform. They had me closing the show because I was what you call some kind of star. We walked in backstage, and I saw an entirely different Hank Williams. He had a wonderful wardrobe and a clean hat, and shiny boots. He looked great. He went on right before me, and that's the last time he ever went on before me. I told the promoter that night, 'Never again will I follow or try to follow Hank Williams.' I knew he was going to be a star."

After being admitted to the hospital several times for false labor pains, Audrey gave birth to Randall Hank Williams Jr. on May 26, 1949. He weighed ten pounds, and Audrey claimed, "He practically killed the both of us." Hank was at the hospital with Clent Holmes's wife, Mamie, and couldn't be dragged away from the delivery room door because he could hear Audrey screaming. An ecstatic Hank sent a telegram at 3:51 a.m. to Fred and Lorene Rose: "10 lb boy borned this morning at 1:45. Both doeing [*sic*] fine." Hank was extremely proud that Hank Jr. was the biggest baby in the nursery, exclaiming, "That's my son. Look how big he is already and imagine how big he's going to be!" Hank affectionately nicknamed Hank Jr. "Little Bocephus," after a stage dummy used by Roy Acuff's comic Rod Brasfield. His godmother was June Carter Cash.

Considering that Hank and Audrey's divorce had been granted one year to the day before their son's arrival, Hank Jr. was born out of wedlock. This legal technicality was resolved on August 9, 1949, when the Circuit Court of Montgomery, Alabama, amended their divorce ruling by eliminating the paragraphs that dissolved the marriage.

When Hank played his last shows on the *Hayride*, the audience wouldn't let him off the stage. Horace Logan said, "He was the first real star we had. The last show he encored 'Lovesick Blues' seven times—he could have encored it ten times, and I never let anybody encore more than seven times, to keep Hank's record. Hank left saying he was coming back, and there was never any indication that he was not coming back—it was just a question of when." Little did Hank know at the time under what circumstances he would indeed return.

"Lovesick Blues" went on to sell 148,242, copies and "Wedding Bells" sold 81,813, together bringing in royalties of over ten thousand dollars, the biggest check Hank had ever received. Money was starting to flow, and so were the accolades. *Cash Box* magazine voted "Lovesick Blues" as the Best Hillbilly Song of the Year, and *Billboard* magazine declared Hank second only to Eddy Arnold for Top Selling Folk Artist. Hank's battle to record "Lovesick Blues" was paying off in a big way. Surprising everyone but Hank himself, this very song would finally land him on the stage of the Grand Ole Opry.

7

THE GRAND OLE OPRY

"Did you know Hank Williams ain't a member, but they keep a Hank impersonator outside their door?"
—HANK III

T HE GRAND OLE OPRY EPITOMIZES THE VERY HEIGHT of success for a country performer and is the longest-running radio show in the history of country music. Debuting as *The WSM Barn Dance* on November 28, 1925, only two months after WSM went on the air, the weekly radio show has broadcast every Saturday evening since.

The idea for the show came from George D. Hay, a former newspaperman from Memphis who became the program manager of WSM. Hay came up with the name Grand Ole Opry one night after broadcasting a weekly segment of classical music when he said, "For the past hour we have been listening to music largely from grand opera, but from now on we will present 'grand ole opree.'" For many years Hay would open the show by blasting a steamboat whistle named "Hushpuckena" and declaring, "Let 'er go, boys!"

When the show first started, it showcased not only country performers, but comedians, (many in blackface), pop quartets, dancers, and harmonica players. Legendary performers over the years include Eddy Arnold, Patsy Cline, Roy Acuff, Ernest Tubb, Dolly Parton, Hank Snow, Ray Price, Chet Atkins, Minnie Pearl, Loretta Lynn, and Johnny Cash.

Even after the success of "Lovesick Blues" and "Wedding Bells," Fred Rose and Oscar Davis spent weeks trying to get Hank booked into the Opry. The Opry management team of Jack Stapp, Harry Stone, and Jim Denny were reluctant to book him, due to his reputation for drinking and missing shows. On the strength of Rose and Davis's promises that Hank would stay sober, he was finally given a guest spot on the non-networked portion of the show.

Leaving Audrey and Lyrcrecia behind in Shreveport, Hank drove to Nashville and checked in to the Hermitage Hotel, and the following night, Saturday, June 11, 1949, he made his debut on the Grand Ole Opry. His house band included Zeb Turner and Jimmy Selph on guitars, Grady Martin on fiddle, Ernie Newton on bass, and Billy Robinson on steel guitar. Hank sang "Lovesick Blues," during the 9:00–9:30 p.m. Warren Paint segment, which was hosted by Ernest Tubb. He then came back out during the Allen Manufacturing segment between 11:00 and 11:15 and sang "Mind Your Own Business."

Many have claimed to have been in the audience that night, and those who actually were jumped to their feet during the first few seconds of "Lovesick Blues." Flashbulbs started going off, girls pushed toward the stage, and legend has it that Hank did seven encores before the audience would let him leave. Hank's reception at the Grand Ole Opry guaranteed him a spot on the nationally broadcast Prince Albert segment of the show the following week.

For his June 18 return, Red Foley introduced him by saying, "Well, sir, tonight's big-name guest is making his first appearance on Prince Albert Grand Ole Opry. He's a Montgomery, Alabama, boy, been pickin' and singin' about twelve years, but it's been about the last year he's really come into his own … and we're proud to give a rousing Prince Albert welcome to the 'Lovesick Blues' boy, Hank Williams."

When Hank walked out onstage, Red said to Hank that he hoped "You'll be here for a long, long time, buddy." Hank shot back, "Well, Red, it looks like I'll be doing just that, and I'll be looking forward to it." Hank once again performed "Lovesick Blues," this time heard by tens of millions of faithful country music listeners all across the nation and Canada. At the tender age of twenty-five, Hank Williams had officially made it.

Four days after his Opry debut, he signed a two-year contract extension with MGM Records. MGM had a star on its hands and couldn't release Hank's records fast enough. His collaboration with Fred Rose proved to be the perfect combination of an accomplished tunesmith and a simple storyteller. Mitch Miller, a record producer for Columbia Records who would end up placing many of Hank's songs on the pop charts, described the team of Williams and Rose by saying, "Every good writer needs a good editor." Together they produced what many regard to be the greatest country music songs ever written.

Now that Hank had been formally hired by the Grand Ole Opry on July 11, 1949, it was time to put another band together. Naturally the first person he tried to find was Don Helms, who was now looking for work in Richmond, Virginia. When Helms's wife informed him that Hank was trying to reach him, he called Hank right away. As soon as he got him on the phone, Hank said, "You remember when I was going to Shreveport, you told me that if I ever got to the Grand Ole Opry you'd go with me? Well, have your ass here next Friday night." Helms replied, "You got it, chief." Along with Helms, Hank hired guitarist Bob McNett, bassist Hillous Butrum, and fiddle player Jerry Rivers, who had been part of Ernest Tubb's Texas Troubadours.

Staying faithful to Hank's penchant for nicknames, Helms was dubbed "Shag" due to his long hair, and Rivers, who sported a crew cut, got stuck with "Burrhead." Hillous was "Bew," because Hank loved his middle name, Buell, and Bob McNett was known as "Rapid Robert," for his ability to play a song called "Fingers on Fire." In return, the band called Hank "Bones" or "Gimly," short for "Gimly-Ass," because he was so skinny he didn't have one.

After only a few rehearsals in an empty WSM studio, the band came together quickly. Hank and his new lineup first played for Jim Denny, who could either approve of the band or insist that Hank use staff musicians. Once he heard them, he had no qualms about letting them play the Opry. Together they would become the most famous version of Hank's Drifting Cowboys. Their wages were only fifteen dollars each per show, but along with selling photos and songbooks during intermission, Hank was grossing at least $250 every Saturday night.

The Drifting Cowboys were on to something very big, and they knew it. Jerry Rivers recalled in Paul Hemphill's book *Lovesick Blues: The Life of Hank Williams,* "As we rolled out of Nashville in Hank's long blue Packard after my first Opry appearance with Hank, I sat quietly in the back knowing I had changed. In those few moments on stage, watching Hank perform and watching the audience respond, I regained a humility I'd lost somewhere along the way."

Now that Hank had made it into the Grand Ole Opry, MGM was clamoring for some new songs to release, so they booked another recording session for him in Cincinnati on August 30. Hank's favorite place to write was out on the road, telling his life story through songs that were more blues than country. When he didn't have the room to break out a guitar in the car, he'd pound out the rhythm on the dashboard and someone would help him scribble words on anything they could find. Often he would come off the road with a billfold thick with scraps of paper he had written lyrics, or just ideas, on. The band would tease him about it by saying, "Hoss, be careful, you'll fall off that billfold, break an arm, and we'll have to get us a new lead singer."

After playing a weeklong stint with Minnie Pearl, Cowboy Copas, and Ernest Tubb at the Palace Theater, Hank drove from Milwaukee to Cincinnati's Herzog Studios, where Rose once again hired Louis Innis, Jerry Byrd, and Zeke Turner to back him up.

The first song they recorded was "I'm So Lonesome I Could Cry," which was originally meant to be spoken and not sung. Hank had been worried about how the song would be received by his fans, and he tried out the lyrics on anyone who would listen. He was going to save it for a recitation session booked for January of the next year but changed his mind, saying, "I think ol' Hank needs to record this." He later claimed that this song was his personal favorite.

While his road band glumly stood around and watched, the lineup continued to record "A House Without Love," "I Just Don't Like This Kind of Livin'," and an old tune that Hank had learned from Tee-Tot, "My Bucket's Got a Hole in It," which is the only song Hank ever played a solo on. Concerned for Hank's image, Rose didn't appreciate the line "I can't buy no beer." Released on November 8, 1949, "I'm So Lonesome I Could Cry" was used as the flip side to "My Bucket's Got a Hole in It," which made it to number two on the charts. "A House without Love" completely sank, and "I Just Don't Like This Kind of Livin'" reached number five.

Within weeks of Hank's smash debut on the Opry, Audrey, Lycrecia, and Hank Jr. followed Hank to Nashville and immediately started shopping for a house. Audrey's dreams of fame and fortune were finally coming true, and before long she fell in love with a house at 4916 Franklin Road in the Oak Hill subdivision south of Nashville. It was a small three-bedroom brick ranch house, set on three acres of land several miles from the Acuff-Rose offices. Hank and Audrey bought it from W. Raymond Denney for $21,000 and closed the deal on September 3, 1949.

Audrey hired Miss Audrey Ragland, through the Nurse's Register, to be a nanny/housekeeper. Once Miss Ragland moved in, Audrey went to work on having the house made larger. The first addition included a new master bedroom, a breezeway, a den, and a two-car garage. Audrey filled it with the best in furniture, rugs, and crystal chandeliers. She decorated the house with an Oriental motif, with gold dragons and black lacquer everywhere, as well as faux waterfalls, beaded curtains, and a jukebox. Some of the seating was so ornate that Hank told his bandmates he was afraid to use it, preferring to lounge around on the floor. Now on her way to becoming the queen of Nashville, Audrey was determined to make a statement, even designing a wrought-iron railing installed at the front of the house depicting the opening chords of "Lovesick Blues."

Right after closing on the house, Hank was sent on a tour of the Northwest with Ernest Tubb and an Opry troupe. He made his first appearance in Canada on September 13 in Vancouver. Later that month, he went out again with the same troupe for a tour through California. Delighted with the ability to share the stage with his idols, Hank stated to Tubb that he had "found me a place right between you and ol' Roy Acuff." That same month, *Billboard* magazine would officially rename its "Hillbilly" music chart "Country & Western."

While in Los Angeles, Hank replaced his ill-fitting clothes with tailored outfits from Nudie's Rodeo Tailors. Nudka Cohn, known as Nudie Cohen, was born in 1902 in Russia and immigrated to the United States in 1913. Starting out as a bit actor and boxer, he found great success designing flamboyant costumes and other accoutrements for entertainers. Some of Nudie's most infamous designs include Elvis's gold lamé suit, Webb Pierce's silver-dollar-laden Pontiac, and Gram Parsons's suit for the cover of the 1969 Flying Burrito Brothers album *The Gilded Palace of Sin*. Hank became one of Nudie's first Nashville clients and would sometimes hide out at Nudie's house to dry out.

Once Hank Jr. was born, and Audrey had someone to look after him, she was bound and determined to again be part of Hank's career. On two successive Sundays in October, Hank, Audrey, and the Drifting Cowboys went into the studio and recorded eight fifteen-minute programs called *The Health and Happiness Shows*, which became Hank's first syndicated radio series. The recordings reveal how "tight" the new Drifting Cowboys had become. Hank was known to not care for guitarists who overplayed, preferring to keep the solos straightforward. He once said, "I know a lot of good guitar players who've educated themselves right out of a job." Keeping things simple had always worked for Hank, and he often reminded the band to "keep it vanilla."

As soon as the *Health and Happiness* segments were in the can, Hank and his band went back out on the road, traveling all the way north to Ontario, Canada. On November 11, 1949, he returned to Montgomery in triumph to perform with Bill Monroe. Two days later, Hank and

Audrey took off to perform in Europe with the Prince Albert Opry revue, whose lineup included Red Foley, Jimmy Dickens, Minnie Pearl, Rod Brasfield, and Roy Acuff.

The performers left Nashville on President Eisenhower's private plane, stopped in Washington, refueled in Newfoundland, and flew all night across the Atlantic. The next day they refueled in Paris and continued on to Wiesbaden, Germany, where the local band welcomed them by playing "Dixie." They visited military base hospitals, playing shows in Munich, Frankfurt, Berlin, and Vienna. The Frankfurt and Berlin shows were recorded to be played on the Prince Albert segment of the Opry. At the time, Hank and Foley had two of the most popular songs on the charts, "Lovesick Blues" and "Chattanoogie Shoe Shine Boy." After weathering a rough trip back across the Atlantic, Hank gratefully bent down and kissed the tarmac in Nashville.

Things were going so well for Hank that his manager, Oscar Davis, had dropped the rest of his clients to concentrate on him exclusively. Hank faced a grueling tour schedule. As soon as he got back from Europe, he was booked for a week at the Hippodrome Theater in Baltimore, then was to play for a Potomac River Cruise, and afterward was slated for a headlining appearance at the Roosevelt Hotel in Washington, D.C. Hank lost money gambling in Dayton, Ohio, while on his way north, and he started on a drinking bender that continued into Baltimore. Davis tried to discourage Hank's drinking by hiring a bodyguard to keep an eye on him. But Hank was extremely resourceful at sneaking alcohol. He would pay bellhops to hide miniature bottles of liquor inside pitchers of ice. Once he even convinced one of the women from a square dance troupe to hide miniature bottles in the hem of her skirt.

Everyone around him knew Hank's pattern: he would take three days to get good and drunk, and three days to recover. When Hank swayed onstage every night at the Hippodrome, Davis took him off the bill and replaced him with yodeler Elton Britt. Audrey was even summoned to fly up to Baltimore to help take care of him. Helms and McNett picked her up at the airport and later found her sitting by herself in the hotel lobby. She told McNett, "I'm so upset and discouraged; I think I've lost the love I had for Hank."

Within days Hank straightened out and managed to break attendance records with Cowboy Copas on December 16 in the Victory Room at the Hotel Roosevelt in Washington, D.C. Nine hundred people showed up, and five hundred had to be turned away. Once Audrey was back on the road with Hank, she insisted on singing with him, and this time he flatly refused. Audrey responded by storming home, and Hank followed her a few days later to celebrate his first Christmas in Nashville with his family.

Nineteen-forty-nine turned out to be a momentous year for Hank. He was the proud father of a baby boy, whom he missed greatly while on the road. He once told McNett, "You don't know what it's like to have a Bocephus waiting for you at home."

Sadly, Hank Jr. would recall only a couple of vague memories of his father from when he was a toddler. Hank Sr., who longed for a father himself, set in place a pattern of paternal neglect that would span three generations. Hank Jr. wrote, "There are pictures in my mind not quite memories of Daddy. More like snapshots, without any captions. Once, on an airplane, his long lanky frame sprawled out on the floor. He wasn't wearing a hat, and he was balding. Once at an early morning radio show in Nashville, or maybe backstage at the Opry ... I remember the place was packed and Daddy was all decked out—fit to kill—big white hat and big five-inch tie, looking good. The audience just went crazy."

Hank Sr. had finally made it into the Grand Ole Opry, had placed eight songs on the charts, had toured Europe, and was ranked the second-best-selling country singer of the year according to *Billboard* magazine.

"Lovesick Blues" had now sold two million copies and "Wedding Bells" a million. Hank's future couldn't have been any brighter, as long as he stayed clean and sober. Something he just wasn't able to do.

8

LONG GONE DADDY

"I don't know what you mean by country music. I just make music the way I know how." —HANK SR.

HANK WAS BACK IN CASTLE STUDIOS on January 9, 1950, to record "Why Should We Try Anymore," "My Son Calls Another Man Daddy," "Why Don't You Love Me (Like You Used To Do)," and "Long Gone Lonesome Blues." For this session Fred Rose didn't hire outside players, making it the first time the Drifting Cowboys got to record with Hank in the studio. The next day he recorded his first spiritually inspired recitation songs, "Beyond the Sunset," "Too Many Parties and Too Many Pals," "Everything's Okay," and "The Funeral."

Anything with Hank's name on it was quickly bought up by jukebox operators, and Fred Rose was concerned that Hank's spiritual songs would be too morose for the jukeboxes. In 1950, the jukebox operators were a very powerful force in the music industry, with more than four hundred thousand jukeboxes in service across the United States. Wesley Rose once estimated that out of 250,000 copies of Hank's records sold, 150,000 were bought by jukebox operators. Mindful of this revenue, Hank always made sure that his song titles were never more than five words so that they would fit onto the jukebox cards, and he kept the length of his songs under three minutes, twelve seconds long, the exact time it took for a record to be automatically ejected from the jukebox turntable.

To accommodate the situation, Rose convinced Hank to release these songs under the name Luke the Drifter. Once the public found out that Luke was really Hank, the songs sold regardless. Hank never hid the fact that he was Luke, often saying, "And here's a little number by one of my closest relatives, Luke the Drifter." Or, "Here's one by my half brother." Luke the Drifter gave Hank an outlet for his strict gospel upbringing and his constant quest for personal redemption. Hank truly had a big heart, and his battle with alcohol filled him with remorse.

Hank was a walking contradiction, a hard-drinking man who loved to have a good time but who had spiritual longings. He wrote about partying, love, and heartache, and also penned songs that cried for salvation and forgiveness. Recording under two names epitomized Hank's split persona. No matter how hard he fought to live the life of a God-fearing man, he constantly succumbed to the mortal temptations that everyone could relate to.

As William Gay wrote in the liner notes for the CD *Alone with His Guitar*, which was released on Mercury Records in 2000, "The voice was coming from the radio, but it had such an easy affable tone that it could have been coming from the swing at the end of the porch, just the familiar voice coming out of the summer darkness where the shadow of the climbing roses fell. All across the south, [folks] were gathered before a makeshift electronic shrine whose god was Hank Williams ... for nobody was kidding anybody. The rest were the supporting cast ... Hank was the real thing. It was rumored that he had his problems, but hell, we all had our problems. That just made him more surely one of us."

Hank's stepdaughter Lycrecia also remembered, "(Hank) thought as Luke the Drifter he could express his understanding of the pain and despair in the life of the ordinary person and maybe bring some comfort to a few of those lost souls along the way." His own included.

Calling in MGM's Frank Walker to listen in on the session, Rose concentrated on the "Hank Williams sound," teaching Don Helms the golden rule of playing with Hank. Helms stated, "Fred said it was useless for me and Hank to be in the same register. 'When Hank is singing something low why don't you play something high, and if he's singing high, you play something low,' so the steel was always in a different register." Rose also instructed Jerry Rivers to fiddle double-stop style, meaning the harmony and the melody were played on two strings. Hank played rhythm on acoustic guitar, which Rose discouraged him from doing. He wanted him to just focus on singing, but playing the guitar helped Hank keep time, so he stuck with it.

Bob McNett was in the studio when they recorded "The Funeral," although he didn't play on it. He remembered that by the time they were finished, Helms and Hank were both crying. He said, "I've formed an opinion of Hank over late years that I had never thought of when I was working with him. Hank had a deep personal feeling for his fellow man. This didn't show on the outside. You had to get to know him, and then he'd give himself away every now and again about his deep concern for people who were less fortunate. 'The Funeral' touched him. When he did it, he lost himself in it." The lyrics, credited to Hank and sometimes to Fred Rose, are particularly heart wrenching, depicting the death of an African American boy and how he will be lovingly cared for in heaven.

"Long Gone Lonesome Blues" was the kissing cousin of "Lovesick Blues," something Hank had been working on for some time. Hank had set out on a fishing trip on the Tennessee River with songwriter Vic McAlpin but was unable to sleep on the drive there, instead working out the lyrics to the new song. After the men got into the water, Hank was still preoccupied with the lyrics, and McAlpin said, "You come here to fish or watch the fish swim by?" Hank replied, "That's it, that's the first line!" All of a sudden the song just came together, with McAlpin coming up with a few lines, which Hank bought from him.

The song did exactly what Hank thought it would do. It shot straight to number two when it was released on March 25, 1950, and stayed there until April 29, when it bumped Red Foley's "Chattanoogie Shoe Shine Boy" out of the number-one position, and it remained on the charts for twenty-one weeks. In less than a year, Hank had followed up his smash hit "Lovesick Blues," which had sold 150,000 copies by the end of the summer. In comparison, "Too Many Parties and Too Many Pals" sold 20,000 copies and "The Funeral" sold only 6,600, results not surprising to anyone who knows that sinning has always been more profitable than salvation.

"Too Many Parties and Too Many Pals" was shockingly progressive for the times, considering that in it, Hank defends ladies of ill-repute by stating, "If she drinks, well you taught her and, if she smokes you showed her how. So gentlemen do you think you have the right to condemn her now? … For every fallen woman why, there's a hundred fallen men."

As Hank's star rose, so did Audrey's frustration. Unable to fulfill her dreams through Hank, she managed to get herself a record deal with Decca after they missed snagging Hank away from MGM. Hank and the Drifting Cowboys backed Audrey up in the studio while she sang seven tunes. Three were her own compositions ("I Like That Kind," "Model-T-Love," and "My Tight-Wad Daddy"), and two were religious songs by Hank ("How Can You Refuse Him Now" and "Help Me Understand"). The set also included "What Put the Pep in Grandpa," a song about a medicinal product, Hadacol, which was laced with alcohol, and Audrey's own version of "Honky Tonkin'." Predictably, her record didn't sell very well and the critics had a field day.

Compounding the strain their marriage was already under, Hank hid in the bottle, and Audrey took to running around in retaliation for Hank's indiscretions while out on the road. She often locked Hank out of the house if she knew he was coming home drunk, so one night he fell asleep with a lit cigarette at the Tulane Hotel, setting his room on fire. Hank was accustomed to reminding the band, "Just don't tell Ordrey," and many times they would drop him off at a sanitarium in Madison, just north of Nashville, while on their way back from touring. Most of them had families of their own and couldn't take him home with them.

Helms recalled how Hank would wake up on his way to the sanitarium compound, which consisted of a row of small stone cottages each outfitted with a cot, a toilet, and barred windows. As soon as he would see the place, he would say, "Oh, no, not the hut! Not again!" Before long he would sleep, eat, and enjoy the comic books and candy bars Helms would leave for him. After a couple of days, he would be ready to hit the road again, saying to Helms, "Reckon when they're gonna let us out?" and Helms would reply, "*We* ain't in, hoss."

Helms, who worked with Hank the longest and knew him the best, defended Hank's drinking problem in Paul Hemphill's book *Lovesick Blues: The Life of Hank Williams*. "Nobody could have had that kind of career, drunk. He was sober ninety-eight percent of the time, but when he started drinking it was over. The thing is, he couldn't have just a drink. A couple, and he was drunk. Everything he did, in fact, was bad for him: the drinking, the smoking, not eating. He wasn't a pill-head or junkie, but if he read on a label where it said to take one pill every four hours he'd take four pills every hour, figuring it would work four times faster. They never saw Hank drunk in the studio, and they usually managed to get him off the stage before he'd get into trouble."

Hank III said the same thing. "How [Hank Sr.] wrote those songs, getting up at 5:30am and having a great singing voice on the Mother's Best shows. It is unbelievable the hours he kept, especially when he was doing the radio shows. Just try to sing when you're just waking up. Or be happy and cheerful, and energetic. All those things, that's when it starts getting pretty complicated. It makes you wonder how he was pulling it off, and being an alcoholic and drug addict. If he was wasted all the time that much work wouldn't have been done.

"Many people around him have said that. If he was drunk all the time, he wouldn't have been able to do all that writing, and he was never messed up when he went in the studio. Plus, you consider most of his songs were recorded within a couple of hours. And he only had one shot."

With all the radio shows, and the recordings, and the touring, Hank Sr. lived three lifetimes in his twenty-nine years. Hank III agreed, "Absolutely. When you see that much work and energy coming out of it, it's pretty hard to grasp. As far as being a musician, with his addictions, and all those things, it's *beyond*, that's for sure."

Considering all of his personal strife, Hank never forgot his friends who had helped him along the way, in particular his old pal Braxton Schuffert, who was still working for Hormel Meats in Montgomery. Every time Hank traveled through Montgomery, he would try to convince Schuffert to get back into the music business. He was determined to help him, and in January 1950 Hank bought a train ticket for Schuffert to come to Nashville and audition for Fred Rose. After playing several tunes, including Hank's "Teardrop on a Rose," they were asked to write something together, and while sitting on the settee at Hank's house they came up with "Rockin' Chair Daddy." That evening Rose came back to hear their new song and signed Schuffert on the spot. Schuffert quickly released four songs under the name Braxton Shooford.

It was the middle of June before Hank went in to record during a half session. This time he covered a Leon Payne song, "They'll Never Take Her Love from Me," and made his third attempt at recording "Honky Tonk Blues." "Why Don't You Love Me (Like You Used to Do)" replaced "Long Gone Lonesome Blues" in the number-one position, but "They'll Never Take Her Love from Me" stopped at number five. Hank's fans were making it clear that they preferred his up-tempo honky-tonkin' songs to his more heartfelt numbers.

This preference was fine with Hank, since the money was flowing in and he was enjoying every penny of it. After all his years of struggling, he was finally able to indulge his passion for fishing and hunting, buying a dozen fishing poles and enough weaponry to launch a war. Hank loved guns so much that he would look up local police officers on the road to buy up their personal collections, including antique pistols. Hank added to his family's already established stable of horses by buying Lycrecia a black-and-white pony for her ninth birthday. He also bought a green limousine for himself and a yellow-gold convertible for Audrey. Hank had declared that no married woman had any business driving a convertible, and Audrey made sure she always drove one after that.

Don Helms remembered Hank coming over just after he bought his new cars. Helms had also just bought himself a new car and a new house. Being able to buy whatever he wanted humbled Hank, and he said to Helms, "Shag, we've come a hell of a long way, haven't we?" Helms explained to Lycrecia many years later, "[Hank] never stopped to put in perspective how big he was getting at the time. He just knew he had money coming in and a big handful was a lot of money and a little handful was a little money. That's the way he put it."

Bob McNett left the Drifting Cowboys to start a band with his brother and was replaced by Sammy Pruett, who originally played with Hank back in 1944. Hank also said good-bye to his manager, Oscar Davis. For a while Hank booked himself, an approach that culminated in a disastrous date at the July Fourth Watermelon Festival in DeLeon, Texas. Hank was scheduled to play at 10:00 that morning, but he didn't show up until midafternoon, too drunk to get out of his limo. The local police handcuffed a man who claimed to be Hank's personal manager to the steering wheel of the car and dragged Hank up onstage. Hank was practically falling to his knees, so the men let him go and he staggered back to his ride while the audience booed.

After this fiasco, a sad reminder that he had enough trouble handling himself without the added pressure of booking his own dates, Hank signed a deal with promoter A. V. Bamford, who immediately sent him out on another tour through Arizona and Texas with Ernest Tubb and Minnie Pearl.

By August 31, 1950, Hank was back in the studio to record "Moanin' the Blues," with Jack Shook playing the rhythm on acoustic guitar and big-band drummer Farris Coursey playing the snare with brushes, only one of two songs that Hank ever recorded using drums. The second song was "Nobody's Lonesome for Me," followed by two songs released as Luke the Drifter: "Help Me Understand" and a song written by Fred Rose called "No, No, Joe," a direct message to Joseph Stalin.

Now Hank had two new major competitors to battle with on the charts. First was Hank Snow, whose first hit, "I'm Moving On," spent twenty-one weeks at number one, setting an all-time record in country music. Snow had also stolen Hank's bassist Hillous Butrum after the disaster in Texas. The other newcomer was Lefty Frizzell, whose song "If You've Got the Money, I've Got the Time" shared top billing with "Moanin' the Blues." Hank still beat out the both of them to rank as the third-best-selling artist of the year, coming in right behind Red Foley and Eddy Arnold.

While Hank was away on tour, Audrey, who was pregnant again, chose to have an abortion performed in her home. An infection set in, and Hank was called off the road to come see her in the hospital. He brought flowers and jewelry with him, and when he went to kiss her, she turned away and yelled, "You sorry son of a bitch! It was you that caused me to suffer this." Hank's response was, "That woman's got a cold, cold heart," giving him the idea for yet another song about love gone wrong.

Comparable to today's stars reading about their dirty laundry in the tabloids, Audrey's marriage troubles were being exposed in songs for the whole world to hear. Especially since her idea of being an entertainer in the music business wasn't working out the way she had hoped it would. Helms claimed she never demanded to sing with Hank but would be ready to go on if he called her out onstage.

Jim Denny's wife, Dollie, once told Lycrecia how one Saturday afternoon Hank and Audrey had had an argument, and Hank called Jim Denny to say he didn't want Audrey on the show that night. "Then, by the time showtime came around, they'd made up, so he had to call back and say she was on again. And that's the way it was. Whatever Hank wanted. If he wanted her, she was there; if they were on the outs, she wasn't. He didn't think she had the greatest voice in the world, but she loved to do it. That was a form of punishment, you see. If he said, 'No, you can't sing tonight,' well she didn't get to sing. It was just that simple because he had the upper hand there."

Four days before Christmas, Hank recorded "Dear John" and "Cold, Cold Heart," with Jerry Rivers, Don Helms, and a new guitarist in town by the name of Chet Atkins. He also cut two more Luke the Drifter songs, "Men with Broken Hearts" and "Just Waitin'." "Men with Broken

Hearts" was, in Hank's own words, "the awfulest, morbidest song you ever heard in your life."

"Cold, Cold Heart" was yet another testament to how his marriage to Audrey was failing. Everyone knew this song was going to be another hit for Hank, but no one realized at the time just how big it was going to be.

9

COLD, COLD HEART

"It had to have been hard on him, coming home from touring, in severe back pain and watching Audrey get dressed up to go out on the town." —HANK III

HANK BEGAN ONE OF THE BIGGEST YEARS of his career by headlining a New Year's Eve bash in Indianapolis that drew over sixteen thousand people. As always, A. V. Bamford kept him out on the road, touring with Little Jimmy Dickens through Oklahoma and Texas. Hank had great respect for Dickens and nicknamed him "Tater," after his song "Take an Old Cold Tater (and Wait)." Dickens remembered flying with Hank and Minnie Pearl in her husband Henry Cannon's plane. He claims Hank wrote "Howlin' at the Moon" and "Hey, Good Lookin'" while on a flight to Wichita Falls, Texas.

Dickens was amazed at how fast Hank would come up with lyrics. When an idea came to him, Hank would write it down in ten or fifteen minutes, saying, "Got a piece of paper, Tater? Write this down." Hank once said about his ease with the written word, "If a song can't be written in twenty minutes, it ain't worth writing."

Dickens also marveled at the way Hank was a master at pleasing his fans, describing how all Hank had to do was bow his legs and bob his head and the audience would go wild. He also liked to wear his suits loose, with a dress tie that he would tie to one side, deliberately trying to look a bit disheveled. Hank was smart enough to know that his audience related to him being a poor boy from Alabama who didn't always have the best of clothes. When Dickens would try to straighten his tie for him before he walked out onstage, Hank would yank it back, saying, "You're too particular."

When Hank wasn't on tour, he was in the studio, this time pre-recording seventy fifteen-minute radio shows sponsored by Mother's Best flour, with WSM announcer Louie Buck as host. Broadcast from 7:15 to 7:30 a.m., every show opened with "Lovesick Blues," and Buck would pitch Mother's Best over the instrumental backing. Hank would always feature a country song, an instrumental, a gospel number, and a long closing pitch for Mother's Best, including Hank's theme song for the product, which went, "I love to have that gal around, her biscuits are so nice and brown, her pies and cakes beat all the rest, 'cause she makes them all with Mother's Best." These shows included over forty songs Hank never recorded anywhere else. For more than fifty years these tapes went unheard, but luckily they were found and then rereleased, in 2008, revealing Hank as an unguarded twenty-seven-year-old who enjoyed laughing at himself.

"Cold, Cold Heart" was released on February 2, 1951, with "Dear John" as the B side. As predicted, "Cold, Cold Heart" made it to number one. It peaked there for a week in May, then remained on the charts for the rest of the year. What really catapulted it into the stratosphere was the trend of pop artists covering country songs. At the time, pop music was selling more records than country, and Acuff-Rose saw proof of this sales power when Frank Sinatra covered Red Foley's "Chattanoogie Shoe Shine Boy" in 1949.

According to Wesley Rose, he took "Cold, Cold Heart" to every record company in New York to pitch it for pop crossover and was told, "That's a hillbilly song, and there's no use kidding yourself otherwise." That was until he talked to Mitch Miller, who was head of pop music A and R for Columbia Records. Miller has a different version of the story, saying that it was Jerry Wexler, then a columnist for *Billboard*, who alerted him to the song. Miller felt the song was perfect for Tony Bennett, who had to be pressured into recording it. Miller said, "When I heard the song, I thought it was made to order for Tony. I thought the last four lines were particularly poetic, and so I played Hank Williams' record for Tony, with the scratchy fiddle and everything. Tony said, 'Don't make me do cowboy songs!'" Miller told him, "'Tony, listen to the words. It's only a record. If it doesn't work out, I won't put it out. I'm not here to hurt you.'"

Miller once said of Hank's lyrics, "He had a way of reaching your guts and head at the same time. No matter who you were, a country person or a sophisticate, the language hits home. Nobody I know could use basic English so effectively. Every song socks you in the gut." Hank had a more down-to-earth way of viewing himself: "You got to have smelt a lot of mule manure before you can sing like a hillbilly." Spoken like a true prophet.

On March 16, 1951, Hank recorded "Hey, Good Lookin'," "My Heart Would Know," "I Can't Help It (If I'm Still in Love with You)," and "Howling at the Moon." A week later, he and Audrey recorded two gospel songs, singing duets on "A Home in Heaven," and "The Pale Horse and His Rider." When Dickens later saw him at the Opry's Friday Night Frolic, Hank told him, "I recorded your song today, Tater," referring to "Hey, Good Lookin'." He liked to tease Dickens saying that the song was written about him. When they were about to perform together, Hank would always pull the curtain back to check out the audience, saying, "Look out there, Tater. You drew me a good crowd."

Tony Bennett's version of "Cold, Cold Heart" was recorded at the end of May and went straight to the top of the pop charts, eventually selling over one million copies. As soon as the song hit, every record label in town had to have a cover of it, including Tony Fontane and Dinah Washington for Mercury Records, Louis Armstrong and Eileen Wilson for Decca, and Perry Como and the Fontane Sisters for RCA. The song has since been covered by artists including Frankie Laine and Jo Stafford, Tennessee Ernie Ford and Helen O'Connell, Lucinda Williams, Norah Jones, the Cowboy Junkies, and Rosemary Clooney.

Watching the success of this song was a huge delight for Hank, who loved to razz Bennett about it. Bennett told Crook and Chase in 1993, "I got a call one night from Hank Williams. We had never met. I called him Mr. Williams. He said, 'Tony, what's the idea of ruining my song?'" Of course he was joking. Hank was known for playing his own recordings on the jukebox, and now he was having fun spinning Bennett's.

Starting on April 1, A. V. Bamford booked Hank on a tour with Lefty Frizzell, surprising everyone due to the fact that Hank considered Frizzell a competitor. In 1951, Frizzell had four songs in the country top ten at the same time, a record that would remain unbroken until The Beatles did it in 1964. Hank wasn't the biggest fan of Frizzell's singing and told him, "Here, boy, why don't you stay down in Texas, this is my territory up here." Frizzell shot back, "Hank, the whole damn country is the back yard of both of us, can't you realize there's enough room for all of us?" Hank replied, "Well, I was just kidding. It's good to have a little competition. Makes me realize I gotta work harder than ever, and boy you're the best competition I ever had." Hank and Frizzell became mutual fans and would stand in the wings to watch each other perform. Together they played shows in Little Rock, Arkansas; Monroe, and Baton Rouge, Louisiana; Corpus Christi, Texas; and New Orleans.

Even though Frizzell never saw Hank take a drink during their tour together, his sobriety didn't last long. Hank was sent north to Canada to play a show in Ottawa on May 8. While performing somewhere in Ontario, he fell off the stage, aggravating his back problems. Big Bill Lister, who was Hank's opening act, drove him home to Nashville. Lister was known as "Radio's Tallest Singing Cowboy," reaching over six feet seven inches tall without his boots and hat on.

When Audrey heard what condition Hank was in, she forbade Lister to bring Hank back to the house. Lister was told by Jim Denny to take Hank to the huts in Madison, but Hank didn't stay there long.

On May 21, Hank was transferred to the North Louisiana Sanatorium in Shreveport. There he complained of severe back pain and was fitted with a back brace, then discharged three days later. The brace did little for the pain and made it very difficult for him to ride in a car for long periods of time.

On June 1, he was back in the studio, where he recorded four more Luke the Drifter songs, "I've Been Down That Road Before," "I Dreamed About Mama Last Night," "Pictures from Life's Other Side," and "Ramblin' Man." Slowly he went back to touring, playing a July 4 date at a park in Huntingdon, West Virginia.

On July 15, Hank was honored in Montgomery with a "Hank Williams Homecoming Day," sponsored by the Jaycees. The event included an early-afternoon appearance at the Veterans Hospital, a parade, and a 3:00 p.m. show at the Montgomery Agricultural Coliseum, where Hank headlined along with the Carter Family, Hank Snow, Chet Atkins (who was billed as "the Teenage Tantalizer"), and Braxton Schuffert.

For some reason, Hank had forgotten to bring a guitar, so before the concert at the coliseum, Hank's cousin Walter McNeil took him to borrow a guitar from French's Music Store. When Hank offered to pay for it, they refused to take his money. When the men climbed back into the car, Hank said to Walter, "You know, I tried to buy a guitar on credit there once when I was comin' up and they wouldn't have nothin' to do with me. Now they want to give me one."

During the festivities, Hank was presented with a gold watch for his contributions as "Alabama's Goodwill Ambassador," and his mother and Audrey were both given bouquets. Hank's entire family was there, including his father, Lon, whom he had managed to forge a friendly relationship with over the years. Whenever Hank and his band were in the area, he would always make a point of stopping by Lon's for a visit.

Hank became a doting stepbrother to Lon's daughter Leila, who, when she was small, once accidentally called him a "half of my brother." Hank thought that was the funniest thing ever, and from that point on Hank referred to her as "half of my sister," even dedicating songs to her over the radio. Leila once said that Hank's favorite food was tomatoes—he would make a meal from a whole quart of them. He spoiled her with gifts like a cowgirl suit, cap pistols, a Hank and Audrey doll set, and a teddy bear she named Lum, after Hank's bass player Lum York.

While Hank was waiting backstage at the coliseum to go on, a young boy walked up to him and asked him if he could be part of the show that day. Hank told him that he already had his show worked out. The boy replied, "Aw Hank, all I do is sing your songs. Please let me sing just one song on your show today." When Hank asked him what song he wanted to do, the boy told him, "I want to sing 'Hey, Good Lookin.'" Hank said, "Well, that's my current song. I was planning on plugging that myself." The boy continued to beg him to let him play it, so Hank gave in and decided to sing something else. Allowing a young boy to sing your current hit isn't something every major star would do, but Hank let the boy sing it that day. By an even stranger twist of fate, the boy's name was Lamar Morris, and he would later end up marrying Lycrecia.

After the show, Hank took the whole band to his favorite barbeque place, which was run by a black couple, where he treated everyone to sandwiches. Bill Lister remembered how as they were getting into their car, the lady came out with Hank's money clip, saying that he must have dropped it. He told her how much he appreciated that, took the clip off, and handed her back the money as he thanked her. Lister told biographer Colin Escott, "Hank didn't drop it accidentally. That was his way to give them old people a little bit of what he had. Hank helped a lot of people like that and gets very little credit for it. He was just thinking back to when he'd be hard up for a fifteen-cent sandwich."

It was true that Hank no longer had to worry about money, but his spending had become a pastime in itself, rivaled only by Audrey's. She kept adding on to their house on Franklin Road. Now it contained a chandeliered ballroom, seven bedrooms, six and a half bathrooms, a well-stocked bar, a fully equipped music room, and an apartment over the garage. One time, Hank and Jimmy Dickens went shopping in a store in Oklahoma City where Hank came across cufflinks that looked like miniature .45 pistols with pearl handles. When he asked how many they had, the clerk told him, "We have a lot of them." Hank replied, "That's what I want, I want a lot of them." Hank ended up buying twelve pairs of cufflinks that day and probably gave most of them away as gifts.

Hank even went out and bought a 507-acre ranch south of Nashville, in Williamson County. Adding a Tennessee walking horse, he moved the kids' ponies to the farm and hired a manager to look after the place. His dream was to refurbish the rundown farmhouse and become a gentleman rancher, but with his schedule and bad back, all he did was spend time there alone drinking and firing his guns. Audrey showed up only periodically for photo ops or to let the kids ride their horses. The only benefit was that the farm ended up being a tax write-off, making its purchase by default a good business decision.

A bigger house and a farm in the country wasn't enough for Hank. He had always envied Ernest Tubb's Record Shop, and that gave him the idea to open a western gift shop called Hank and Audrey's Corral. He rented a store two doors down from Tubbs, at 724 Commerce Street, and stocked it with $7,000 worth of records, songbooks, signed photographs, clothing, Hank and Audrey dolls, postcards, and anything else a visitor to Nashville might want. Hank and Audrey even performed there on Saturday afternoons, hoping to broadcast the shows live on WSM, just like Ernest Tubb's post-Opry shows. That plan drew so many people who wanted to hear Hank for free that the show had to be moved to the WSM studios.

Before long, the Corral became more trouble than it was worth, turning into a hangout for musicians wanting to meet and pitch their songs to Hank. Audrey hired Mac McGee to manage the store, and within a year he bought it from the Williamses. Hank hardly had time for it anyway—he played more than two hundred dates during that year alone.

Without a personal manager since parting ways with Davis, Hank hired William R. "Bill" England to handle his business affairs. England had previously worked for WSFA in Montgomery, before relocating to

Nashville. The first thing he did for Hank was to organize a collection of promotional materials to be sent out before each of his shows. He also designed advertisements promoting "The Sensational Radio-Recording Star Mr. Lovesick Blues Hank Williams with his Entire Grand Ole Opry Show." This partnership didn't last long, and right after the Homecoming in Montgomery, England returned to his old job at WSFA.

During an evening session on July 25, 1951, Hank cut "I'd Still Want You," "Baby, We're Really in Love," "Crazy Heart," and "(I Heard That) Lonesome Whistle," where Hank mimics the sound of a train whistle when he sings the word "lonesome." Hank was scheduled to go out on a six-week tour with the Hadacol Caravan, so Rose scheduled another recording session for August 10. This time Hank recorded "Half as Much" and rerecorded "Baby, We're Really in Love" and "I'd Still Want You." Rose played piano on "Half as Much," and the songwriting credit went to Hank and his friend songwriter Curley Williams. A month later, Curley recorded it himself for Columbia Records.

Over the years, Hank had given plenty of songs to other artists to record, but none of them ever saw any real success. Rose had always been sensitive regarding Hank's writing about alcohol, but Big Bill Lister's career always included a drinking song. When Lister asked Hank for help to come up with something to follow his "Beer Drinking Blues," Hank told him, "Don't worry 'bout it, Big un, I got you covered. I got one that's hotter'n a pistol." The song he gave him was called "There's a Tear in My Beer," and Hank recorded a demo of it the night before Lister recorded it. This single tape would turn into a momentous discovery for Hank Sr.'s fans and family. It became a number-one hit for Hank Jr. and gave the world a song by Hank Williams Sr. that no one had ever heard before.

Right after recording the song himself, Lister threw Hank's demo acetate into a box of records at his house. After resigning himself to the fact that his career wasn't going to take off, Lister moved back to San Antonio, taking the box of records with him. For several years the box sat under a tarp in his yard before being moved to a loft in his house that got hot enough during the summer to fry eggs. A couple of decades later, Lister came across the box while cleaning house and found Hank's demo recording. Lister's son had worked on some guns for Hank Jr., who had inherited his father's passion for weaponry. The next time Hank Jr. came through San Antonio, they gave him the acetate, saying, "Here's one they ain't never heard your daddy do."

Hank Jr. took it back to Nashville and, in September of 1988, over-dubbed himself onto the recording. He also shot a video of the song superimposing himself onto a performance of his father's. Video engineers had to slow down the footage of Hank's singing to match the tempo of the song, and new lip movements were pasted on Hank's mouth by an actor who lip-synched the words. Hank Jr. was superimposed over four thousand frames that lasted forty-six seconds, creating the "duet" with his late father. "There's a Tear in My Beer" became a hit for Hank Jr., who gave some of the song's revenue to Lister. He also flew Lister to Nashville to appear on TNN and awarded him with a gold record.

The success of Bennett's version of "Cold, Cold Heart" had started a whole new trend for Hank. Before the end of the year, Polly Bergen and Theresa Brewer had both covered "Honky-Tonkin'," Kay Starr recorded "Lovesick Blues" for Capitol, and Guy Mitchell did "I Can't Help It (If I'm Still in Love with You)" for Columbia Records, prompting *Billboard* to report that Hank had "blossomed out as a full-fledged pop writer."

Asked to play the last of the great traveling medicine shows by his friend Dudley LeBlanc, Hank was sent out to headline the Hadacol Caravan, a tour by train through eighteen states across the South and Southwest. Hadacol was a "patented medicine" that was actually an elixir laced with alcohol. LeBlanc had already lost two million dollars that year, and the government drug enforcers were breathing down his neck. Little did the performers know that this tour was his final attempt to salvage his company.

Hank, his Drifting Cowboys, and Big Bill Lister drove to Lafayette, Louisiana, in mid-August to meet up with the Caravan. There they did a full dress rehearsal with over 150 entertainers and crew members, including beauty queens and circus acts. Hank was paid to live on the train, which included nineteen air-conditioned Pullman cars, and perform forty consecutive one-night stands. In the larger cities some of the biggest stars in the entertainment business would stop by, including Jack Benny, Rudy Vallee, Cesar Romero, Tony Martin, Jimmy Durante, Milton Berle, and Bob Hope.

Jerry Rivers questioned how they would fit into a medicine show, writing in his own book, *Hank Williams: From Life to Legend*, "At first I wondered where a Tennessee fiddler would fit into all this, but I soon learned that once again I was underestimating Hank Williams' booming popularity and uncanny hypnosis of even the largest audience."

No matter who was performing, the crowds would scream so loudly for Hank that no one wanted to follow him onstage. When they played in Louisville, Kentucky, Bob Hope was paid a reported ten thousand dollars to close the show. After Hank walked off, the audience screamed so loudly, the emcee couldn't introduce Hope. Eventually Bob Hope was brought out, unannounced. As soon as he could be heard, Hope pulled a cowboy hat down over his ears and said, "Good evenin', folks, this is Hank Hope."

Afterward, Hope grabbed LeBlanc and made him promise never to make him "follow this Hank Williams again."

No expense was spared on this tour. The performers enjoyed steak dinners, laundry services, and plenty of free refreshments. The total cost of the Caravan was running close to ten thousand dollars a day and totaled over one million dollars by the end of the tour.

When Braxton Schuffert showed up to visit Hank when the train came through Montgomery, he found Hank was pretty unsatisfied with how things were going. Schuffert remembered in Lycrecia's book that he sat down beside Hank and asked him how he was doing. Hank told him he wasn't doing very well at all. It was right about sundown, and Hank said, "You know, this is the lonesomest time of the day." Schuffert pointed out all the beautiful dancers and movies stars walking around, saying, "Boy, what are you talking about being lonesome? All these pretty women on the train, and you're lonesome?" Hank said, "I don't want to have nothing to do with them folks. They think they're better than I am." Schuffert replied, "Hank, don't you never think that. You're better'n every one of them that walked by." Hank pulled out a pink check from LeBlanc for 7,500 dollars, saying, "Looky here, Brack. Everybody on the train has got one of these checks that just bounced and came back."

The Caravan played its last date in Dallas, just short of the original plan to play forty days straight. LeBlanc ended up selling his interest in Hadacol to the Tobey Maltz Company in New York, which eventually filed for bankruptcy.

During the Caravan tour, Hank kept up his appearances at the Opry, flying back and forth to Nashville to perform every Saturday night. His constant touring and recording was taking a toll on both his health and his home life. Schuffert remembered one time Audrey and Hank Jr. drove out to say good-bye to Hank, and as soon as Hank Jr. saw his father, he started to climb out the driver's-side window of the car. Hank just grabbed him and held him while tears streamed down the boy's face, before handing him back to Audrey so he could take off again.

A WSM engineer once remembered that one time Hank left Nashville for Jackson and realized halfway there that he had forgotten to say good-bye to Hank Jr., so he turned around and drove all the way back. Ernest Tubb also recalled the time he, Minnie Pearl, and Hank played the Tri-State Fair in Amarillo, Texas. Hank had bought every stuffed animal he could find, barely leaving enough room in the car for the band to sit. Tubb said, " 'Hank, that kid ain't big enough to play with them,' 'cause Hank had a stuffed dog as big as a man, but he worshipped that boy. Never knew a man worshiped a child like that. He just couldn't buy enough things for Bocephus."

Hank was so proud of his son, and had a hard time reconciling the fact that he couldn't spend much time with him. Little did anyone know that Hank Williams didn't have that much time left at all.

10

WHY DON'T YOU LOVE ME LIKE YOU USED TO DO?

"If you really want Audrey back, get a haircut, buy a new suit, wash your face and throw that damn whiskey bottle out the window, and become a man that she would be proud to have back." —FRED ROSE

HANK HAD CONQUERED THE OPRY, topped the country and pop charts, and drawn thousands of fans wherever he went. He was so popular that the police would have to guard his door whenever he stayed in a hotel. One time he tried to go out wearing a disguise of an overcoat, hat, dress shoes, and sunglasses. He only made it half a block before the first person he passed said, "Hi, Hank, how ya doin'?"

The next logical step for someone of Hank's caliber would have been a film career, and on September 24, 1951, the *Nashville Banner* announced that MGM's Joe Pasternak had signed Hank to a four-year movie contract. *Billboard* reported that Hank was to "get straight dramatic and singing roles in featured dramatic and musical productions. It's estimated that his salary will be graduated from three thousand to five thousand dollars per week if he makes good." Hank's movie debut was to be a co-starring role with Esther Williams in "Peg o' My Heart."

Between touring through Georgia, Alabama, Mississippi, Pennsylvania, Michigan, and Ohio, flying back to Nashville every weekend for the Opry, and performing his early-morning Mother's Best radio shows, there wouldn't be enough of Hank left to make it to the silver screen. Besides, Hank wasn't completely sold on becoming a movie star. When he flew to Hollywood to meet with Pasternak, the movie executive asked him if he had any hair, to which Hank replied, "Hell, yes, I have a dresser drawer full of it." Audrey had pushed Hank into wearing a toupee to hide his thinning crown, but he didn't tolerate that nuisance for very long.

Luckily he had no problems with TV, and Hank made his first national television appearance on *The Perry Como Show* on November 14. Hank sang "Hey, Good Lookin'," and the following week, Como opened the show with his own version of the song and then apologized to Hank afterward.

Hank's back had been giving him trouble for too long, and the final straw was accidentally falling into a ditch while hunting with Jerry Rivers, causing him excruciating pain. Unable to endure it any longer, Hank agreed to let Dr. George Carpenter and Dr. Ben Fowler at the Vanderbilt Medical Center perform surgery. Hank had a mistrust of people in general and definitely did not have a lot of faith in big-city doctors. At first he checked into St. Jude's in Montgomery, feeling more comfortable there, but was referred to Vanderbilt. He later said he told his doctors, "Cure me or kill me, Doc. I can't go on like this."

Right before being admitted into the hospital, Hank went into Castle Studios to record, which would be the last session to include all of the Drifting Cowboys. This time Hank cut an old song, "Let's Turn Back the Years," from his 1946 WSFA songbook, along with another try at "Honky Tonk Blues." Rose had originally held back on releasing that song, concerned that it would be confused with "Honky Tonkin'." "Honky Tonk Blues" finally came out in February of 1952 and was backed by "I'm Sorry for You, My Friend," written by Hank for Lefty Frizzell.

Only days after his grueling back surgery, Hank insisted on being moved home for Christmas Eve, which wasn't the best idea. Especially when he and Audrey got into a fight over this decision and Hank threw a chair at her, aggravating his condition and sending him back to Vanderbilt. His recuperation also wasn't helped by the fact that Hank was forced to record an apology to audiences in Washington and Baltimore for missing two concerts due to his surgery. What the promoter really wanted was proof that Hank didn't miss the shows because of his drinking.

In the message to his fans, Hank sadly explained his surgery and how much pain he had been in, saying, "On December thirteenth, I had to have an operation that I'd been putting off for about a year. ... The first and second vertebrae was no good, it was just deformed or broken when I was a child, or wore out or something. ... So he went ahead and fixed it, so after I came to, after the anesthetic wore off he told me it'd be impossible for me to be out of here before the first of February."

Jim Denny hired Jimmie Davis to take Hank's place, booking Audrey to come in and sing with the Drifting Cowboys and then play Hank's message to the fans. On December 29, Audrey accused Hank of physically attacking her, moving herself and the kids to their friends the Garretts' home. When she returned home that Sunday to pack for her trip, Hank fired a gun four times as she left the house. Audrey recalled, "I could hardly walk. I was scared to death. Thinking back, I don't know if he was shooting at me, or wanting me to think that he was shooting himself. Anyway, I went on to Washington, and New Year's Eve night I called him and said, 'Hank, I will never live with you another day.'"

When Kitty Wells, along with Johnnie and Jack, stopped in on Hank, they found the screen door of the house riddled with bullet holes and one of his guitars, smashed, out on the porch. Hank was in extreme pain, both physically and emotionally. His back surgery had made his condition worse. Audrey was done with him. It seemed the harder Hank worked, the faster everything was falling apart.

The year-end edition of *Billboard* named "Cold, Cold Heart" the top country song of the year, which epitomized where Hank's life was at. Even though he was suffering greatly in his life, the songs that came from his personal pain couldn't have been doing better.

At Audrey's request, Hank moved out of their house on Franklin Road on January 3, 1952. At first he stayed at the Andrew Jackson Hotel and then moved back to Lillie's boardinghouse in Montgomery for a couple of weeks. While he was staying with his mother, he called Lon and asked him to come pick him up. When Lon finally got there, Hank was being taken to St. Jude's Hospital on a stretcher. The doctors told Lon that Hank had overdosed on painkillers and would have to stay until the drugs were completely out of his system.

When he recovered, he moved in with Ray Price, who had rented a house at 2718 Westwood Avenue. Hank lived in the downstairs, while Price took the upstairs. Hank and Price had become fast friends when they met backstage at one of the Opry's Friday Night Frolics show. While traveling to a date in Evansville, Indiana, Hank and Price wrote "Weary Blues from Waitin," Hank taking the copyright for the song and Price recording it. Shortly after moving in with Price, Hank began seeing an attractive blonde by the name of Bobbie Jett. Bobbie was less than a year older than Hank and was working as a secretary in Nashville. She had been raised by her grandparents after her mother left her to move to California and, just like Audrey when he met her, was a single mother, with a daughter named Jo.

On January 10, Audrey filed for divorce from Hank for the second and last time. Alleging physical abuse, Audrey claimed that "cohabitation was unsafe and improper," asking for a full disclosure of Hank's income so he could provide for child support for Hank Jr. and separate maintenance for her. Hank countered her complaints by stating that her "extravagant living and carousing" required him "to keep [his] nose to the grindstone continuously to keep the bills paid." Hank also claimed he had proof of her infidelity, stating that she had become pregnant while he was away on tour and confirming that she had had an abortion in September of 1950, which led to an infection that required treatment at St. Thomas' Hospital. The document concluded with a request for custody of his only son.

Not wanting to keep the Drifting Cowboys on salary during his recovery, Hank had let the band go, and most of them found positions elsewhere. Without his band or Audrey to answer to, Hank started mixing alcohol with too many painkillers. On top of that, he wasn't eating properly or sleeping much. Hank was thin as a rail and looked much older than his twenty-eight years. As soon as he could, he went back out on the road, playing two dates at the Mosque in Richmond, Virginia, on January 29 and 30. Ray Price performed with him and practically had to do the first show by himself because Hank was too sick to handle it. After the first night, Edith Lindeman, a reporter for the *Richmond Times-Dispatch*, wrote a critique of Hank's show, and on the second night, Hank dedicated "Mind Your Own Business" to her. He may have been in a lot of pain, but at least his sarcasm was intact.

Hank and Price continued through Charleston, South Carolina, and Macon, Georgia, but after the Macon show, Hank disappeared. Price believes he went out to the West Coast, judging from a phone call to Jim Denny from a banker saying that a man by the name of Hank Williams was trying to cash a check.

Hank managed to pull himself together to appear on *The Kate Smith Hour* in New York City on March 26, to sing "Hey, Good Lookin'," and with the rest of the cast he played "I Saw the Light." This is the same footage Hank Jr. would use for the video "There's a Tear in My Beer" thirty-seven years later. Don Helms recalled of playing on the *Kate Smith* show, "I remember a lot of preparation went into the show. Kate Smith and her staff gave us first-class treatment. She congratulated everyone on a great show after it was over and shook hands with us. I felt like we had really done something spectacular."

The response to Hank's appearance was so tremendous that he was asked back for a second time on April 23. For this show Hank began with the introduction, "I've got a song here that I'd like to do that has been awful kind to me and the boys, it's bought us quite a few beans and biscuits, it's the best song we've ever had ... financially. A little tune called 'Cold, Cold Heart.'" Afterward, he joined Anita Carter on "I Can't Help It (If I'm Still in Love with You)." This would be Hank's last televised performance. The only footage remaining of Hank Sr. live are his appearances on the Perry Como and Kate Smith shows. Also stored in the vaults of the Country Music Hall of Fame are home movies of Hank singing with Ernest Tubb and showing off his collection of Cadillacs.

Hank and Audrey's property settlement was concluded on April 3, granting Audrey full custody of Hank Jr., the house on Franklin Road and all of its furnishings, her yellow convertible Cadillac, and half of Hank's royalties, as long as she didn't remarry. Hank was given the clothing store, which he sold to Mac McGee in June; the farm in Williamson County; and his cars. Their divorce became final on May 29, 1952.

The second time Hank went to Tinsel Town to meet with one of MGM's biggest executives, Dore Schary, he sat with his boots on the man's desk and mumbled "Yep" and "Nope" to all of his questions. Hank was clearly unimpressed with Schary and had no intentions of trying to fit into Hollywood. The thought of becoming a movie star was something he couldn't fathom. The day before he was to report to work for MGM, a letter arrived through Fred Rose "to notify you that, for good and sufficient cause, your employment under said contract is hereby terminated." At least Hank no longer had to worry about becoming an actor.

Now that he was mixing painkillers with his drinking on a regular basis, Hank could barely keep up with his touring schedule. In late April, he flew out to California to appear in San Diego with Minnie Pearl. When she saw what condition Hank was in, she tried to convince the promoters that he was too sick to work. During the intermission, they took him out for a drive to try to sober him up. Pearl remembered, "We started singing. He was all hunkered down, looking out of the side of the car, singing, 'I Saw the Light,' and then he stopped and he turned around, his face broke up and he said, 'Minnie, I don't see no light. There ain't no light.'"

From April 29 through May 2, Hank performed with an Opry package show that included Ernest Tubb, Carl Smith, and the Carter Family.

They played concerts to sellout crowds in Corpus Christi, Beaumont, and Houston, Texas. Hank was in no shape to be on the road, but that didn't stop his promoter from booking him into Las Vegas at the end of May.

Most of his band had left him, but Don Helms and Jerry Rivers were still around, and they drove Hank to his two-week engagement at the Last Frontier Club. Jim Denny sent along Charlie Sanders, an ex-policeman, to keep an eye on him. Locking him in his room between performances didn't keep him from drinking, since Hank figured out a way to lower his boots down to the ground using a bed sheet and paid a bellboy to fill them with bottles of liquor. Within five days, his two-week appearance in Las Vegas was canceled. Hank, no more comfortable in Vegas than he was with becoming a movie star, was relieved to be let out of his contract.

After miraculously completing a successful tour through Illinois and Indiana, Hank went back into the studio in Nashville for his first recording session in six months. On June 13 he laid down "Settin' the Woods on Fire," "Window Shopping," "Jambalaya," and "I'll Never Get Out of This World Alive." Hank performed "Jambalaya" for the first time on the Opry the day after he recorded it, saying, "I got a brand-new song ain't never been aired." The song was released a month later and made it to number one by September 6, then stayed on the charts until the end of the year.

A few weeks later, on July 11, Hank recorded "I Won't Be Home No More" and "You Win Again," along with two Luke the Drifter songs, "Why Don't You Make Up Your Mind" and "Be Careful of Stones That You Throw."

Hank's relationship with Bobbie Jett didn't last long, and one night while playing at the Opry, Hank ran into Billie Jean Jones, a nineteen-year-old redhead who at the time was dating Faron Young. Once Hank laid his eyes on her, he asked Young if he was going to marry her, and Faron told him no. Hank replied, "Well, if you ain't gonna marry her, ol' Hank's gonna marry her." Billie told him that she used to live four doors down from him when he and Audrey first moved to Shreveport in 1949 and had told her mother that someday she would marry Hank Williams.

In March 1952, Faron signed a record contract with Capitol Records, and his breakthrough song, "Goin' Steady," was recorded in October. It was the only time that a song Hank gave to another artist became a hit, although it was credited to Young. It's possible that Hank gave the song to Young in trade for stealing Billie Jean away from him.

Right after meeting her, Hank proposed to Billie Jean, while driving to Shreveport in August to meet her parents. In the car Hank looked over at Billie Jean and remarked, "I can say one thing baby, I could never be ashamed of you." During the trip, Hank dictated thirteen songs to her, asking her to "write this down for ol' Hank, baby." When they returned to Nashville, Hank had an old girlfriend waiting at his house for him, Audrey was refusing to let him see Hank Jr., and Bobbie Jett was claiming she was pregnant with Hank's child. Within a few days, Billie Jean packed her bags and left for home, telling Hank, "I'm going back to Louisiana. This is wrong and I don't want any part of it." Falling in love with one of country music's biggest stars was clearly not turning out to be what Billie Jean had expected.

Hank was drinking heavily, and Jim Denny advised Helms and Price to take him to the hospital to dry him out. Hank was so angry that he ordered Price to move out of the house. As Price was packing up his belongings, Hank pulled up wearing a hospital robe and told Price that he didn't really have to leave. Price told him that he couldn't take it anymore, believing that Hank was trying to drink himself to death. Hank had been diagnosed as a spree drinker, but all that meant was that he was able to keep from drinking for days at a time. His band members knew how surly he would get when he was drinking. Helms once said, "He was a pain, a real pain. If you wanted to leave, he wanted to wait, if you wanted to wait, he wanted to leave."

This was decades before the country music industry would embrace the image of a hard-drinking, fast-living outlaw cowboy. Every time

Hank missed a show or appeared drunk onstage, the squeaky-clean image of the Grand Ole Opry was at stake. For years, Hank worked every roadside honky-tonk he could get himself booked into, just to make his way to the hallowed stage of the Opry, and now it seemed that none of it mattered anymore. Audrey and the kids were gone, along with his home and half of his income. On June 12, 1952, he played "Jambalaya" and "Window Shopping" on his last night with the Opry. Feeling used and exploited, Hank complained, "They're slicing me up and selling me like baloney."

The final insult came when Hank missed an Opry performance on August 9 and two days later received a phone call from Jim Denny. Denny had warned Hank that he would be in serious trouble if he kept missing performances. Ernest Tubb remembered being in the office the day Denny made the call. Denny said, "Hank, that's it. You gotta prove to me. You call me in December, and I'll let you know about coming back to the Opry next year." When Denny hung up the phone he had tears in his eyes, telling Tubb, "I had to do it. I had to let Hank go." He later admitted that it was the toughest thing he ever had to do in his life. Johnnie Wright was at Hank's house when the call came in. Wright claims Hank said, "You can't fire me, 'cause I already quit!" Little did Hank realize that his expulsion from the Mother Church of the South would be the downward turning point of his meteoric career. Stripping him of his membership in the Opry would also spark a battle that echoed with his equally rebellious progeny.

Hank immediately had Wright drive him to the National Life Building to pick up his final paycheck. Then he packed up most of his belongings and had Wright and Wright's brother-in-law drive him to Lillie's boardinghouse in Montgomery. Don Helms and his wife, Hazel, went over to see him before he left town. Helms remarked to Hazel that he didn't expect to see Hank live another six months. Four days after his firing, Hank made an appearance at the Greenville Homecoming in front of 8,500 people. Riding in the parade in his new powder-blue Cadillac convertible, with his father Lon and uncle Robert in attendance, Hank publically acknowledged Tee-Tot, the black street musician who had taught him so much, not realizing that he had been dead since 1939.

As soon as Billie Jean was out of the picture, Bobbie Jett showed up at Lillie's boardinghouse. Lillie called Bob McKinnon, a friend who lived in Alexander City, asking him if Hank could come out to the country to rest. On the afternoon of August 17, McKinnon drove Hank and Bobbie out to a lodge on an area of Lake Martin known as Kowaliga Bay, arriving around 4:00 p.m. Hank was sober and looking forward to spending some time relaxing. By midnight, McKinnon received a phone call from the police department informing him that Hank had been arrested for running up and down the halls of the local Russell Hotel, screaming that someone was beating old ladies and he needed to stop them. McKinnon showed up and posted bail for Hank, taking him to a motel to sleep it off. He then took Bobbie back to the lodge to get her things, and she explained to him how Hank had met up with some locals the day before, who produced a five-gallon jug of liquor, and that's when all the trouble started.

The next night Hank went right back to partying at the lodge, and this time, while picking up more liquor from a bootlegger, Hank pounded out a rhythm on the dashboard and started singing, "Kowaliga, Kowaliga." That morning he called for Fred Rose to come down and help him work on songs with him. Over the next few days, Hank composed "Kaw-Liga," "Lonesomest Time of the Day," and "Your Cheatin' Heart."

In "Kaw-Liga," it was Rose's idea to make the forlorn lover a dime-store wooden Indian who falls in love with the "Indian maid over in the antique store." "Your Cheatin' Heart" turned out to be Hank's signature song—it was written about Audrey, although she spent the rest of her life refuting it.

Hank once stated about his own writing, "People don't write music, it's given to you; you sit there and wait and it comes to you. If [a song] takes longer than thirty minutes or an hour, I usually throw it away." Rose often helped Hank with his songs but rarely took credit for it. Rose once stated, "Don't get the idea that I made the guy or wrote his songs for him. He made himself, don't forget that!"

Don Helms told *Guitar Player* in November 1996 that "Hank didn't let Fred change his songs, but he would accept a better way to say 'I love you' from him. Hank would be the first to tell you that he learned a lot from Fred."

Now that Hank was off the Opry, Rose convinced the Louisiana Hayride to hire him back. "Jambalaya" had already sold two hundred thousand copies, necessitating the record plant to add on a Saturday shift just to keep up with the demand. At the end of August, Jo Stafford's version of "Jambalaya" hit the top of the charts, and *Billboard* declared Hank to be a leader of the pop field.

During Hank's career, he recorded sixty-six songs, writing fifty himself, with thirty-seven of them hitting the *Billboard* charts. That brought up Hank's total record sales of thirty-one singles to over ten million copies sold in just under five years. With "Jambalaya" at number one, Hank's record sales had still dropped from $22,574 in 1950 to $13,869 in 1952. But his income from pop covers helped to balance that out by rising from $18,040 in 1950 to $55,044 in 1952.

The Opry's loss was the Hayride's gain, and the *Shreveport Times* announced on August 30 that Hank Williams had signed a three-year contract. In September, Hank sold his farm for $28,500, less than half of what he paid for it, cutting his final ties to Nashville—except for to his son, Bocephus. Hank Jr. would do the same in the 1970s, and Hank III has been in a constant struggle with being accepted into Nashville's music community, continuing a battle waged by three generations of Williams men in the very city they helped build.

Before Hank left for Shreveport, he called Billie Jean and talked her into joining him there. He had asked her to marry him, and he was serious about it. Once they found a place to stay, Hank tried to put together another version of the Drifting Cowboys, but this time it just didn't work. When he toured, he ended up using a house band or sometimes Red Sovine's band, which at the time included guitarist Tommy Bishop, steel guitarist Jimmy Day, and pianist Floyd Cramer. Similar to how Chuck Berry never used his own band, Hank figured everyone knew his songs well enough that he didn't have to work them in anymore. Once onstage, to start the band off he would say, "Gear of C, boys," and the last verse would be signaled by the lift of his foot.

Making a brief appearance on the Hayride on September 13, Hank played "Jambalaya," "Honky Tonk Blues," "Lovesick Blues," and a song he hadn't recorded yet called "I Could Never Be Ashamed of You." The crowd was so thrilled to have him back that their applause kept him onstage for twenty minutes. Hank promised to come back to sing every week, and a week later he made his official return to the Hayride in three years.

On his twenty-ninth birthday, Hank performed in front of a record audience at Charlie Walker's club, the Barn, in San Antonio, Texas. Walker had arranged for a birthday cake to be brought out at the end of the night. It was decorated with the notes to "Jambalaya," and written around the edge were the words "Happy Birthday Hank from All Your Friends." Hank was so overcome by this gesture that he cried. At the end of the night, a three-hundred-pound oil field worker burst into Hank's dressing room after the show, trying to attack him. Billie Jean's brothers were able to protect him, but it was an eerie occurrence considering it would be Hank's last birthday.

Hank went back into the studio for the last time in Nashville on September 23, 1952, to record "Your Cheatin' Heart," "Kaw-Liga," and "I Could Never Be Ashamed of You," the song that he had written for Billie Jean. To finish off the session, Hank cut one of the best songs Fred Rose ever wrote for him, "Take These Chains from My Heart." "Kaw-Liga" needed a drummer, and Rose brought in Farris Coursey, who had also played on "Moanin' the Blues." Hank is best known for songs that spoke of real heartbreak, but he also had a great sense of humor, evident in "Kaw-Liga," about a wooden Indian in love with an Indian maid "over in the antique store," who loses her because his heart is "made of knotty pine."

All four songs were recorded in less than three hours, and "Your Cheatin' Heart" would become Hank Williams's signature song. He once told Braxton Schuffert," "Brack, I just wrote a song and recorded it, and it is the best song I ever wrote." Schuffert insisted, "Hank, it'll never beat 'Cold, Cold Heart.'" Hank replied, "Yeah, this is the best one," as he started singing the words to "Your Cheatin' Heart."

Billie Jean claimed he wrote it on their drive to Shreveport in August, and it was definitely written about Audrey. Not surprisingly, Audrey spent the rest of her life declaring that Hank had written it about himself. The song is a testimony to how much the two had hurt each other, and once apart, Hank and Audrey would never again find a love like the one they had shared together.

11

I'LL NEVER GET OUT OF THIS WORLD ALIVE

"Hank was different things to different people. A lot of people liked him because they liked his songs. Some of them liked his sincerity, and some of them liked him because he was skinny." —DON HELMS

WHILE BILLIE JEAN DID PUBLICITY for their impending marriage, Hank played shows in Oklahoma City on October 13 and 14. The next day he flew back to Montgomery to sign legal papers taking responsibility for his and Bobbie Jett's baby. The document stated that "Hank Williams may be the father of said child" and provided for medical expenses, Bobbie's room and board in Montgomery, and a one-way plane ticket to California one month after the baby was born.

The child was to be placed in the care of Lillie and Bill Stone for the first two years, with Hank paying for a nurse. The agreement gave both Hank and Bobbie visitation rights, and beginning on the child's third birthday, Hank would assume custody until his or her fifth birthday. After that point, custody would be shared, with Hank having the child during the school year and Bobbie having custody during the summer months. Even though the agreement questioned Hank's paternity, it is doubtful he would have signed such a paper if he were truly uncertain that he was the father.

Billie Jean finally filed for divorce from her first husband, Harrison Eshlimar, and went on tour through South Carolina and Georgia with Hank and her ex-boyfriend Faron Young. Hank had briefly hired back Oscar Davis to work with him, and Davis came up with a way Hank could make some money off of his marriage to Billie Jean. His idea was to have them tie the knot in public at the Municipal Auditorium in New Orleans on October 19.

Two days before their wedding, Billie Jean went to court in New Orleans with her father, Judge Louis Lyons, representing her. She was told that her divorce would be final on October 28, and she could not get remarried before that. She still went ahead and exchanged vows with Hank on October 19, but their public marriage was invalid. When the court reconvened on the 28th, the judge informed Lyons that Hank and Billie Jean would need to get married again.

While Billie was busy in court, Hank was allegedly in a hotel room fighting with Audrey and his mother, who flew to New Orleans to talk him out of marrying Billie Jean. Audrey threatened that he would never see Hank Jr. again, and in his wedding photos, taken two days later, Hank appears to have a giant welt on his head. It's anyone's guess which woman clobbered him, but my money would be on Audrey.

Hank's idea of having a public wedding to spite Audrey didn't work out the way he had planned. After Hank appeared on the Louisiana Hayride on Saturday, October 18, he and Billie Jean were married privately by a justice of the peace in Minden, Louisiana. They figured if Audrey tried to disrupt the public wedding, they could say they were already married. At least they thought they were, although all three wedding ceremonies ended up being invalid, considering Billie Jean's divorce from her first husband wasn't yet finalized.

On top of that, the original minister backed out when he discovered that they had already been married by a justice of the peace. After searching around, Oscar Davis persuaded Reverend L. R. Shelton, who was from the First Baptist Church of Algiers, to fill in. Tickets were sold for prices ranging from $1.00 to $2.80, and fourteen thousand people saw Hank get married at a 3:00 rehearsal and then again at 7:00 p.m. No one from Nashville had been invited except for Audrey, who had the good manners not to show up.

The couple planned to fly to Cuba for a honeymoon, but Hank passed out in their room at the Jung Hotel that night, thanks to plenty of champagne and medication for his back. The surgery hadn't really done him any good, and now he was more dependent on painkillers than ever. Even though Billie Jean tried to care for him and saw that he was eating better, photos show Hank to be bloated, although he seemed to be happier than he had been in a long while, telling one of his Hayride costars, Paul Howard, "Billie is the best thing that ever happened to me. I was way down and she brought me up out of the ditch."

Hank was also showing signs of heart disease, complaining to Red Sovine that he had chest pains so bad that sometimes he couldn't sleep and couldn't catch his breath at night. On October 31, Billie and her brothers admitted Hank into the North Louisiana Sanatorium to dry out, and he complained again of chest pains. Incontinence started to become a problem; Hank would wet himself almost every night, regardless of whether he had been drinking or not. Clearly this was not what his young bride had in mind, and Billie Jean quickly realized she was in over her head. She desperately tried to keep Hank from drinking, but he had mastered a multitude of ways of finding alcohol when he really wanted it.

At this point in his life, alcohol was the least of Hank's problems. As bad as his drinking was, alcohol would take a back seat to something much stronger. While he was playing in Oklahoma City, he was introduced to a man claiming to be a doctor who specialized in working with alcoholics. His name was Horace Raphol "Toby" Marshall, and he treated Hank with chloral hydrate, a powerful narcotic. It was a new drug to Hank but had been around since 1860.

Chloral hydrate was potentially lethal, especially when combined with a depressant like alcohol. It was also the drug most often used to make a Mickey Finn and was particularly dangerous for anyone suffering from heart disease. Known at the time as a hypnotic sedative, it became notorious for killing a leopard that had gotten loose from the zoo in Oklahoma City three years earlier. After eating meat that had been laced with the drug, the animal soon died from a collapsed lung.

Marshall was a questionable figure at best, having done time in San Quentin for armed robbery, and an alcoholic himself. He had been paroled from the McAlester Penitentiary in Oklahoma on October 8, 1951, and started to pass himself off as a doctor with a diploma from the Chicago University of Applied Sciences and Arts, something he bought off a traveling salesman whom he had met at a gas station. But Marshall offered Hank the empathy that no real medical doctor had shown him regarding his alcoholism, and Hank put Marshall on the payroll as his personal physician, paying him three hundred dollars a week.

Hank spent most of November headlining a tour with Tommy Hill, Tommy's sister Goldie Hill, and Claude King and Red Sovine. Billie Jean went on the road with him, and he introduced his new bride at every show. He tried his best to stay sober, but one night in Opelousas, Louisiana, the crowd demanded their money back when Hank showed up drunk. The next morning his hotel was surrounded by angry fans. Nonplussed by the whole situation, Hank walked out, sat down on the sidewalk, and opened up his suitcase filled with money. As dollar bills floated up into the air, Hank laughed it off and promised to come back and make it up to them.

The folks in Lafayette weren't as lucky. Hank was so drunk that night that he staggered up to the microphone, saying, "I bet y'all drove a long way to see ol' Hank, didn't you?" When the crowd cheered, he continued, "Well, now you've seen him." Laying his guitar down on the floor, he turned around and walked offstage. That move epitomizes the original country outlaw swagger emulated by everyone from Willie Nelson to Hank Jr. and Johnny Cash.

Hank's bitterness wasn't surprising when you consider he had records in the top ten and had been a major star on the Opry for the past three years, and now he was back to playing high school gyms. His ego was taking a beating, and so was his body. Hank spent the ride back to Shreveport lying on the floor in the back seat of the car, in tears from back pain.

On November 21, "I Could Never Be Ashamed of You" hit the stores with "I'll Never Get Out of This World Alive" on the flip side. Rose had sent the tapes of Hank's latest recordings to Frank Walker at MGM, and Walker sent them out to his pop acts. Singers Frankie Laine and Joni James both cracked the top ten with their versions of "Your Cheatin' Heart," and Dolores Gray recorded "Kaw-Liga" for Decca Records, making it up the pop charts to number twenty-three in the spring of the next year. Over the years "Kaw-Liga" has also been covered by Marty Robbins, Roy Orbison, Charley Pride, Loretta Lynn, Johnny Cash, and Hank Jr.

A. V. Bamford arranged another tour of Georgia and Florida for Hank, slating him to perform with Radio Dot, Smoky Swan, and Ray Edenton; Edenton later became a well-known rhythm guitarist in Nashville. While in Florida, Hank stopped in to visit his sister, Irene, who was living in Jacksonville. After seeing how badly Hank was doing, Irene accurately predicted that she would never see her brother again. Bamford recalled Hank complaining of chest pains, but that didn't stop him from securing two more dates for Hank, in Charleston, West Virginia, on New Year's Eve and Canton, Ohio, on New Year's Day.

When Hank returned to Shreveport in late November, he was drinking so heavily that he was once again admitted into the North Louisiana Sanatorium. Over the next two weeks, Hank left the hospital to play at the Big D Jamboree in Dallas on December 6, along with a few dates in the Mississippi Gulf. Less than a week later, Hank was back in the hospital, but he left immediately to continue his binge in downtown Shreveport. By late afternoon he was arrested for being drunk and disorderly, and after bailing him out of jail, Billie Jean took him right back to the sanatorium.

Hank's recovery lasted all of two days, and on December 13, he performed on the Louisiana Hayride before taking off for a one-week tour through Texas. This time Hank was appearing with Tommy and Goldie Hill, Al Rogers, Charlie Adams, and Billy Walker. On their way to Houston, Hank groaned and slumped over in the back seat. Goldie turned around and screamed that Hank wasn't breathing. Tommy Hill pulled over and dragged Hank out of the car, carrying him around on his shoulders until he could catch his breath. Then they drove him to the Rice Hotel in Houston, where they took Hank up to his room on a stretcher. Refusing to have Hank see a local doctor, Toby Marshall wrote Lillie of Hank's condition, and she immediately flew to Texas to be with him.

Marshall was the original "Dr. Feelgood," liberally doling out medication to Hank without the slightest concern of what it was doing to him physically. Years later, both Elvis and Michael Jackson would lose their lives in pretty much the same way.

Instead of taking Hank to a hospital, Marshall shot him up, and Hank went onstage in Houston. That night the audience booed him off, and backstage he ran into Sergeant F. D. McMurry, who had hired Hank to play a benefit for the police in Beaumont a couple of months earlier. When Hank saw McMurry, he said, "Man, they're killin' me, they're killin' me. They're workin' me to death." Judging from the routine he was now living, which involved drinking, being shot up, performing, and then given downers to sleep it off, Hank knew what was happening to him, but didn't have the will or the strength to do anything about it.

Faced with shows booked every night of the week, Hank missed the first date in Victoria on Monday due to an overdose or a possible heart attack. Marshall noted that Hank was "too goofed up" to perform, so they just continued on to the next city.

While on the road, Hank tried to reach out by calling Big Bill Lister (who wasn't home), Ernest Tubb, and Jimmie Rodgers's widow, Carrie. He also ran into his old roommate Ray Price, while playing the Sportatorium in Dallas. Price's song "Don't Let the Stars Get in Your Eyes" was doing well on the charts, and Hank started to sing it as he walked up to him. Price invited Hank to spend the holidays with him, but Hank told him he didn't know what he was doing. They agreed to meet up in Ohio after Hank's concert in Canton. Regarding Nashville, Hank told Price, "I'll be back with you before you know it."

Billy Walker recalled for Lycrecia that he spent a lot of time talking to Hank on that tour, and Hank realized how sick he was. His plan was to rid himself of Marshall and check in to a place in the Bahamas to rest and recuperate. Hank had confessed to Walker that he was going to leave Billie Jean and go back to Audrey, because "he could never love no one but her." Lycrecia claims that Hank called Audrey and asked if he could come home. Audrey agreed and asked Miss Ragland to help get the house ready for him.

Hank played his last night in Texas on December 19, 1952, at Stark's Skyline Club in Austin. Tommy Hill opened the show around 8:00, followed by Charlie Adams, Goldie Hill, and then Billy Walker. Around 9:00, Hank took the stage, and instead of doing his usual thirty to forty-five minutes, he played until 1:00 a.m. During an intermission, running a temperature and sweating profusely, Hank went back into an office and was given several shots by Marshall before playing a second set. Tommy Hill recalled how Hank had put on one of the best shows he had ever seen, playing every song he knew, more than once, including some gospel numbers. Hank always relied on the songs that he grew up on. As soon as he finished, he was driven directly back to Shreveport, where he was admitted into the Highland Hospital and treated for pneumonia.

That same morning, Lillie called Horace Logan at the Louisiana Hayride and told him Hank was too sick to appear that night. As a matter of fact, she said, she was taking him back with her to Montgomery. Logan stated that he never insisted on releasing Hank from his three-year contract but asked him to only make personal appearances booked by A. V. Bamford and, considering he was being paid two hundred dollars a week, to fly into Shreveport every weekend to play on the Hayride. When Logan realized Hank was physically unable to fulfill that agreement, he granted him an indefinite leave.

Billie Jean packed up their belongings, and Lillie, Hank, and Billie drove back to Montgomery, moving into one of Lillie's boardinghouses. She now owned two and wasn't too happy with Billie when she found out that she was responsible for talking Hank out of giving her the money to buy a third boardinghouse. Hank still suffered from severe back pain, and Marshall made sure he had a prescription of chloral hydrate delivered to the house. Causing yet another argument with Billie Jean, as soon as he was able, Hank went out and bought a train set for little Bocephus, shipping it to him at the Franklin Road house in Nashville. Hank Jr. was living with Audrey, and unfortunately, Hank hadn't seen his son in months.

Just before Christmas, Hank took Billie Jean on a trip to Advance, Alabama, to visit his uncle and aunt, Taft and Erleen Skipper. That night they went to the East Chapman Baptist Church, where Hank declined their requests to hear him sing. Afterward, he played the Skippers an acetate of his latest song, "The Log Train," written about his father's days on the railroad.

On Christmas Day, Hank and Billie drove to Lon's place in McWilliams, but he was away visiting family in Selma. Hank left a cigarette lighter for his father and a five-pound box of candy for Ola and his "half-of-my-sister" Leila on the porch. It had been Lon's last chance to see Hank alive, and Lon saved the wrapping paper and box, and for years he was afraid to leave the house for fear he would miss a visit from someone he would never see again.

During that trip, Hank stopped to see the owner of the Journey's End Inn, a place he had played when he first started out. He also visited with Lon's sister Bertha and ate Christmas dinner with her family in Pine Apple before heading back to Montgomery. Two days later, Hank and Billie took in a football game at the Crempton Bowl but left early because of the cold.

On Sunday, December 28, Hank performed for 130 people at the eighth annual holiday party held at the Elite Café, for Montgomery's American Federation of Musicians Local 479. The *Alabama Journal* reported, "Another star of the show the musicians put on for themselves was a thin, tired-looking ex–country boy with a guitar. He got up and sang (or howled) a number of his tunes that started out to be hillbilly and ended up as pop numbers, played and sung by every band in the land. The boy who once worked here for eleven dollars a week in the Depression sung 'Jumbalaya' [*sic*] 'Cold, Cold Heart,' 'You Win Again,' and 'Lovesick Blues.' There was thunderous applause as he went back to his steak. He was, of course, Hank Williams."

Hank had originally planned on flying to his New Year's Eve gig in Charleston, West Virginia, but the weather reports were bad. When Billie found out he would be driving, she claims to have agreed to meet up with Hank in Nashville on January 3. Lillie recounted a different story, saying that Hank and Billie had fought over the news delivered via a phone call from Billie's father a few days earlier, stating that they weren't legally married. Lillie said Billie packed her things and moved back to Shreveport.

At first Hank had asked Braxton Schuffert to drive him to Virginia, but Brack had to be at his job at Hormel. After several other friends were unable to help him, Hank went down to the Lee Street Taxi Company. The owner, Daniel Pitts Carr, suggested as a driver his seventeen-year-old son, Charles, a freshman at Auburn University, who was home for the holidays. Charles Carr had driven Hank before, but Hank didn't particularly care for his driving technique, thinking he was a bit reckless. The young man seemed to be the only one able to take the time to make the trip, though, so Hank agreed to hire him.

The morning he left, Hank visited the chapel at St. Jude's Hospital, saying, "Ol' Hank needs to straighten up some things with the Man." He also gave his cousin Marie Glenn forty dollars to pay for the taxi and other expenses for Bobbie Jett's delivery. When he said good-bye to her, he told Marie, "Ol' Hank ain't gonna be with you another Christmas. I'm closer to the Lord than I ever been in my life."

Around 11:30 a.m., Charles Carr picked Hank up at Lillie's boardinghouse, helping him load his baby blue Cadillac with clothes, guitars, photos, songbooks, and records. Hank was wearing a navy blue overcoat, a blue serge suit, blue suede shoes, and a white hat. Right after they drove off, Hank asked Carr to turn around and go back so he could change into white cowboy boots. On their way out of town, they stopped at WSFA, where Hank got talked into attending a highway contractor's convention being held in the same hotel where WSFA had their studios.

Even though he had a few drinks at the hotel, he stopped at the office of a Doctor named Stokes for a shot of morphine for his back. Smelling alcohol on his breath, Stokes refused, so Hank talked another physician, Dr. Black, into giving him the injection. At around 4:00 p.m., Hank ran into Leo Hudson at the Hollywood Drive-In on Bell Street. Hudson was a member of the Musicians Federation and had organized the party on Sunday night that Hank had just played. Hank thanked him for a good time and asked him to drive him to West Virginia. When Hudson told him Carr was a good boy, Hank said, "But I don't trust his driving like I trust yours." Hudson was on his way to Selma and told Hank he couldn't help him out. They picked up a six-pack of Falstaff beer, and he and Charles Carr took off on Highway 31 headed north on the 650-mile drive to Charleston, for what would turn out to be Hank's last road trip.

12

THE SILENCE OF A FALLING STAR

"Kept my fingers crossed, hoped it wasn't true. But it was true. It was like a great tree had fallen. Hearing about Hank's death caught me squarely on the shoulder. The silence of outer space never seemed so loud." —BOB DYLAN

H ANK WAS IN NO SHAPE TO BE GOING BACK ON THE ROAD, and his determination in wanting to make this trip was certainly questionable. He knew he had to clean up his reputation, and perhaps playing these dates would have helped that. Carr remembers Hank being in a good mood, talking and singing as they drove north through Alabama. On the evening of December 30, Hank and Charles stayed overnight at the Redmont Hotel in Birmingham. It was unseasonably cold that night, and a snowstorm made their trip even more difficult. Shortly after the men checked into their room, a couple of female fans were invited inside, and when Hank asked them where they were from, one of them said, "Heaven." Hank quipped, "Well, in that case, you're the very reason I'm goin' to hell."

The next morning they took off early, stopping for lunch in Chattanooga, where Hank left a fifty-dollar tip and played Tony Bennett's version of "Cold, Cold Heart" on the jukebox. According to Mary Wallace, Hank asked the waitress if she had ever received that large of a tip before, and she said yes. When he asked by whom, the waitress answered, "By you, Mr. Williams."

At the rate they were going, it was obvious that Hank wasn't going to make his show in Charleston, unless he could fly the rest of the way. He had two shows booked that night, one at 8:00 p.m. and the second at 10:30. They made it to Knoxville by 1:00 p.m., drove to the airport, and found a flight leaving at 3:30 p.m. Hank asked Carr to book it for him and also had him make a phone call to Cas Walker, a DJ at WROL, telling him he would be able to make an appearance on his noontime *Dinner Bell Show*.

Hank, along with Charles Carr, boarded the plane and took off for Charleston on schedule at 3:30, but the flight was turned around due to bad weather, and they landed back in Knoxville at 6:00 p.m. Shortly after 7:00, Carr checked them in to the Andrew Johnson Hotel, where Hank had to be helped to his room by two porters. Hank ordered steak dinners for himself and Carr from room service, took a few bites, fell asleep, and rolled off the bed hiccupping, then going into a fit of convulsions. Carr called the front desk and immediately sent for Dr. Paul H. Cardwell, who injected Hank with two shots of morphine mixed with vitamin B12.

Dr. Cardwell later described Hank as being "very drunk" and also noticed he had some chloral hydrate capsules but didn't realize at the time what they were. After the doctor left, Carr called A. V. Bamford and told him they would have to cancel the New Year's Eve show in Charleston and drive directly to the 2:00 p.m. matinee of the *Western Style Revue*, scheduled in Canton, Ohio. Bamford informed him that four thousand tickets for the show had already been sold at $2.50 a piece, and if Hank didn't make it, he would owe Bamford a one-thousand-dollar fine.

Hank was carried out of the hotel unconscious and put into the back seat of his Cadillac, where Carr covered him with his overcoat and a blanket. The porters who helped carry Hank said they heard him making coughing sounds but disregarded them. Charles Carr and Hank weren't twenty miles outside of town before Carr almost hit a police car while trying to pass a truck, and he had to follow the cop into Rutledge to pay a twenty-five-dollar ticket for reckless driving. When Officer Swann H. Kitts asked Carr who was lying in the back seat, and if he was all right, Carr told him it was Hank Williams and that "he's been drinking a beer and the doctor gave him a sedative."

Kitts stated in his police report, "After investigating this matter, I think that Williams was dead when he was dressed and carried out of the hotel. Since he was drunk and was given the injections and could have taken some capsules earlier, he couldn't have lasted over an hour and a half or two hours. A man drunk or doped will make some movement if you move them. A dead man will make a coughing sound if they are lifted around. Taking all this into consideration, he must have died in Knoxville in the hotel." This explains the cryptic comment that Hank III made to his audience in Knoxville in July of 2009, stating "that those of you who know the true story, this is where my granddaddy really died."

Around 4:30 a.m., Carr stopped in Bluefield, West Virginia, at a gas station and asked about hiring a relief driver. He was directed to the Doughboy Lunch Restaurant, where he claims he asked Hank if he wanted something to eat. Hank refused and told him he just wanted to get some sleep, which is very unlikely considering what the police officer observed. At the diner Carr hired Donald Surface, a cab driver who had just finished his shift, to help him drive the rest of the way. After Surface drove several hours, Carr paid him seventy-five dollars and dropped him off somewhere in West Virginia.

When Carr got back behind the wheel, the weather had let up and he only had 300 miles to make it to Canton. Hank was lying stretched out in the back seat, with his hands folded across his chest. Carr noticed that his coat and blanket had fallen off, so he reached around behind him to pull the blanket up. When he did, his hand brushed over Hank's hand, which felt stone cold. Carr panicked and drove as fast as he could to Burdette's Pure Oil station in Oak Hill, West Virginia.

Carr pulled up, ran inside, and asked the man on duty to come out and check the passenger in the back seat for him. When he did, he told Carr, "I think you got a problem," and directed him to the Oak Hill Hospital. Carr rushed Hank to the hospital, running inside to get two interns to come and help. They followed him to the car, and after just glancing at Hank one of the interns said, "He's dead, all right." Carr begged them to do something, and the intern just replied, "It's too late, the man's dead." Next to Hank in the back seat were empty beer cans on the floor and the verse of a song expressing the bittersweet turn of events in a love relationship, most likely his own tumultuous marriage.

Hank was carried into the hospital by the two interns and placed on a stainless-steel table in the emergency room, where he was officially pronounced dead at 7:00 a.m. on January 1, 1953, by intern Dr. Diego Nunnari. The doctor estimated the actual time of Hank's death at approximately 1:00 that New Year's morning. Distraught, Carr called his father with the news. Hank was then moved across the street to the Tyree Funeral Home, where an autopsy was performed by Dr. Iven Malinin, who worked as a pathologist at a larger hospital in Beckley, West Virginia. The autopsy showed that Hank had suffered hemorrhages in both his neck and heart. When a state trooper was called in to rush some of Hank's internal organs over to the lab in Charleston, he was so sickened by the sight that he threw up.

The doctor noted that Hank had fresh needle marks on his arms and that he seemed to have recently been severely beaten and kicked in the groin. There was evidence of alcohol in his blood, but they didn't test for drugs. The coroner declared that Hank died of "a severe heart condition and hemorrhage."

The official cause of death was documented as "acute right ventricular dilation." Leaving behind the classic blueprint for living fast and dying young, Hank Williams, at twenty-nine years old, one of the most influential artists in the history of country music, was gone.

13

THE SHOW MUST GO ON

"When he walked on stage, and started bending his knees, kind of humped over in the shoulders, and started singing those old songs he had written, the audience just came unglued." —LITTLE JIMMY DICKENS

A S SOON AS LILLIE WAS CALLED, she sent a telegram to Hank's sister, Irene, saying, "Come at once Hank is dead." Then she called Charles Carr and told him, "Don't let anything happen to the car." Billie Jean broke down when she heard the news but was also equally concerned about the well-being of the car, as was Audrey, who had been partying the night before with A. V. Bamford's wife, Maxine, at the Plantation Club in Nashville. Carr took the Cadillac over to the Pure Oil station in Oak Hill, where it was shortly impounded before being moved to N & W Motors, the local Ford dealership.

Toby Marshall had traveled to Charleston to meet up with Hank and kept on driving to Canton when he realized that Hank wasn't going to make the New Year's Eve show. When he arrived in Canton, he was greeted by A. V. Bamford, who broke the news of Hank's death. Akron DJ Cliff Rodgers from WHKK walked up to the microphone and announced to the audience of four thousand, "Ladies and gentlemen, I've been in show business almost twenty years, and I've been called upon to do many difficult things in front of an audience, but today I'm about to perform the most difficult task I have ever done. This morning on his way to Canton to do this show, Hank Williams died in his car." When some audience members chuckled, not believing what they had just heard, he continued, "Ladies and gentlemen, this is no joke. Hank Williams is dead."

When everyone realized he was telling the truth, people started weeping. Don Helms was also at the theater in Canton waiting for Hank, and he took the news harder than anyone. They had been friends and bandmates since 1944, and no one knew Hank as well as Helms did. He once said, "Hank was a good friend. Some people liked him because he could sing. Some people felt sorry for him because he was skinny and humped over. But to me, he was my fishing and hunting buddy. Plus, he wrote and played the type of music I love."

The lights were dimmed, and a spotlight was pointed toward the middle of the stage, and cast members from behind the curtain starting singing, "I Saw the Light." Some of the audience sang along. The *Canton Repository* wrote that "while a single spotlight played on the drawn curtains, fans … joined with the entire cast to sing 'I Saw The Light!' Then the show went on … That was the way he would have wanted it."

Performer Hawkshaw Hawkins played his heart out that day and eventually made a name for himself in Nashville, only to die ten years later in the same plane crash that killed Patsy Cline and Cowboy Copas.

Within hours, Lillie had flown into Beckley with Carr's father and took a taxi to Oak Hill. She immediately collected Hank's clothing, boots, guitars, jewelry, money, and wedding ring. Someone had already snatched his white Fedora and the pearl-handled pistol he was carrying. Supposedly Burdette, the owner of the Pure Oil gas station, had stolen Hank's hat and later lost his hair due to a fungal disease. Of course everyone blamed it on the hat being cursed, and years later he committed suicide out behind his station.

Billie Jean and her father arrived with nothing to do but go back home and wait for the funeral. Toby Marshall drove in from Canton and unceremoniously presented Lillie with a bill for "services rendered," of $736.39, which she threw back in his face. Hank had died without a proper will, designating Lon as executor of his estate even though Lillie listed Lon as "deceased" on the Oak Hill death certificate.

On January 3, 1953, Hank's body, dressed in a white stage outfit, was taken to Montgomery in a hearse. Lillie, Charles Carr, Carr's father, and Toby Marshall followed in the powder blue Cadillac. In the main room of Lillie's boardinghouse, Hank's body was laid in state, after the mortician broke his ankles, at Lillie's request, so they could bury him with his boots on. The Drifting Cowboys stood honor guard, Wesley and Fred Rose drove in from Nashville to serve as pallbearers, and dozens of Nashville celebrities flew in on chartered planes.

Before the funeral, Billie Jean was fighting with Lillie over Hank's belongings. Audrey, Lillie, and Hank's sister Irene spent their time searching the house for any of Hank's unfinished lyrics that he might have left behind. They found a notebook in Billie Jean's bedroom, grabbed it, and eventually gave it to Fred Rose. Lon hitchhiked in from McWilliams and bought a bouquet of flowers for his dead son with the last five dollars he had. Once he got there, he and Lillie fought over who would act as the executor of Hank's estate. Willing to do anything to get her out of his life for good, Lon gave in to her demands.

Hundreds of cards and letters flooded Lillie's mailbox, and on Sunday, January 4, between fifteen and twenty thousand people showed up for Hank's funeral. Only 2,750 were allowed inside the City Auditorium to view the open casket and pay their respects to one of the greatest country singers of all time. The *Nashville Banner* reported that "the thousands who streamed past his open casket ... were proof that the followers of Hank Williams knew no class barriers." Hank was flanked by two guitar-shaped floral arrangements, with a tiny white Bible placed in one of his hands. Fighting back tears, Ernest Tubb sang "Beyond the Sunset"; the Southwind Singers, a black gospel quartet, sang "My Record Will Be There" and "Precious Memories"; Red Foley sang "Peace in the Valley"; and Roy Acuff led everyone in singing "I Saw the Light."

Dr. Henry L. Lyon of the Highland Avenue Baptist Church gave Hank's eulogy: "Hank had a message. This message was written in the language of all the people. It was a message of the things that everyone feels—life itself. Years ago, one of America's greatest doctors said, 'If you have something which represents a genuine need of humanity, though you live in a cottage, deep in the forest, mankind will beat a trail to your door.' Hank Williams did have something that humanity universally needs—a song with a heart-felt message."

Among the guests were Opry performers Johnny Wright, Jack Anglin, Webb Pierce, Bill Monroe, Ray Price, Little Jimmy Dickens, Carl Smith, and June Carter. The Drifting Cowboys performed, and Don Helms remembered, "It was the eeriest thing I ever had to do in my life. I had to stand up there and play with Hank's coffin right below me. I can never explain how I felt playing the songs for somebody else the way I played for him with him laying in his coffin."

Horace Logan had flown in from Shreveport and sat behind Jim Denny from the Grand Ole Opry. Denny turned around and said, "Logan, if Hank could raise up in his coffin, he'd look up toward the stage and say, 'I told you dumb sons of bitches I could draw more dead than you could alive.'" The Statesmen Quartet, who would later appear at Elvis's funeral, sang "Precious Memories" before the final benediction. Afterward, everyone traveled to Oakwood Cemetery Annex for Hank's burial.

Hank was unable to find any peace while he was alive, and even in death they wouldn't leave Hank alone. Although he was laid to rest that day, a new site was dug for him on January 16, and in the middle of the night his casket was moved to a new grave, which would become the family plot. Marking his final resting place was a white marble tower with a replica of his signature cowboy hat sitting in front. Hank had packed several lifetimes into his twenty-nine years and left the world some of the greatest songs ever written.

Two days after Hank's funeral, Bobbie Jett gave birth to a baby girl at St. Margaret's Hospital in Montgomery. She was named Antha Belle Jett and within days was dropped off at Lillie's boardinghouse. On January

28, Lillie went to the Montgomery County Department of Public Welfare and stated that Antha was Hank Williams's child and that she was willing to adopt the baby, as "this was what her son would want her to do." After the legal adoption of Antha Belle, Lillie changed her name to Cathy Yvonne Stone, after the character in *Wuthering Heights* and Hank's song "Jambalaya."

While Lillie and Audrey went to court to make sure Billie Jean didn't share in any of Hank's estate, Audrey and Billie Jean hit the road separately as entertainers, both billing themselves as "Mrs. Hank Williams." Audrey's all-girl band was called the Drifting Cowgirls, and she managed to get A. V. Bamford to book dates for her. This curious situation lasted until August 19, 1953, when Billie Jean signed a legal agreement with Audrey to stop performing as Mrs. Hank Williams, giving up any and all rights to Hank's estate and any future income from it, and accepting a lump sum settlement of thirty thousand dollars. Audrey still received half of Hank's royalties as per their divorce, with the other half now going to Hank Jr., to be administered by Lillie. Of course, no one realized at the time just how valuable Hank's songs would become.

"Kaw-Liga" became the biggest-selling country song of 1953, and the B-side, "Your Cheatin' Heart," hit the top of the charts, as well. His next single, "Take These Chains from My Heart," also went to number one. By March, MGM released two albums, *Hank Williams as Luke the Drifter* and the *Memorial Album*. Hank's income from MGM in 1952 was $13,869, and his Acuff-Rose income was $55,044. After his death, his income rose to $60,636 from MGM and $72,762 from Acuff-Rose.

In late January, *Billboard* reported that the MGM plant in New Jersey was having a hard time keeping up with the demand for Hank's recordings, including fifty singles and two albums. The radio airwaves were flooded with Hank's music, and Acuff-Rose was overwhelmed with demands for copies of his songbooks.

On March 18, 1953, "Kaw-Liga Day," the first of many tribute shows to Hank, was held at Lake Martin, where he had written the song. The event helped to promote the new Kowaliga State Park. Hank's friend

Jim Watley and the Alexander City DJ Bob McKinnon came up with the plan. Opry performers Autry Inman, Stringbean, George Morgan, Radio Dot, and Smoky Swan played three shows for twelve hundred people each that day, with the featured guest being Audrey Williams, who would become a regular spokeswoman for Hank's memory.

Audrey kept a strong image in public, but Lycrecia revealed in her book that her mother took the blame for Hank's premature death. She wished she had not divorced Hank and had done more for his illness, and her regrets would shape the rest of her life. Of course, that didn't stop her from traveling the country billed as "the girl for whom the late, great Hank Williams wrote his famous songs."

Hank III doesn't have any memories of his grandmother at all. "The closest I have ever came to her besides the pictures, are of talking to her daughter, Lycrecia, and hearing those stories. [Audrey] didn't like my Mom very much, and there aren't very many pictures of her with me. She was in a pretty tough spot, at that time, also." Audrey suffered in her last years, and as Hank III explains, "It was pretty tough on her, she was a ball of fire, that's for sure."

Audrey was a very savvy businesswoman, despite some of the derogatory things that have been written about her. She helped Hank Williams become the star he was meant to be, even if he was so talented he would have made it on his own.

Hank III agreed. "No doubt. The foundation was there. It was a fifty–fifty thing, after awhile, that lifestyle catches up with you and it starts showing the bad side of itself. But she had the drive, the creativity and the vision in her. Where it got kind of messed up is when Hank would be in bed with a bad back, and she was still going out there and making the rounds, and doing the business. That probably wasn't the smartest move on her end, she should have been there. There was already enough fame that she didn't have to go and make him more jealous. She was the Sharon Osbourne back then.

"I'm always envious of those music people that I know who have that kind of relationship, you had Waylon Jennings and his wife, Johnny and

June, Hank and Audrey, Ozzy and Sharon, I know there's a few others, I think Johnny Rotten's wife has been pretty solid in his career, and Tom Waits, his wife has been pretty deep in with him. And hats off to 'em, because it takes a very strong woman to stand by any musician, that's takin' it on full-time. There's a lot of jealousy, of not being home, alone time, head games, the highs and the lows, and it takes a toll." It must have been hard on Audrey to step aside, considering she wanted a career of her own. After Hank's career took off, it had to be very difficult for her when she realized hers wasn't going to do the same. She did perform, and she was onstage a lot. Audrey was the Lucille Ball (as her character in *I Love Lucy*) of her time. All the schemes Lucy came up with to be included in Desi's nightclub act. It must have been hard to let that go. Hank III concurs, "I'm sure it was, and even after Hank was dead and gone, she always wanted to have the best parties, with the most important people showing up, and keeping that kind of name around."

Most people don't realize how young Hank and Audrey really were during his rise to fame. Hank III continued, "Yeah, most people think Hank was probably forty when he died. It shows how tapped in and tuned in he really was, and how he was an old man in a young man's body, pretty much. He grew up fast, had a lot of wisdom, had the voice, was pretty arrogant, and knew he was the best. That's why he was such a troublemaker."

Hank Sr.'s life wasn't really any different from a lot of performers' who reached a certain level of fame. It had a lot to do with the times, the late 1940s and early 1950s. Hank Sr. was one of the first rock stars of his time. Hank III said, "Especially in such an uptight community. That's probably why there are still problems to this day. That's part of the song, 'the good die young'—it's just part of the mystery."

Many claim that the Williams family has been cursed, but their problems, including alcoholism and drug abuse, plague so many families. Of his grandfather, Hank III said, "[It was] alcohol and drugs. Absolutely, he might have had a longer life if he hadn't had the back pain and the injury wasn't there. That's a huge thing.

"In those days they just threw you in a loony bin." After his back surgery, "the pain was worse and the drugs were harder. He got into some stuff he'd never done. It's a huge factor. A lot of bands don't realize that the road will always be there, as long as you wanna keep doing it. The crowds might not be as big, but you'll always have a little bit of a chance to go back to it. If that's what you want to do."

It's hard to fathom that no one around Hank Sr. was taking care of him. Although he was sick, he was also obsessed with proving that he was on top and was going to stay on top. "Well, I'm sure the obsession was there," said Hank III. "I know he was tuned in to also knowing when he was going to die. There's those stories with Billie Jean, where he had said that this is the last time you're going to see me. He was dealing with it pretty heavy. It's hard to speak for him, but he kind of knew, and everyone around him tried their best in the music world, I guess at that time, to help. When you've got that much of the demons in you, or whatever, a lot of people just get frustrated and walk away."

Some may have walked away when he was alive, but in death Hank remained a huge star. One of the biggest tributes to Hank was held in Montgomery on September 20–21, 1954. "Hank Williams Day" drew almost fifty thousand people, including over one hundred country music artists and three state governors. Hank Jr. and Lycrecia placed wreaths on Hank's grave, and a parade featured Audrey, Hank Jr., Lycrecia, Lillie, and Miss Ragland riding in Hank's blue Cadillac. For the opening night, Ernest Tubb, Hank Snow, and Roy Acuff hosted a three-hour show celebrating Hank's life.

At the end of the two-day event, a ten-foot marble monument was unveiled at the gravesite. On the front is engraved, "I Saw the Light," and the back inscription is a poem written by Audrey:

Thank you for all the love you gave me
There could be no one stronger
Thank you for the many beautiful songs

114

They will live long and longer
Thank you for being a wonderful father to Lycrecia
She loved you more than you knew
Thank you for our precious son
And thank God he looks so much like you
And now I can say
There are no words in the dictionary
That can express my love for you
Someday beyond the blue.

Less than two years after Hank left this world, his mentor/ songwriting partner Fred Rose followed him. Rose's Christian Science beliefs prevented him from seeking help for his heart disease, and he suffered a heart attack while in the studio and died on December 1, 1954. Regardless of the trials and tribulations that he went through with Hank over the years, after Hank's death, Rose had said, "Whatever people say about Hank, he never hurt anybody but himself. He was his own worst enemy … but one thing he had—and all his friends recognized it—was loyalty. I don't give a hang whether he drank or not, I appreciate the fact he was loyal. … [If someone tried to bribe him away], he'd say, 'I started with Rose and I'll stay with Rose.'" And that he did.

Lillie turned Hank's old bedroom into a shrine and shared the raising of Cathy Yvonne with Hank's cousin Marie. She also wrote a booklet called *Life Story of Our Hank Williams*, which she hawked over the radio. On February 26, 1955, her maid called Marie to tell her that she couldn't get Lillie up. Lillie had died in her sleep, and Marie found her slumped across the bed.

Hank's sister, Irene, became the new executor of his estate but declined to take over the care of Cathy Yvonne, putting her up for readoption. Attempting to save Cathy from another adoption, Marie located Bobbie Jett in California, who informed her that she had remarried and her new husband didn't know anything about her having a child with Hank, so she refused to take her daughter back.

In March, Cathy Yvonne went to live with Mr. and Mrs. J. H. Cook of Pine Level, Alabama, and in February of 1956 she was permanently adopted by Wayne and Mary Louise Deupree in Mobile. They changed her name to Cathy Louise Deupree, and if Hank's mother Lillie hadn't willed Cathy $2,200 to be paid when she turned twenty-one, she might never have figured out who her father really was.

14

LITTLE BOCEPHUS

"Of the two of us [children], I always considered myself to be the luckiest one because I got to do things with Daddy. [He] was a fun person. He would take me bowling a lot. He would go horseback riding and fishing with me." —LYCRECIA WILLIAMS

L ITTLE BOCEPHUS WAS NOT QUITE FOUR YEARS OLD when his father died, and he has only a few faint memories of Hank. What he does remember is being aware of who he was, as he wrote in his autobiography, *Living Proof:* "See, I was Hank Williams' son, and I lived in Hank Williams' house and Hank Williams' wife was my mother … I knew that the people who came to my Mother's parties were important in some way … and all they could do was tell me how good I was, how smart I was, how much I looked like Daddy, and what a great man he was … I learned to idolize my father … His memories were all over the place … There were times, I remember, when I was sure that Daddy wasn't dead at all."

Over the years, Audrey was very fond of throwing parties with guests that included Red Foley, Perry Como, Brenda Lee, Jerry Lee Lewis, Fats Domino, Earl Scruggs, and Johnny Cash. They all had advice for Hank Jr. and were always very much impressed with the idea of Hank Jr. being able to carry on his father's legacy.

Audrey attempted to continue a solo career recording for Decca Records, although none of her sessions were ever released. Instead she moved into management and promotion and started working with

Eddie Crandall. *Billboard* reported in August 1957, "Eddie Crandall, former personal manager to Marty Robbins, and Audrey Williams, 'Grand Ole Opry' performer, have opened offices at 2508 Franklin Road to book 'Grand Ole Opry' and other c & w talent." Over the next two years, together they formed the Audrey Williams National Talent Search, the Audrey Williams Musical Caravan, and the Hank Williams Memorial Foundation.

When Hank Jr. was just eight years old, he performed his first concert in front of a packed audience at the Nancy Auditorium in Swainsboro, Georgia, on March 22, 1958. With slicked-back hair and wearing a black suit, he sang "Lovesick Blues." The crowd went crazy for "Hank's little boy," and that year Hank Jr. was included in the Audrey Williams Musical Caravan, a recurring show that featured his mother, his half-sister Lycrecia, Carl Perkins, and the Big Bopper. Occasionally, artists like Grandpa Jones and Ernest Tubb would pop in to sing a few songs.

At the time, Hank Jr. felt that performing his father's music was "like the most natural thing in the world. No different from going to school and learning cursive writing. No different from reading, writing and 'rithmetic. Stage presence, delivery, and style." He did so well that Audrey put him onstage every chance she got. Hank Jr. remembers traveling around when he was still small enough to sleep in the space behind the back window of the car.

Audrey worked religiously with Hank Jr. on his singing and made sure to teach him all of Hank Sr.'s mannerisms, especially his stage banter, which Audrey believed was Hank Sr.'s secret weapon. Every weekend Hank Jr. would sing his father's songs, and during the week he taught himself how to play rock-and-roll by listening to Elvis, Chuck Berry, Ray Charles, and Chubby Checker. Hank Jr. learned to mimic his father's mannerisms and practiced in front of the mirror until he had it right.

By late 1958, Hank Jr. had his own band backing him. Audrey had hired Buddy Spicher to play fiddle, Howard White on pedal steel, and

Goober Buchanan on bass, with Ken Marvin, who was Lonzo in the Lonzo and Oscar comedy team on the Grand Ole Opry, fronting the band and playing guitar. Regarding working with Audrey and Hank Jr., Howard White told Lycrecia in her book *Still in Love with You*, "She never interfered with the musicians or tried to tell us how to play or anything. We played mostly Hank Sr.'s music. The crowds liked Hank Jr., and I thought he did a good job. He was a nice little boy."

Goober Buchanan also recalled to Lycrecia that "Audrey prompted little Hank—we called him Randall then—on the shows. He played the drums and he wanted to be a rock 'n' roller. She had him do the Hank Williams tunes; she would let him do one rock 'n' roll song, but the rest she picked. I was so surprised at him. Even as a kid, he seemed to be born to the stage."

It also helped Hank Jr. to have the pleasure of performing with some of country music's future icons. In 2006, Hank Jr. talked to CMT about being on the road as a kid: "People don't realize that [when I was] on tour with Audrey Williams's caravan of stars—and there's a guy named Merle Haggard and one named Waylon and a little bitty kid out there, Hank Jr. And they're wondering which of those two guys is going to make it? And I'm in [Waylon's] Dodge motor home so I can get over there and sneak cigarettes to get away from Mama. Yeah, we were pretty close."

Hank Jr. was so comfortable onstage that he was only eleven when he made his debut at the Grand Ole Opry. He was clearly destined to become a star, and he believed that it was his birthright. One of the defining moments of his early career was the night he performed in front of twenty thousand people at Cobo Hall in Detroit along with Marty Robbins, Red Foley, and Minnie Pearl. He easily captured the audience and afterward ran into Foley backstage. Hank Jr. remembered Foley was pale and almost shaking and said that when he broke into "'Long Gone Lonesome Blues,' I thought I heard a ghost. I thought for a second that was Hank out there!"

The next night Hank Jr. made his first television appearance on the *Ed Sullivan Show*. The gig was set up by Elvis's manager, Colonel Tom Parker. When Hank Jr. was introduced, Ed Sullivan said, "Colonel Tom Parker, who of course, got us together with Elvis, sent this young man up here to sing for us. His father was a famous singer in his own right. Hank Williams Junior, let's hear it for him!"

Hank Jr., playing a Gibson Dove guitar and wearing a glittery Nudie suit, sang two of his father's songs, including "Long Gone Lonesome Blues." The audience loved him, and the girls were screaming for him. Sullivan was very happy and immediately asked him to come back. Parker stated that Hank Jr. would never be as big as Elvis but had "all the stuff from which headliners are built. Hank Williams Junior could be the next BIG teen star."

After Lillie's death, Hank's sister, Irene, being the executor of his estate, became Hank Jr.'s guardian in the state of Alabama. In June of 1963, Audrey and Hank Jr. went to court and petitioned to have Audrey appointed his legal guardian in the state of Tennessee. The Chancery Court of Davidson County granted their motion, and for the first time Audrey was able to officially handle Hank Jr.'s legal agreements and contracts. At the same time, Audrey started working with Buddy Lee, who was an ex–professional wrestler turned promoter.

Lee booked a show in Columbia, South Carolina, for Hank Jr. at the Township Auditorium for three hundred dollars. Audrey agreed to the booking but also asked for an extra one hundred and fifty dollars to cover herself for singing and driving Hank Jr. to his performance. They both went over really well and played three more dates for Lee before Audrey asked for more money, getting Hank Jr.'s fee raised to five hundred dollars. While Hank Jr. was busy honing his skills on the stage, Audrey was busy talking MGM into giving Hank Jr. a recording contract.

Since he was so young, MGM wasn't sure Hank Jr. would be successful, so Lee booked him on a sixteen-city tour of the South, starting in the Carolinas and ending up in New England. Almost every show was sold out, and as soon as the tour ended, MGM signed Hank Jr. to a recording contract, paying him three hundred thousand dollars over the next three years. They also arranged for the prestigious talent agency William Morris to represent him. Hank Jr. quickly went into the studio and recorded his first single for MGM, a cover of his father's "Long Gone Lonesome Blues," which became his first hit record.

The demand for Hank Jr.'s live performances was steadily increasing, so Audrey talked Buddy Lee into moving to Nashville and forming a company with her called Aud-Lee Agency. She would continue to manage Hank Jr., while Lee would do the booking, including handling all the merchandising and advertising.

With royalties pouring in from Hank Sr.'s estate, money was no object, and Audrey continued to expand the house on Franklin Road. The new additions included a Japanese garden, swimming pool, and bathhouse. She also built a new home for her parents in Banks, Alabama, and a chalet for herself in the Great Smoky Mountains in Gatlinburg, Tennessee.

A lot has been said about Audrey Williams, most of it being negative, but Buddy Lee told Lycrecia, "She was a very sharp businesswoman, and her word was her bond. If she made a deal and there was ten thousand dollars in it, she'd pay the ten thousand dollars. We became real tight because I depended on her and she depended on me. She was a good friend. If she liked you, she'd give you the shirt off her back."

Along with her booking agency, Audrey formed Marathon Pictures, her own movie company, producing three major motion pictures. *Country Music on Broadway* was the company's first feature-length movie, made in Nashville and filmed in the summer of 1963. It premiered at the Tennessee Theater in November and featured Audrey, Hank Jr., and Lycrecia, along with over twenty major country music artists. The idea came from Hank Sr.'s appearance on the Kate Smith show and included that black and white footage, where Hank Snow asks Hank Jr. if he'd like to see a "home movie" of his late father.

Marathon Pictures' second release, the following year, was *Second Fiddle to a Steel Guitar*, featuring Kitty Wells, Johnnie Wright, Lefty

Frizzell, Little Jimmy Dickens, Faron Young, Bill Monroe, Webb Pierce, and Minnie Pearl.

Within a year of Hank's death, MGM began talking about making a movie about his life, and in the spring of 1964, production began on *Your Cheatin' Heart: The Hank Williams Story*. George Hamilton would star as Hank, Susan Oliver was to play Audrey, Red Buttons was cast as Hank's manager, and Arthur O'Connell would play Fred Rose.

Hamilton himself petitioned to sing Hank's songs on film, and MGM considered letting him lip-synch to Hank Sr.'s original recordings. Of course Audrey had her own ideas. She was so convinced that fifteen-year-old Hank Jr. should sing his father's songs for the film that she took him into the studio to record a demo for MGM to listen to. As soon as she had the tapes in her hands, she flew to Hollywood and persuaded the movie executives to let Hank Jr. sing the soundtrack.

Another aspect in the decision to let Hank Jr. record the soundtrack for the film was the fact that Acuff-Rose, the sole licensing agent for Hank Sr.'s music, had to approve who was going to sing it; otherwise they wouldn't have let MGM use the songs in the first place. Audrey knew what she was doing, because when you watch the film, you would swear you were listening to Hank Sr., and not his teenage son.

Your Cheatin' Heart: The Hank Williams Story premiered in Montgomery on November 5, 1966, and the next day opened at the Country Music Association convention in Nashville. Audrey served as a consultant on the film and allowed the movie to portray her in a less-than-flattering light. She later said in an interview in 1973, "Hank was gone and he could not protect himself, and I did not want the people walking away from the theatre and not liking Hank. I wanted them walking away loving him, as they do today. I am still alive, and I can kind of protect myself. So that's one reason I threw it in the light I did and I could have changed it if I had wanted to because I had all the say-so on it." Audrey also explained that she originally wanted Hank Jr. to play his father as a boy in the picture, but by the time they had begun filming, he was too old for the part. That's why she wanted him to sing the soundtrack, so he would somehow still be included in the movie.

During the making of the film, Audrey kept demanding to change her part to show how much she pushed Hank to become a star. Wesley Rose tried to advise her against it, because the picture depicts her as a very controlling, overbearing woman, something she didn't mind at all. Her viewpoint was that Hank wouldn't have succeeded without her, and she didn't want that fact taken away from her. *Your Cheatin' Heart: The Story of Hank Williams* was a box-office success, and its soundtrack sold over one million copies.

Audrey later stated to a Nashville newspaper, "I feel sad and happy at the same time. George Hamilton plays Hank and Susan Oliver plays my part. But hearing Hank Junior on the soundtrack reminds me of his father. He sounds so much like his dad, and his mannerisms are the same."

When the movie came out, Lycrecia, who was now married to Lamar Morris, the little boy who got to play Hank's new song that night at the Hank Williams Homecoming Day in Montgomery, had moved back to Nashville. Audrey asked Lamar to help her put a band together for Hank Jr., so he could go out on the road full-time.

Forming the Cheatin' Hearts, the band consisted of Bill Aikins on piano, Charlie Norrell on bass, and Larry Joe Williams on drums. Lycrecia noticed that Audrey had started drinking more and had begun to date younger men, who wound up living in the apartment above her garage. Some of these men were singers looking for help with their careers, and Audrey was never serious about them, considering she would lose her rights to Hank's royalties if she remarried.

Making sure Hank Jr. would be comfortable on the road, Audrey bought him a used two-level Trailsways Scenic Cruiser that they christened "The Cheatin' Heart Special." Tommy Cash, the brother of Johnny Cash and a singer who had signed with Aud-Lee, started riding on Hank Jr.'s bus and told Lycrecia how he remembered Audrey always being around. "She was at the shows, she was at the hotel, she was on the bus, she was everywhere. She insisted on the sound being good and everyone dressing sharp.... Many times I'd look over and see her watching Hank Jr. I remember one night I caught her looking at him like she stood in awe of him. Her eyes were partly closed, and her head was back. I think she knew there couldn't be another Hank Williams, but that Hank Jr. could be just as big in a different way."

Hank Jr. was becoming country music's biggest draw, so Audrey took him into the studio to record duets with his late father. Stripping off the accompaniments and adding harmonies from Hank Jr., listening back, the studio engineers deemed the duets as "eerie." This latest recording project garnered Hank Jr. his first bad reviews, which declared that enough was enough. A few critics asked if his next project would involve taking Hank Sr.'s coffin out on tour with him. Johnny Cash even commented to Hank Jr.'s mother, "Loosen up a little, Audrey. Let him be Hank Williams Junior for a while." It would take a few years, but that was something Hank Jr. would have to figure out for himself.

15

STANDING IN THE SHADOWS

"My daddy, he was somewhere between God and John Wayne." —HANK JR.

BEFORE LONG, JUST LIKE HIS FATHER, Hank Jr. started to write his own songs. One of his first original hits was called "Standing in the Shadows," which he wrote in about twenty minutes while riding on his tour bus. It was about his life spent living in the shadow of Hank Williams Sr. "The people they're all hollerin' and clappin' real loud … I look up toward the ceiling, and say … 'Just listen Daddy … to Bocephus and probably some of your old crowd."

When he showed the lyrics to his mother, she smiled, and in his autobiography, *Living Proof*, he remembered that "the front section of the bus lit up with that smile." But as he watched her read, her smile turned into a frown and she started to cry. The song was released in 1966 and made it to number five on the charts.

That same year, Audrey hired Nudie to customize a Pontiac for Hank Jr., creating the first country music "Silver Dollar Car." The car was covered with 547 silver dollars, fifteen silver horseshoes, three rifles, ten small pistols, twelve large pistols, seven silver horses, and seventeen silver horse heads, along with a saddle installed between the driver and passenger seat. Even though Hank Jr. was extremely embarrassed by it, he drove it around Nashville just enough to get his picture taken in it.

The custom job cost $22,000 and, as Audrey said, "it was great publicity." The car now sits in a museum in Pigeon Forge, Tennessee.

Following the success of the film *Your Cheatin' Heart*, Hank Jr. decided he wanted to become a movie star himself, an ambition Audrey was fully behind. MGM signed him to a three-picture deal, and his first major motion picture was called *A Time to Sing*, a story about Grady Dodd, a tobacco farmer who wanted to become a country music singer. Hank Jr.'s costars were Ed Begley and Shelley Fabares, and his band in the picture was called the Cheatin' Hearts. Elvis happened to drop by the set one day and told Hank Jr., "I just want to tell you that your daddy was really something, man. ... I want you to know that I thought about Hank when I walked out on that Opry stage for the first time. All I could think about then was, 'This is the same stage Hank Williams was on, and now I'm here.'" Elvis was such a fan of Hank Sr.'s that if you watch the movie *Jailhouse Rock*, you will see a picture of Hank Williams on the wall of Elvis's jail cell.

When the producers of *A Time to Sing* balked at the fact that the eighteen-year-old star wanted Sharon Martin, his seventeen-year-old high school sweetheart, to live with him in Hollywood while they filmed, he promptly left Los Angeles and flew home to Nashville to marry her.

Running off and eloping with Sharon without telling Audrey completely devastated his mother, and her drinking increased. Just like Hank had before her, Audrey was mixing her pain medication with alcohol. She was also suffering from digestive problems, and *Billboard* reported in March of 1967 that "Audrey Williams was recently released from the hospital following an extended stay for treatment of a stomach ailment." Audrey had been admitted to Miller's Clinic complaining of external bleeding and not being able to keep food down. Exploratory surgery found a blood vessel bleeding into her stomach, so the surgeons rerouted her intestines and removed part of her stomach.

After the surgery, her health was never the same. It took several days before Hank Jr. even called his mother while she was in the hospital, only after being scolded by Audrey's friend, singer Jean Shepard. She once told Lycrecia that Audrey admitted to her, "I know a lot of people don't like me, but I'll still make my son into a star."

Her estrangement from the son she loved so much didn't help Audrey's drinking at all. Hank Jr. needed his independence just as much as she needed him to stay. And those around her easily took advantage of her. Her accountant, Ed Neely, neglected to see that her taxes were paid every year, which eventually put her house on Franklin Road in jeopardy.

It doesn't seem to make sense that Hank Jr. wasn't there for his mother financially, although the reasons are clear to Hank III, who said, "But [Hank Jr.] wasn't really gettin' along with her. She definitely lived a pretty extravagant life, with the parties, the house and the clothes and all that. When you put your trust and money into someone else, it's tough."

In spite of Audrey's pushing, when Hank Jr. turned eighteen, he went to court and was granted the "removal of the disability minority." He agreed to his mother's final accounting of his business affairs and removed her from any and all obligations. In an article that appeared in *Billboard* on January 27, 1968, under the heading "Audrey Williams to Exit Aud-Lee," Hank Jr. told the reporter, "Buddy Lee now will handle all my affairs, and my mother will have no connection with the agency." He also started to receive half of his father's royalty income and used to joke that the hardest work he had to do was to walk out to the mailbox and then cash the checks.

Hank's sister, Irene, was still the executor of Hank's estate and guardian of Hank Jr. in the state of Alabama. Acuff-Rose went to court to ensure that Hank Sr.'s copyright renewals would be reassigned back to them. The law required copyrights to be renewed every twenty-eight years, and Acuff-Rose was concerned that once Hank Jr. became eighteen, he might go with another music publisher. The lawsuit showed that up to that point, Hank Sr.'s estate had earned over 1.6 million dollars, and Audrey had already spent half of that.

Irene ended up convicted of smuggling drugs and served several years in a federal prison in West Virginia, not far from where her brother Hank Sr. was pronounced dead. Hank III revealed, "She could barely afford toilet paper. I heard her new husband called her up and said, 'Hey, honey, I bought you a new car, I want you to come pick it up.' She went across the border into Mexico and picked it up, and it was full of drugs. And they never saw him again."

By the time he was nineteen, Hank Jr. was co-headlining concerts with Johnny Cash. Both being fascinated with the Civil War, Hank Jr. and Johnny spent a lot of time together searching for Civil War artifacts to add to their collections. They also loved to explore caves and investigate anything that had the slightest potential for danger. Johnny Cash was the perfect companion for Hank Jr., and he was also one of the few people in the music business that Audrey actually approved of.

Although Hank Jr. and Johnny Cash were two of the biggest stars in country music, the world and the music were changing around them. Americans were in conflict over the Vietnam War, and in 1968, Hank Jr. had twenty-five shows canceled due to rioting. Hank played a few benefit concerts for George Wallace's presidential campaign but couldn't support him after Martin Luther King Jr. was assassinated. When one of his band members remarked that King's death "was a good thing considering all the trouble he stirred up," Hank Jr. was no longer proud to be living in Tennessee. Racism was one thing Hank Jr. would never tolerate.

Scheduled to play an afternoon and evening show at Cobo Hall in Detroit in 1969, Williams and Cash sold them both out. When the receipts were added up, the gate totaled almost one hundred thousand dollars, making it the biggest-grossing show in the history of country music. Now Hank Jr. had started singing songs by George Jones and added playing the banjo to his performance. A multitalented musician, Hank Jr. also played guitar, bass guitar, standup bass, steel guitar, Dobro, keyboards, fiddle, harmonica, and the drums. Their reviews were stellar, declaring, "Cash got the audience with his great records, and Hank Jr. with his incredible virtuosity."

In 1970, Hank Jr. signed the biggest recording contract in the history of MGM Records, for $500,000 per year. But while his career was soaring, his personal life was falling apart. He had inherited his father's formidable talent, but also his weakness for drugs and alcohol. Hank Jr. had developed a taste for whiskey and cocaine, and the Nashville gossips were tearing him apart. He stopped trusting the media when the *National Enquirer* misquoted him as saying he thought his music was better than his daddy's. What he actually said was the recording techniques of the day were better than they had been in his daddy's time.

By the early 1970s, Hank Jr. wanted to play rock-and-roll, becoming a fan of southern rock bands like the Marshall Tucker Band, the Allman Brothers, and Charlie Daniels. He was slowly losing the fans who wanted to hear him play his father's music. He recorded "Meter Reader Maid," one of his first rock numbers, under the name Bo Cephus—he also occasionally performed his new music as Rockin' Randall. The more Hank Jr. moved away from his mother's influence and turned his back on being a "Hank Williams clone," the more his songwriting developed, and he enjoyed his first two number-one hits, "All for the Love of Sunshine," which appeared on the soundtrack for the film *Kelly's Heroes* in 1970, and "Eleven Roses," which was released in 1972.

During his first marriage, to Sharon, Hank Jr. began an affair while on tour with a feisty brunette, a former model by the name of Gwen Yeargain. She had pursued him while he was out on the road, and before long he was flying her around the country to meet him in different cities. The sneaking around didn't last long with Sharon, so Hank Jr. and Gwen moved in with his friend Merle Kilgore, the same man who as a teenager was in the audience the night Hank Sr. debuted at the Grand Ole Opry. Hank Jr. had left Buddy Lee and hired Kilgore as his manager.

Sharon was determined to prove that Hank Jr. was living with his girlfriend, and she actually had the police show up at Kilgore's house one night, and they arrested him for unlawful cohabitation. He pled not guilty, the case was dismissed, and Hank Jr. took off for Bermuda, arranging to have Gwen meet him there.

When his divorce from Sharon was finalized, she was awarded a $100,000 house, $90,000 in cash, and a new Cadillac, along with the money she made selling off Hank Jr.'s gun collection even though he had it hidden in a pickup truck parked at a friend's house. As soon as he could, he married Gwen on April 7, 1971, at the First Presbyterian Church in Nashville and honeymooned in London, where he performed at the third International Festival of Country Music. On December 12, 1972, they welcomed a son, Shelton Hank Williams III.

The baby was named after his grandfather Hank Sr. and Audrey's father, Shelton. Newspapers across the country heralded his birth. The headlines read, "Latest Music Heir Premiered at St. Thomas," and one article stated, "Hank Williams and Son: Hank Jr. got a close look at his son, Hank III, not long after he was born. The baby's mother is the former Gwen Yeargain, daughter of Mr. and Mrs. T. A. Yeargain, Jane [Missouri]. The baby was born December 12. Mr. and Mrs. Yeargain, their daughter Gayle and son Tom Jr., spent Christmas with the Williams. Mrs. Yeargain stayed for two weeks to help with the new baby. The other members of the family returned immediately home after Christmas. Mr. Williams is an MGM recording artist." The coverage included a picture of the beaming parents, with Hank Jr. holding Hank III up for the camera.

What started as a passionate affair turned into a grind for Gwen, who grew tired of waiting for Hank Jr. to come home from touring. She made the best of raising her son and recorded in his baby book that for his first Christmas he received a chair giraffe, a gun, a play garage, a top, trucks, a Noah's ark, and a train. His favorite gift was the chair giraffe. She also noted that his first holiday dinner consisted of game hens, wild rice, mashed potatoes, corn, gravy, and tea rolls, and that Santa paid a visit to their house on December 19, and Hank III didn't care for Santa at all.

In *Living Proof*, Hank Jr. revealed that Gwen told him, "There has to be more to life than just sitting home waiting for some damn country

Hank Williams Sr. and his Drifting Cowboys, January 1, 1940. (GAB Archive/Redferns/ Getty Images)

Audrey, Lycrecia, and Hank Sr. holding Hank Jr. during happier days, New Year's Eve 1948. (Michael Ochs Archives/Getty Images)

Hank Jr. enthralled by his famous father, Hank Sr., January 1, 1950. (GAB Archive/Redferns/Getty Images)

Billie Jean Jones marries Hank Sr., October 18, 1952. (GAB Archive/Redferns/Getty Images)

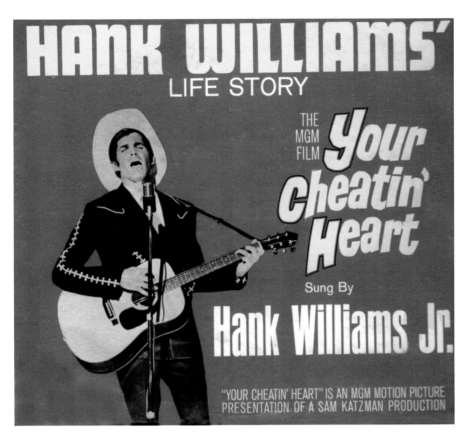

Film poster from the movie *Your Cheatin' Heart*, starring George Hamilton. (GAB Archive/Getty Images)

(Michael Ochs Archives/Getty Images)

Top: Hank Williams Jr., a 1960s country-and-western star. (GAB Archive/Redferns/ Getty Images)

Right: (Michael Ochs Archives/Getty Images)

Gwen Yeargain (the second Mrs. Williams) and Hank Jr., April 12, 1972. (Evening Standard/Hulton Archive/Getty Images)

Hank Williams Jr. rockin' thousands, January 1, 1970. (Michael Ochs Archives/Getty Images)

Hank Williams Jr. picking up a Country Music Award, accompanied by his son Shelton Hank Williams III, April 10, 1989. (Ron Galella/WireImage/Getty Images)

Shelton Hank Williams III, the spitting image of his grandfather, January 1, 2000. (Nicky J. Sims/Redferns/Getty Images)

Pamela Anderson, Kid Rock, and Hank Williams Jr. at the Country Music Awards, May 22, 2002. (Trench Shore/WireImage/Getty Images)

Hank Williams Jr. rockin' the Arena at Gwinnett Center in Duluth, Georgia, September 20, 2003, five decades and counting. (Rick Diamond/WireImage/Getty Images)

Superjoint Ritual with Hank Williams III (far right) on bass, January 1, 2004. (Mick Hutson/Redferns/Getty Images)

Top: Hank III rippin' up
the stage with Superjoint
Ritual at Ozzfest in Hartford,
Connecticut, July 10, 2004.
(Theo Wargo/WireImage/Getty
Images)

Right: Hank III displaying
the Williams attitude at the
Masquerade in Atlanta, Georgia,
March 30, 2005. (Frank Mullen/
WireImage/Getty Images)

Left: Hank III playing his own brand of "hellbilly" at the Sunset Junction Street Fair, August 28, 2006. (Paul Redmond/WireImage/Getty Images)

Bottom: Hank Williams Jr. campaigning for John McCain, October 13, 2008. (Chip Somodevilla/Getty Image News/Getty Images)

Hank III carrying on the family tradition on tour in the Netherlands, August 22, 2009.
(Dimitri Hakke/Redferns/Getty Images)

singer to come in off the road." He begged his wife to come on tour with him, but after Shelton was born, she spent more time at home raising her son. After seeking help from marriage counselors, and living separate lives under the same roof, Hank Jr. and Gwen divorced in 1975.

His son would lose the presence of a full-time father at the same age Hank Jr. had lost his. Hank III remembers, "Growing up I didn't see him much, but I can see why. He was drinking and drugging and being with women."

At twenty-five, Hank Jr. was still battling with his father's legacy. The southern-rock movement was bringing together rock and country music, and Hank Jr. wanted to be a part of that development. He wrote, "I could feel, even through the haze I was living in, that a fusion between rock and country music was not only possible, it was inevitable. A lot of people had tried to make that kind of music and failed—rejected by either one camp or the other. But I knew I could try and succeed. For once, damn it, I'd make this Williams name work for me instead of against me!"

One day, after Hank Jr. had stopped to put gas in his new decked-out Ford truck, it wouldn't start back up, and he went to the closest bar to drown his sorrows. He plugged the jukebox and played Linda Ronstadt's version of "I Can't Help It (If I'm Still in Love with You)," then broke down at the bar. When he went outside to try to start his truck again, the song "Stoned at the Jukebox" came pouring out as fast as he could scribble it down. As soon as he finished writing, he was able to start the truck right up after realizing he'd forgotten to turn on the electric fuel pump switch.

Like many tortured artists, Hank Jr. drew vast inspiration from the depths of his pain. He was writing great music, but his personal life was in shambles. Many nights he would sit alone in his apartment, drinking too much and crying his eyes out to his father's music. A psychologist he and Gwen had gone to told him, "Number one, Hank. I don't know how you've made it this far in your situation. You've always expected to act like Hank Williams, to be like Hank Williams, to sing like Hank Williams, to look like Hank Williams—the whole thing. I don't really see any outs. They've almost succeeded. You're almost like Hank Williams—deceased at an early age."

He was advised to save himself and leave Nashville altogether. Hank had always enjoyed his visits with J. R. Smith, a fishing buddy who lived in Cullman, Alabama, so he moved in with Smith and his family while he looked for a place of his own. The Nashville press exclaimed, "Hank's son leaves music city; vows to give up business!"

When he arrived in Cullman, twenty-six-year-old Hank Jr. was broke and in debt to just about everybody. Not only did he have his own bills to worry about, but he was supporting Gwen and paying Sharon alimony, he owed money to the IRS, and he had to cover road expenses. After living with Smith for a year, Hank Jr. found himself an A-frame cabin next to the city reservoir. He spent much of his time drinking and pleading to Gwen over the phone to get back together again. One day, engulfed in his misery, Hank Jr. downed a bottle of Darvon painkillers, made a quick good-bye call to Gwen, and was ready to give up and go down just like his daddy. A handyman showed up at his house that afternoon and called J. R. Smith for help. Smith rushed Hank Jr. to the hospital to have his stomach pumped. Gwen flew down to see him but stayed only for the afternoon.

Hank wrote of that time, "The only thing I had left to me was my music, and I finally threw myself into the idea I'd been nurturing in my head for so long. I wanted to do a special album of my own music, done my own way. It would be totally different from anything I'd ever done before, and I knew I was taking a hell of a risk—I'd even had hit songs in 1974. 'Last Love Song,' was a number-one song. I walked away from that, there was a chance I'd never get it back. … Still, I was totally determined."

Audrey was also wrestling with her own demons, and her future plans for opening a country music museum was shot down by the

Nashville city council. Her attempt at holding the "biggest and best" garage sale in Nashville's history backfired when the *Nashville Banner* ran an article headlined, "Cleaning Out Hank Williams' Attic." She spent most of the sale drunk, sitting in a chair with a cardboard cutout of Hank Sr. standing close by.

16

AJAX MOUNTAIN

"Hank, please think about my job before you ever do anything like this again!" —MERLE KILGORE

INSTEAD OF GOING BACK INTO THE STUDIO IN NASHVILLE, Hank Jr. chose to record in Muscle Shoals, Alabama, where the studios had a "funkier rhythm-and-blues feel to them." The first person he called was Phil Walden, president of Capricorn Records, the label that had launched the Allman Brothers and the Marshall Tucker Band. Walden was all ears and quickly introduced Hank Jr. to both the Tuckers and the Allman Brothers.

Toy Caldwell, vocalist and lead guitarist for the Marshall Tucker Band, and Hank Jr. were fans of each other, and Caldwell had told Hank how he used to get thrown off the stage for playing Hank Williams songs.

When Hank asked him if he and his band would like to work together, the answer was a resounding, "Hell, yeah!" Hank Jr. told them, "Before you start practicing those Hank Williams songs, wait a bit. This album is going to be something special, it ain't gonna be *old* Hank, it's gonna be *new* Hank." Hank Jr. also wanted to cover a couple of Caldwell's songs that had been recorded by the Marshall Tucker Band, "Losin' You," and "Can't You See," two tunes that he knew would become country hits.

Up until that point, no one in Nashville had looked at the material coming out of Macon, Georgia. Hank Jr. was clearly at the forefront of southern rock, stating, "I knew that the artificial barriers between the music couldn't last much longer—they just couldn't! Kids aren't that dumb. One day they're going to turn on the radio and realize it was time to change the dial and find some of the originals. I knew the kids were going to come looking for country music, and I intended on being there."

Along with the two songs from Caldwell, Hank Jr. included "Stoned at the Jukebox"; his last love song to Gwen, "I Really Did"; "On Susan's Floor," a song written by Shel Silverstein and Vince Matthews; "Montana Song"; "Clovis, New Mexico"; "Brothers of the Road"; and one he had been working on for a very long time, called "Living Proof," a song that intended to be, in his own words, "the exclamation point at the end of the old Hank Williams Jr."

The album was to be called *Hank Williams Jr. and Friends.* Joining him in the studio were Toy Caldwell, Chuck Leavell, and Dickey Betts from the Allman Brothers, and Charlie Daniels. They started recording, at Music Mill Studios in Muscle Shoals, in February 1975 and finished up in July. The album turned out to be everything Hank Jr. had hoped it would be, and everyone who had worked on it was equally excited. He was so optimistic that he considered going back out on the road even though he knew he wasn't strong enough to start touring again. He had yet to kick the drugs or alcohol, and he definitely wasn't over Gwen.

To keep himself busy, Hank Jr. took flying lessons and had his pilot's license within a month. His plan was to begin touring again in September, giving him just enough time to try to get in shape for the road. He called his friend Dick Willey in Montana, to plan a trip to go hunting and climbing in the mountains the first week of August. His friend J. R. Smith had helped him get his finances back in order, and now Hank Jr. stopped off in Nashville to shop for an airplane.

While looking over some planes and visiting with his old friend C. F. Lautner, he was stopped in his tracks by a picture sitting on Lautner's desk. It showed a blonde named Becky White, and she worked for ABC Records. After much cajoling, Hank Jr. got his buddy to call Becky and convince her to meet him. Their first date was dinner and seeing the movie *Jaws*.

Becky had also just had her heart broken, and the two of them ended up talking for hours. They saw each other every night for a week before Hank Jr. left for Montana. His trip to visit Willey and climb mountains didn't go as planned, though. Northwest Airlines was on strike, and they happened to be one of only two airlines that flew into Missoula, Montana. All the available flights out of Nashville were booked solid, and the harder Hank Jr. tried to leave for Montana, the more forces conspired to keep him in Tennessee.

Hunting and fishing in the mountains of Montana had always been a sweet refuge for Hank Jr. This adventure would clear his head, get him back in shape, and help him prepare to perform again once his new album came out.

J. R. Smith advised him, "I'll tell you, Hank. Maybe somebody's telling you you ought to stay in Nashville and not go out there." His business manager even said, "It's fate; someone upstairs just doesn't want you to go to Montana. Forget it, and get ready for your next tour." Believing this trip was crucial to him, Hank Jr. was unwilling to give up on his plans. In his biography he wrote, "I couldn't forget it any more than I could forget the next tour. I had to get to Montana, or maybe there wouldn't *be* a next tour."

After finally booking a flight to Missoula, Montana, with a stopover in Billings, Hank Jr. said goodbye to Becky, telling her that he loved her and wanted to see her as soon as he got back. Then he boarded a plane headed for what was to be a rejuvenating vacation before he had to face the road again. Instead, this trip nearly cost Hank Jr. his life, and it would completely change him forever.

At 8:00 in the morning on August 8, 1975, Willey, his eleven-year-old son Walt, and Hank Jr. started scaling the mountains along the edge of Idaho and Montana, called the Continental Divide, which soars eleven thousand feet into the sky. Ahead of them was Ajax Mountain, covered with an icy blanket of snow. Willey's plan was to make their way over the top through the snow field, across to the lower peaks on the other side, and then back down into the valley. After climbing for several hours, they stopped to take a break, and Hank Jr. could see Salmon, Idaho, miles below, where people didn't "worry too much about who my daddy was and think Nashville might as well be on the moon."

As they talked about hunting, guns, and how Chief Joseph of the Nez Perce got his people through the mountains while being chased by the U.S. Cavalry, Hank Jr. told Willey about his new album, and the song he had written called "Montana Song."

Feeling philosophical in the cold mountain air, Hank Jr. was wishing he could have brought Gwen and Audrey along with him. In *Living Proof*, Hank Jr. confesses, "I'd like to sit around the campfire and exorcize, once and for all, the ghost of my father, Hank Williams, Sr. I'd like to calmly explain who I am, what I do for a living, and why I don't intend to die in the back of a blue Cadillac on the way to a one-night stand.... I won't be billed as the reincarnation of Hank Williams, and old men won't spit on me because I don't do enough of Daddy's songs."

This trip was more than a way to get back in shape for the road. Hank Jr. wanted it to give him the strength to finally face his true legacy, which wasn't to be an impersonator or just the son of a country music legend, but to become a trailblazing country rock-and-roll outlaw in his own right.

When they approached the snow field, Willey looked over at Hank Jr. and Walt and said, "Be careful, now." As they slowly held on to the edge underneath the icy overhangs, Willey laughed and said, "I'll tell you one thing, Hank, this is the truth. I don't give a damn what John Denver says, you're the only SOB in your business who's ever been up this high, and I'll swear to that!"

Without being equipped with proper climbing gear, and agreeing not to go back they way they came, they decided to work their way around the snowdrifts and climb back up the peaks and keep hiking. All they had to do was cross one flat snow field and continue on their way. As Hank Jr. remembered, "That's all you have to do, except that there's no way of knowing how sturdy the ground is underneath the snow, or whether the snow is melting underneath or whether it's all ice or anything."

Once they reached the edge of the snow field, Willey decided to walk across it first, followed by his son, and then Hank Jr. Willey, who weighed 165 pounds, carefully made his way across the snow without dislodging anything. Then he turned to his son and said, "When you come across, walk in my footsteps. And be damned careful not to slip, 'cause it's a long way down!" Walt made his way through the snow, stepped back onto the rocks, and turned around to wave. Hank Jr. waved back and smiled as he started to cross the field.

As the snow crunched beneath his hiking boots, Hank Jr. was careful to stay within the footprints, although the snow was packing down a bit deeper than Willey's original steps. Just as he was halfway across, he suddenly realized that the rocks under his right foot had started to shift. As soon as he felt the rocks move, Hank Jr. tried to switch his weight to his left leg, and as he stepped back, he could feel the ground start to drop away. As he watched the snow around him slide and the rocks start to rearrange, he could see Walt screaming while Willey stretched out his arms in a panicked effort to grab him, but Hank Jr. was a good seventy yards away from them when he started to fall.

As he slid down the side of the mountain, Hank Jr. could see everything. He saw the lake below, his friends frozen in horror, and the rocks coming up at him. He remembers being two people, one insane with fear clawing at the air and looking for an escape, the other very rational and calm, realizing there was no escape, thinking, "You're going to die here. You're already dead."

From what seemed like a million miles away, Hank Jr. could hear Walt screaming, "My God! He's going to die! He's going to die!" Then he heard Willey yell, "Turn around, Hank! Get turned around! The boulders, man! The boulders!" Hank Jr. could see the boulders coming up at him, and he struggled to turn himself around, trying to slow himself down by digging his heels into the earth. He managed to get turned around, and, bringing his knees up to his chin, he kicked out off the mountain, sending himself sailing into the air. For a few seconds Hank Jr. actually believed he was going to make the "longest swan dive in the history of the world, and land in that icy lake."

After hitting the ground, he continued to tumble and slide, continually smashing his face into the rocks. Ahead of him, he could see a giant boulder with a ridge that lined right up with his nose. He collided with the mass of stone headfirst, and he remembered it as a thud that seemed to go on forever. Then he landed on his knees, with his head slumped forward between them. The first thing he did was look at his hands and realize that he was still alive. He managed to mumble, "I'm all right; I'm all right." Hank Jr. had fallen 442 feet.

Willey frantically scaled down the mountainside, reaching him within what seemed like no time at all. When he finally got to him, all he could do was stare. Hank Jr. miraculously declared that he was all right and wanted to know what was wrong with him. Willey lied and just told him his nose was broken. Hank Jr. replied, "Then I'm going to walk off this mountain. I've got to walk off this mountain." Trying to get up, he quickly sank back to his knees just as Willey's son Walt came running up. As soon as Walt saw Hank Jr.'s injuries, all he could do was scream.

Putting his hand up to his face to feel his nose, Hank Jr. found nothing where his nose should be, and some of his teeth and parts of his jaw fell off into his hands. When he went to touch his forehead, all he could feel was something squishy. He asked Willey what it was; it was his brain. Hank Jr. recalled, "My cheek is gone. My eye is hanging down. My head is shattered, and the warm stuff I feel is my blood. 'Oh, God,' I think, 'Oh, dear God. After all this, the mountain's going to win anyway.'"

Willey quickly laid Hank Jr. down into the snow and took his hands off of his face. Then, with his own hand, he pushed the exposed part of Hank Jr.'s brain back into his skull, making a sound that Hank Jr. swears he can still hear to this day. Willey proceeded to push some of the shredded parts of Hank's face back where they belonged, taking off his shirt and tying it around Hank's head.

Willey and Walt together moved Hank to a clearing out of the snow, laying him facedown. As Hank Jr. wrote, "Dick and Walt carry me to some higher ground, which is all rocks and no snow—not much of an improvement, if you ask me." Much to his son's horror, Willey talked Walt into staying with Hank while he ran for help, telling him to keep Hank Jr. talking and not to let him go to sleep.

Valiantly keeping him awake, young Walt sat with Hank and talked about every subject he could think of, including fishing, football, and basketball season. Hank Jr. actually tried to answer him back, not wanting to be impolite. What he was actually thinking was, "I don't think Walt has seen how banged up I am—that's the only way to explain this conversation. He doesn't know that I'm going to die, and he doesn't know that he's going to end up on this godforsaken mountain with a corpse. I feel sorry for him. … It's odd, you know, but I've wanted to die a lot of times. I tried to kill myself once, and I even screwed that up. I've wanted to die a lot, but I never wanted to die on this godforsaken mountain…. It's just not musical enough, damn it."

Lying there in the cold, Hank Jr. kept thinking of his son, Hank III, his wife Gwen, his mother Audrey, his father, and his friends. At the same time, reconciling himself with why he grew up the way he did, and how he wanted to be just like Hank Sr., he fell in and out of consciousness. Hank Jr. said it best when he wrote in *Living Proof*, "I'm alone on this mountain. And I'm dying. The despair comes like a savage animal—to find your soul and lose your life in the same afternoon! I look across the lake, and sleep is both seductive and insistent. Come, it says, let go. Rest."

As the sun started to sink into the horizon, and the wind howled, with tears streaming down his cheeks, Walt just kept right on talking, telling Hank Jr. that he was going to be all right. As Hank listened, all of a sudden they both heard Willey yell for Walt, asking if Hank Jr. was still alive. Walt screamed back, "Dad, Dad! He's still talking! He's alive!"

While Walt kept vigil with Hank Jr., Willey had made his way down the mountain to his Toyota Land Cruiser station wagon, which barely fit the fire trail he had to navigate to get help. It's usually a fifteen-mile-per-hour journey, but at times Willey says he was going eighty. Upon reaching the base of the mountain, they were still twelve miles from any civilization. It would be two years before Willey admitted to Hank Jr. that he actually wrecked his vehicle on the way down, smashing into the side of a bridge and landing in the middle of a creek bed. Using his four-wheel drive, he got back out on the road, but he was still ten miles from his cabin and a phone to call for help. Luckily, Willey happened upon a Forest Service vehicle; he claimed you could drive those roads for months without seeing another vehicle, much less one from the Forest Service.

The forest ranger radioed for a helicopter to come and rescue Hank Jr., and as soon as Willey had confirmation that they were on their way, he took off back up the mountain. Amazingly, he was gone for only two hours. As soon as he got within half a mile of the spot where he'd left Hank and Walt, Willey hollered as loudly as he could to see if Hank was still alive. As they waited for the helicopter to arrive, they both kept reassuring Hank Jr. that he was going to be fine. Walt had constructed a wall of rocks around Hank Jr. to keep the wind away, but the more Hank Jr. became aware of each part of his body, the more the pain set in.

After a couple of attempts, the helicopter found a place to land two hundred feet away. A medic named Swede Thorenson changed the bandages (Willey's shirt) on his head and gave him a shot. Strapping him onto a stretcher, the medics carefully made their way across the rocks into the helicopter and flew Hank Jr. to a ranch with an airstrip, where a small plane waited to take him to Missoula. Once they landed there, another helicopter took him to the Community Hospital.

As they prepped him for surgery, Hank startled the doctors by declaring that he didn't want them to call anyone. As he wrote, "My mother is sick, maybe dying, and if she isn't dying, this should just about do it. My wife is just more pain. My friends are after my money, Dick [Willey] cares, and he already knows. Maybe I shouldn't bother anyone else with my problems. Maybe I've spent my whole life bothering other people with my problems. Maybe that's what I learned up on that mountain."

By another incredible twist of fate, on that Saturday afternoon, there just happened to be three surgeons at the hospital. Dr. Richard Dewey, Dr. Don Murray, and Dr. Tom Holshaw spent seven and a half hours cleaning, stitching, and putting Hank Jr.'s head back together. They were grateful for the cold having kept away infection, and for Hank being in good shape to start with. When he woke up in the intensive-care unit the next morning, he had a breathing tube in his throat, and his jaws were wired shut. Dr. Dewey had spent time in Vietnam working on bone fragments and bullet holes, and Dr. Holshaw, the eye, ear, nose, and throat specialist, as Hank said, "was going to have a field day, finding me a new eye, ear, nose, and throat."

They informed Hank that every single bone in his face had been broken. The only reason why he wasn't killed in the fall was that his face, jaws, teeth, even his forehead had protected his brain from the impact. The real danger now for Hank Jr. was an infection of the brain, which they were extremely worried about, considering his brain had been exposed to the elements.

Word quickly spread back to Nashville that Hank Jr. was near death. He scoffed at the reports, saying, "But I don't think I'm near death; I've been near death, and I've got a pretty good idea of what it looks like." As soon as they heard the news, Audrey and Lycrecia flew out to be with Hank Jr.

Even though he was fighting for his life, he wrote a note to Lycrecia, saying, "I know someone that has a birthday in a few days." Her birthday was four days later, on August 13. Gwen rushed to his bedside and declared her love for him. Also staying close by were friends Dick, Betty, and Walt Willey; Bill and Betty Dyer; his manager, J. R. Smith; Merle Kilgore; and Johnny and June Cash. All Hank Jr. needed was to make it eight days without an infection, and he would be on the road to recovery. Only this time it would be the hardest road he had ever traveled.

At the end of those eight days, Hank Jr. picked up a cheap acoustic guitar and, thanking God for preserving his hands, lit right into "Freight Train," Chet Atkins style, and was ecstatic that he remembered how to play. At the time he believed he would never sing again, but as long as he could play, he would still be a part of the music business. He was comforted by that thought until he saw his reflection in a mirror.

17

THE ROAD TO RECOVERY

"June Carter and Johnny Cash were there when I came around and it meant a lot." —HANK JR.

O N HIS WAY BACK TO HIS HOSPITAL ROOM after a whirlpool bath, Hank Jr. asked to stop at a bathroom. Up to this point, he had not seen himself and had no idea what his injuries actually looked like. When he weakly hobbled into the bathroom, there was a mirror on the wall reflecting someone he didn't recognize. His head was swollen, resembling a watermelon that had been crushed. His right cheek was stretched up, his right eye was completely purple, and his left eye didn't move at all. Not to mention he had no teeth and his mouth was wired shut. Quickly his thoughts of performing again, or ever having a woman even look at him again, vanished within seconds. His only consolation was the fact that he still remembered how to play guitar.

The more Hank Jr. mastered his guitar playing, the more he worried about his ability to hunt again. He was used to lining his aim with his right eye using his right hand, but losing the sight in his right eye would force him to learn how to line up a shot with his left. Talking Willey into bringing him a gun without a cylinder to practice on in the hospital, every day Hank Jr. would aim out the window, determined to become as good with his left eye as he had been with his right. His doctors were thrilled with his tenacity in rehabilitating himself. He also kept his spirits up by reading all the mail that flooded into Missoula, Montana, while he was recovering. Hank Jr. received hundreds of letters, from everyone from Ernest Tubb to the Marshall Tucker Band.

Even though his doctors predicted a six-week hospital stay, on the fifteenth day after his fall, a team of doctors walked into his room and told him there was nothing more they could do for him and he might as well go home. As soon as he could check himself out, Hank Jr. went back to Dick and Betty Willey's home in Polson, Montana. Their house sat on the Flathead Lake shoreline at the tip of Glacier National Park, which was a perfect place for Hank Jr. to recuperate. Spending a lot of time sitting outside staring at the mountain he fell off, Hank Jr. reflected on what he had actually learned coming that close to death. He wrote, "I spend a lot of time thinking of that lesson, which is so simple I can't imagine having not learned it a long time ago—if you're going to live, live. Just live your life to the best of your abilities, and if you need strength, it's there for the asking. A simple prayer will suffice."

Along with hiking around the house and drinking enough liquids to float a battleship, Hank Jr. fantasized more about eating solid foods than he ever had about a woman. When Willey asked him to drive back into the mountains to pick up some cattle, he gladly went along, and together they practiced shooting targets. Hank had succeeded in teaching himself to shoot using his left eye, which was a great confirmation that he was going to rebuild his life no matter what. He also had to learn how to chew again once the doctors took the wires out of his jaws. Since he had no teeth, tackling solid foods would be his next challenge.

By October, Hank Jr. was given permission to go back to Cullman, Alabama. Still needing someone to watch over him, he spent one night at his A-frame and then moved in with his manager, J. R. Smith; Smith's wife, Connie; and their three kids. Within weeks he boarded a plane to Nashville to have nine of his front teeth implanted. After taking X-rays of his mouth, his dentist informed him that he would have to have his jaws realigned before any teeth could be restored, something Hank Jr. wasn't happy to hear, but as soon as he could schedule surgery, he was back in the hospital having his jaws fixed. He recalled how funny it was to have to pay for someone to break his jaw, since he knew plenty of people "who'd do it for free." Hank woke up with his jaws again wired shut; he was back on a liquid diet. This was the first of a total of nine surgeries he would undergo in sixteen months to reconstruct his face.

Aside from mastering how to eat solid foods again, Hank Jr. had to teach himself how to talk without any speech impediments. Once he had his permanent teeth implanted and the others capped, he practiced speaking as much as could, including talking on the CB radio to whoever would listen to him. If he could learn to speak clearly, he could sing again.

The most dangerous surgery Hank Jr. had to endure was patching the hole in his forehead. Through all of his recovery, he still had an opening in his head that left his brain exposed. His surgeon, Dr. Dewey, skillfully placed a plastic piece into his skull and had him on his way home to Alabama within days. That November, a full fifteen months after his fall, he went back into a hospital for one of his final surgeries in Charlottesville, Virginia, to have his eyes repositioned.

Just nine months after his accident, Hank Jr. walked out onstage in Delaware in May of 1976. He was still very weak, but a lot more comfortable performing his own songs, his own way. Most of his old friends told him he wasn't the same guy, saying, "The body's sure as hell not the same, and neither is the person in it." Hank Jr. was very happy to hear it. For the first time in his life, he looked out into the audience and saw friends instead of people who wanted a piece of him.

His metamorphosis was complete in 1976 when MGM released his album *Hank Williams Jr. and Friends*, which made it to number seventeen on the charts. All the reviews were raves, including one in *Rolling Stone*, which normally shunned country music. John Morthland wrote in his April 8 review, "These songs are highly personal and intimate, but not obscure; they have the kind of vividness that only the best singer/songwriters can produce. … *Hank Williams Jr. and Friends* marks his emergence as a major contemporary artist—and as his own man."

New York City's *Village Voice* declared *Hank Williams Jr. and Friends* one of the ten best albums of the year, stating, "A lot of people have talked about fusing country and blues and rock and rhythm-and-blues. Now the son of Hank Williams has done it!" Years later, his friend Charlie Daniels told the Biography Channel, "That's when Hank started to blossom. He finally took a turn off of the lost highway."

Hank Jr. begged his record company to release "Can't You See" as a single, but the record executives wouldn't listen and instead went with "Living Proof," which only made it to number thirteen. His buddy Waylon Jennings was so sure "Can't You See" was a hit that, with Hank Jr.'s blessings, he went into the studio and recorded a version of it himself. Jennings's recording was a huge hit, helping to change what most people thought country music was all about.

Hank Jr. also made a critical decision that he wasn't going to be a hermit, especially since he was still hearing from Becky, who faithfully kept writing and calling him. She wanted to see him again, and he was determined to keep her away as long as he could. During his recovery, he made frequent trips to Nashville for physical therapy, staying at the home of Christine Longyear, who was also a friend of Becky's.

One day while he was resting after a rough session, Christine came in to tell him that Becky was there to see him. At first he refused, but she wouldn't leave until he said hello to her. He was completely self-conscious about his appearance, it took about ten minutes to make him forget what he looked like. As he wrote, "What rushed in to fill the void was love."

As soon as Hank Jr.'s divorce from Gwen was final, he and Becky White were married on June 18, 1976, in her hometown of Mer Rouge, Louisiana. Their wedding guests included Jerry Rivers, Merle Kilgore, and Waylon Jennings and his wife, Jessi Colter.

Hank Jr. left MGM and signed a new deal with Warner Brothers, then went into the studio in Muscle Shoals to record *One Night Stands*. The album was released in 1977 and didn't do as well as *Hank Williams*

Jr. and Friends. He immediately followed that with *The New South,* which was produced by Waylon Jennings, who also sang on "Once and for All." Hank Jr. had been working on and off with Jennings since his days with Audrey's Caravan of Stars, and on this record Hank Jr. also included one of his father's songs, "You're Gonna Change (Or I'm Gonna Leave), played as a blues number.

The following year, with his newfound identity and his faithful friend Dick Willey, Hank Jr. returned to Montana and climbed back up the mountain he had fallen off of. He carefully made his way back to the spot where his body had come to rest, where the boulders were still stained burgundy from his blood.

Thankful for his family and his miraculous recovery, Hank Jr. took time off the road to stay with Becky until their first child was born. Despite warnings about how much money he was losing by staying home, Hank had decided that the value of getting to know his new bride and take the time to be with her while she was pregnant couldn't be measured by any amount of money.

Sure of the fact that he wasn't going to end up going down the same road his father traveled, Hank Jr. closed his book *Living Proof* by saying, "And I'll tell you one thing for certain: I'm not going to die a broke, drunk country singer. I've really made my mind up on that point. Even if I'm not a singer, I'm not going to die a broke, drunk *anything.* Period. I will not do it. No matter what my family name is."

Less than ninety days after his horrific fall, the woman who had pushed him into stardom was gone. In her final years, Audrey had opened her home to tourists, sold off most of Hank Sr.'s possessions, and accused Hank Jr.'s manager J. R. Smith of stealing her son away from her. Since Hank Jr.'s accident, she had barely left her bedroom, refusing to eat; diagnosed with epilepsy, she was suffering from seizures. She was so addicted to alcohol and painkillers that sometimes she didn't recognize her closet friends. Shortly before her death, she told her friend Erma Williams how Hank Sr. had appeared in her bedroom in her dream and that they made love and he told her he loved her and that everything was going to be all right. Hank had been dead for twenty-two years, but Audrey never let him go.

Her financial problems had resulted in losing the smaller house next door and her chalet in Gatlinburg to the IRS. The city of Oak Hill eventually won their battle against Audrey opening the museum and closed it down, and Billie Jean was back in court fighting Audrey for half of Hank Sr.'s royalties.

When Audrey found out that the government was going to seize her home on Franklin Road, she told Lycrecia that they would "never take her out of this house alive." She wanted to leave the house to Lycrecia, considering she didn't benefit from Hank Sr.'s estate due to the fact that Audrey had refused to let him adopt her. Yet, fearing she would hurt Hank Jr. with the decision to give Lycrecia the house, Audrey never put it in writing. She also stopped taking her epilepsy medication, and on November 4, 1975, just one day before the government was going to seize her house, Miss Audrey died. She was only fifty-two years old.

Her funeral at White's Chapel was one of Hank Jr.'s first public appearances after his accident, and some reports said he looked like death himself. Bob Harrington, "the Chaplain of Bourbon Street," gave the eulogy and then turned to her chrome and silver coffin and said, "Hey, good lookin', whatcha got cookin'? There will be no more cold, cold heart, no more parting, no more heartache, no more lonely nights. Audrey will never be lonely again."

Because of her death, the house went into her estate, so the IRS wasn't able to take it from her. Appraised at $175,000, the unfinished, piecemeal seventeen-room house was declared "functionally obsolescent." Her estate was in debt for almost a half a million dollars, and the house was sold for $200,000, which the IRS settled for. Eventually Tammy Wynette, known as the First Lady of Country Music, would buy and refurbish the house. In 1998, she would also die there.

Audrey was originally laid to rest some thirty feet away from Hank Sr., but eight years later, Lycrecia and Hank Jr. arranged to have her moved next to him, installing a matching white marble monument adorned with the letter "A." As Lycrecia so poignantly wrote, "Now Hank and Audrey were together—in peace—for all time."

18

ENTERTAINER OF
THE YEAR

"I know a lot of people don't like me, but I'll still make my son into a star." —AUDREY WILLIAMS

A S HANK JR. CONTINUED TO HEAL, he kept right on performing, recording some of his most successful songs on the albums *Family Tradition* in 1978 and *Whiskey Bent and Hell Bound* in 1979. He and Becky welcomed a daughter, Hilary, in 1979, and Hank Jr. kept his life on track with a new family and a new sound. He now sported a beard, dark sunglasses, and a hat to hide his scars—this would become his trademark look.

He became one of the original country outlaws. Hank Jr.'s career as a hell-raising cowboy who rocks landed him a Grammy in 1980 for Best Country and Western Vocal Performance. He also made another big-screen appearance when he played himself in the 1980 film *Roadie*, which starred fellow rocker Meatloaf.

In 1981, Hank Jr. was on a roll with four hit singles: "Texas Women" and "Dixie on My Mind," from the album *Rowdy*; "All My Rowdy Friends Have Settled Down"; and what is now known as his signature song, "A Country Boy Can Survive," from *The Pressure Is On*. On March 12, Hank Jr. and Becky had their second daughter, Holly, who was born in Cullman, Alabama.

Following the success of Hank Jr.'s autobiography, *Living Proof*, his life story was made into a movie starring actor Richard Thomas. The television movie did well in the reviews, although some critics scoffed at Hank Jr. being played by "John-Boy Walton." His manager, Merle Kilgore, played himself, and the groupie who takes his virginity backstage was played by future country superstar Naomi Judd. She was paid the scale sum of $630 and only had to say one line. The television movie traced Hank Jr.'s struggles to get free from his mother's influence and his father's legacy, and his survival and incredible recovery after his mountain fall.

Having successfully carved out his own place in country rock, Hank Jr. still gave credit where credit was due by including nods to his father in songs like "Are You Sure Hank Done It This Way" and "The Ballad of Hank Williams." Now able to make his own music and step beyond his famous father's shadow, Hank Jr. prolifically recorded back-to-back albums throughout the 1980s, sometimes releasing two albums in one year. This era's ouput includes *Habits Old and New*, *High Notes*, *Strong Stuff*, *Man of Steel*, *Major Moves*, *Five-O*, and *Montana Cafe*.

Touring relentlessly took its toll on Hank Jr.'s third marriage, and he and Becky divorced in 1983. Years later Hank Jr. would tell Crook and Chase how he would come home from a long tour, grateful for home-cooked meals and a real bed, to find that his wives were as home-weary as he was road-weary. They would end up fighting the whole time over the fact that he wanted to spend time at home and they wanted to go out and socialize. Before long, Hank Jr. couldn't wait to get back out on the road.

Well known for his high-octane shows and a long string of hits, Hank Jr. took home the Entertainer of the Year Awards from the Academy of Country Music in 1986 and 1987, and the Country Music Association in 1987, 1988, and 1989. As he once said about performing, "I'm going to put the pressure on ya, if you follow me, you're gonna know it."

In his video for the song "Young Country," from his 1987 album *Born to Boogie*, Hank Jr. trades licks with Les Paul and Hank III. A picture of all three of them appeared in newspapers with the caption "Three Generations of Fine Guitar Players."

Accepting the Entertainer of the Year Award in 1988 from actor Patrick Duffy, and the Judds, Naomi and Wynonna, Hank Jr. beamed and said, "Unbelievable. Wynonna said her grandpa had some influence—I'll give you two guesses who had influence on me. It's wonderful. I kind of look at some of these fresh new artists, that great show tonight, and think back over the years—I have been around for a while. And I kind of get the feeling that maybe people were scared of me, or the academy was scared of me. I'm as gentle as a lamb, and just sweet as sugar, you don't have to be afraid of me. I've had a lot of wonderful help from some great names in country music, pop music, rock-and-roll music, and I will do whatever it takes, just like Daddy's plaque in the Hall of Fame, to broaden and expand this thing called country music that I play every night, that feeds all of us! Thank you!"

Upon the discovery of the lost tapes in the attic of Big Bill Lister's house, Hank Jr. and his father sang one last duet together. Using the video footage of Hank Sr. on the Kate Smith show, Hank Jr. recorded a new song from Hank Sr. that no one had ever heard. Another classic ode to lost love, "There's a Tear in My Beer" became a hit in 1989, and Hank Jr. received the awards for Vocal Event of the Year and Music Video of the Year from the Country Music Association, and the Video of the Year from the Academy of Country Music. Chiding the Country Music Association when he picked up his video award, Hank Jr. said, "I also do audio."

Snagging one of the most prestigious accolades in the music business, the song also won a Grammy for Best Country Collaboration with Vocals. "There's a Tear in My Beer" was thought to have been written between the years 1950 and 1952, and the original recording was just Hank Sr. singing and playing guitar.

Thanks to digital magic, for several seconds it appears that Hank Jr. is singing along with his father, and it's a moment in country music history that never fails to bring a tear. It's a striking reminder of where Hank Jr. came from and all he had been through. Hank Jr. won his first Grammys in 1965 for Best Country and Western Artist and Best Country

Music Album. Over twenty years later he had been there, done that, and was still kicking ass along the way.

Hank Jr. was now his own man, bringing in thousands of fans wherever he played. Although he lived apart from Becky, she and Hank Jr. raised their daughters together. Holly would say in a 2009 interview that her parents did the right thing by getting along and never bad-mouthing each other. Hank Jr. continued to speak through his music, and the song that would be the key to a very lucrative deal, "All My Rowdy Friends Are Coming Over Tonight," won him another Grammy in 1985. He hired as his manager Merle Kilgore, who had started out carrying a guitar for Hank Sr., and Kilgore helped Hank Jr. build and sustain a solid reputation as a country music icon over the next two decades.

Hank Jr.'s half-sister, Cathy Yvonne, who changed her name to Jett, had started to search for information in the early 1980s to find out the whole story of her true heredity. After piecing together her early years living with Lillie, and her subsequent adoptions, she was declared in court on October 26, 1987, to be the biological daughter of Hank Williams Sr. The Supreme Court of the State of Alabama reversed a ruling from a lower court on June 5, 1989, declaring that she had been a victim of fraud and judicial error that concealed her identity for financial gain. The courts reopened Hank's estate and made Jett Williams a legal heir, giving her one-half of the estate proceeds, which now meant that Hank Jr. had to split his father's royalty income with Jett.

Having a natural talent for singing and playing guitar, with her newfound identity, Jett Williams went on to make a name for herself in the country music business. Jett has become a regular performer at many of the annual Hank Williams celebratory events and continues to promote her father's legacy.

Jett and Hank Jr. have never been close, and Hank III has never been a big fan of Jett. He explained,

No, her husband made a comment about my mother so I had to make the comment that if I see ya, I'm gonna beat your fuckin' ass.

He probably said something because I said she'd be better at writing a book than singing a song. She's out there sayin', "Oh, poor pitiful me." He didn't like that tone, so he went after my mom and I said, okay, the old tradition is if you're gonna talk shit about my mom,... They've canceled shows when I was [playing] on Broadway in Nashville, because they refused to play if I was on the street.

I've also had an old black man come up to me in New York City and say, "You need to meet Jett. You all should talk." You've got a lawyer standing in the way of that. I remember the days that Hank Jr. didn't have that much good to say about Jett. I've heard more than one story that because of him it's a problem. Even at a funeral, the "boast" was there, the showy/flashy kind of thing. That's okay sometimes, but not all the time.

I've heard her sing enough to know that it's not that natural for her. If you want to really say something, a book is better than going out there and trying to put on the white suit and the white hat and act like you're a Hank Williams. If she had been doin' it from the get-go it would be a little different. The only other reason why I dissed her is she should go and write her own songs.

Seven years after his divorce from Becky, Hank Jr. married his fourth wife, Mary Jane Thomas, on July 1, 1990. At forty-one years old, Hank Jr. wed the twenty-six-year-old former Hawaiian Tropic Suntan lotion model, who hailed from Florida, at the Congregational Church near Missoula, Montana. Planning a delayed African safari as their honeymoon, Hank Jr. told *People* magazine, "I've never been so happy in my life; Mary Jane is truly one in a million." Hank Jr. had diligently taught Mary Jane to hunt and shoot right along with him. He had given her a ring after she visited his Tennessee farm wearing red high heels. Calling her "the Queen of my Heart," Hank Jr. also gave her a new pair of hunting boots along with the ring.

That same year Hank Jr. received two awards from TNN/Music City News for Video of the Year and Vocal Collaboration of the Year. He was also approached by the NFL, to revise his song "All My Rowdy

Friends Are Coming Over Tonight" for use as their theme song for the live televised broadcast of *Monday Night Football*. Apparently, the son of a producer for *Monday Night Football* had a tape of Hank Jr.'s in his tape player, a call was made to Merle Kilgore asking if Hank Jr. knew football, and Kilgore's response was, "He's American—of course he knows football!" That's all it took to seal the deal, which ended up earning Hank Williams Jr. four Emmys, in 1991, 1992, 1993, and 1994, making him the first country music artist to receive television's highest honor.

On what would have been his father's sixty-eighth birthday, September 17, 1991, the city of Montgomery unveiled a statue of Hank Williams Sr., a life-size replica gracing the Lister Hill Plaza downtown. It stands right across the street from the Montgomery City Hall, a place where Hank Sr. performed many times and where his funeral was held.

That same day the statue was introduced, the city dedicated a bronze plaque that stands on a stone pedestal in front of the Oak Hill Library across the street from Burdette's Pure Oil, the gas station that Charles Carr had stopped at looking for help the night Hank Sr. died. Two years later, a Hank Williams tribute concert was held at the Fayette Armory, where the power failed when the band began playing "I Saw the Light."

Hank Jr. and Mary Jane welcomed their first daughter, Katherine Diane, in 1993 and a son, Samuel, in 1997. All five of his children have inherited the hunt-and-gather instinct. Hank III loves to bow hunt, and daughters Hilary and Holly both hunt deer. Hilary brought in her first buck at the tender age of fourteen as her proud father watched. Both Katie and Samuel enjoy fishing, and Hank Jr. loves being able to spend time with them after forty years on the road. He told *WTO* magazine, "Sam and Katie are young and they love the farm and fishing for bream at the lake. I don't want to miss that, because they'e my 'Rowdy Friends' now."

Hank Jr. has circled the world on big-game-hunting adventures, going on eleven African safaris, hunting for bear in Canada and Alaska, and fishing for peacock bass in the Amazon River. Every September 1, he holds an annual Tennessee dove shoot. His whole family and lots of friends share in the activities in their sunflower fields. He maintains two farms, one in northwestern Tennessee and one in the middle of Alabama, and hunting whitetail deer remains his preference.

At seventy-three years old, Hank Sr.'s sister, Irene, passed away in 1995. Just a couple of years earlier, she had sold most of her brother's belongings to country performer Marty Stuart. Her collection contained letters Hank Sr. had written to their mom, as well as hats, pistols, clothes, and the handwritten lyrics to "I Saw the Light" and "Cold, Cold Heart." Hank Jr. sang at her funeral, although they had never been close. Hank III explains,

> There's a huge rift in the family right there. I only got to talk to Irene a few times before she passed away. She was a very deep woman, and you could see the Indian [Native American] side come through a lot more. She was basically struggling, and she respected Marty. [She] really wanted to get this stuff to Hank Jr., but there was a problem there. Marty made a call and [Merle] Kilgore told him no. So Marty, out of his good faith, asked Irene how much money he didn't need. She said, "You've got about thirty thousand that you don't need, and you can just send that to Irene." Out of that, he got all that stuff. It wasn't like he was tryin' to con her out of it or anything. She really trusted him, and at that time in her life, he really helped her a lot. She was going through some things, but that's a real gray area. I just don't understand what it is right there.
>
> But Irene Jr., her daughter, is very close to me, and I look at her words with real deep meaning, you can just tell being around her, the way she looks at you, and the way she talks to you, she's a healer and it's pretty deep. I've gotten to be around her a couple of times, and am very thankful for the relationship. I've always questioned why there is something there. There is a rumor that Irene tried to get custody of Hank Jr., so she could receive Hank Sr.'s royalties.

Considering Irene had the rights to Hank Jr.'s income in the state of Alabama, something happened and the family's never been the same. Maybe it was an unhealthy relationship that she [Irene] was trying to shelter Hank Jr. from. Audrey wasn't in a good frame of mind, but you never know. There was all kinds of things there.

"Well, he [Hank Sr.] didn't have a will. So you have all of that stuff going on. She was just feeling guilty. That was probably the main thing that happened to her, and then her and Hank Jr. fighting didn't help. It goes pretty deep. Who knows what else she had to deal with. It's kind of what we know about, not even behind the scenes of the rest of it. She was tough, but it's all that stress, and the drugs and the guilt."

The following year, Hank Jr. brought three generations of Williams's men together on one album when he released *Three Hanks: Men with Broken Hearts*. Debuting on Hank Sr.'s birthday, the album featured Hank Sr.'s songs, with Hank Jr. and Hank III adding vocals. The tracks included "I'll Never Get Out of This World Alive," "Move It on Over," "Moanin' the Blues," "Never Again (Will I Knock on Your Door)," "I'm a Long Gone Daddy," "Honky Tonk Blues," "I Won't Be Home No More," "'Neath a Cold Gray Tomb of Stone," "Where the Soul of Man Never Dies," "Hand Me Down," "Men with Broken Hearts," and "Lost Highway."

This was the recording debut for Shelton Hank, the eldest son of Hank Jr. At fourteen years old Shelton, later known as Hank III, was already an accomplished musician. Just like his father and grandfather, Shelton naturally gravitated to singing and playing at an early age. Listen to his performance on "Moanin' the Blues" to hear just how similar Hank III's voice is to his grandfather's. Truly making it a family affair, even Audrey's vocals are included, on "Where the Soul of Man Never Dies."

One of the songs is an original by Hank Jr. called "Hand Me Down." Hank Jr. had written the song several years earlier but later couldn't find the lyrics, which turned up in an old guitar case once he started working on the project. The song is based on a note that Hank Jr. had found in one of his father's cases, written to him years before. "Son, this is my old guitar, and it's for you only to play. And I hope you make it ring and talk in our good old family way. And if you make it to the top, Bocephus, boy I'll be so proud. But listen to me son, when the time comes, take this guitar and hand me down."

Hank Jr. told the *Joplin Globe* on August, 24, 1996, "I can't tell you what a thrill it is to do this album. I've done projects before where I've sung with daddy's old recordings, but to have my son alongside me on this one was extra special. When people hear this, there will be no doubt that he's more than worthy to carry on the Williams musical tradition." Hank III added, "I wanted to do this project to pay my respects. The whole thing just felt natural."

Forty-four years after Hank Sr.'s death, the Alabama State Legislature voted to christen a stretch of Interstate I-65 as the Hank Williams Memorial Lost Highway. The portion starts in his hometown of Georgiana and travels north to Montgomery. It was officially dedicated on August 20, 1997, and on that occasion Hank Jr. stated, "It probably should have been done several years ago, but good things take time."

To celebrate Hank Sr.'s seventy-fifth birthday, the Country Music Hall of Fame unveiled a bronze statue of him on September 17, 1998. Because of his strong resemblance to his grandfather, Hank's grandson, Hank III, had posed for the artist.

In 1999, Beth Birtley founded the Hank Williams Museum in Montgomery, Alabama. Birtley is the daughter of Cecil Jackson, who rotated and balanced the tires on the 1952 Cadillac a week before Hank Sr. was found dead in the back seat. When Jackson was eight years old, Hank Sr. bought a Coke from him when he stopped at the gas station across the street from Cecil's house. Three years later, Hank Sr. dedicated a song to Cecil and his "Lightwood Flat Fixers" when he performed at the Lightwood Community.

Along with the *Three Hanks*, Hank Jr. released nine studio albums in the 1990s, including *Lone Wolf, America, The Way I See It, Pure Hank, Maverick, Out of Left Field, Hog Wild, A.K.A. Wham Bam Sam*, and *Stormy*. In 2000, Alan Jackson hit the top forty on the country charts with one of Hank Jr.'s songs, "The Blues Man."

In honor of Hank Sr.'s live appearances at the Almeria Club in Alabama, Hank Jr. recorded thirteen songs in 2002 for an album called *The Almeria Club*. The tracks included both a live and an acoustic version of "Last Pork Chop"; "Go Girl Go"; "The 'F' Word," featuring vocals by Kid Rock "If the Good Lord's Willin' (And the Creeks Don't Rise)"; "X-Treme Country"; "Big Top Women"; "The Cheatin' Hotel"; "Outdoor Lovin' Man"; "Almeria Jam"; "Tee Tot Song"; "Cross on the Highway"; and "America Will Survive."

The last song was a version of "A Country Boy Can Survive," rewritten as a post-9/11 anthem, and it pushed the album up the charts to number nine. *The Almeria Club* garnered Hank Jr. some of his best reviews in years. Writer Stephen Thomas Erlewine stated that Hank Jr. "has a talent for raw, hardcore honky tonk that's genuine, so genuine that it gives the rockers passion and the ballads a real melancholy streak."

Released in November of 2003, Hank Jr.'s album *I'm One of You* made it to number twenty-four the following year for Top Country Albums. Although two of his highest-charting songs, "If It Will, It Will" and "Don't Give Us a Reason," were both released in 1990, Hank Jr. remained a top-drawing performer into the twenty-first century with the help of his weekly Monday-night declarations asking America if they were "Ready for some football?" Originally a one-year deal with two one-year options, the Monday Night Football theme has lasted for over two decades, and in Hank Jr.'s own words, "It's become an American sports signature."

Making an appearance at the annual Country Radio Seminar held at the Country Music Hall of Fame, Hank Jr. shared his memories of Merle Kilgore, who passed away in 2005. Kilgore had been his manager, his best friend, and a second father to him. He spoke of the healing power of time and entertained the crowd with his unbridled stage presence, giving the impression, as one reviewer said, "that enough time, a good shot of whiskey and a little bit of faith could just about cure anything. Hank's been there. He knows, and he's taken us all along for the ride."

19

A COUNTRY BOY
CAN SURVIVE

"My family's music has always been my psychiatrist."
—HILARY WILLIAMS

N OT ONLY HAD HANK JR. SURVIVED AND THRIVED as the son of country music's biggest legend, but he continued to set the standard
for keeping it real. In the wake of Hurricane Katrina, Hank Jr. donated
$125,000 to the city of Biloxi, Mississippi.

He also made a personal visit in January 2006 to the comatose miner
Randal McCloy and his wife, Anna. McCloy was the only survivor of
the Sago Coal Mine tragedy, after an explosion in Sago, West Virginia,
trapped thirteen miners underground for two days. While McCloy was
in the hospital recovering from his injuries, his wife played music by
Hank Jr., his favorite artist, especially the song "A Country Boy Can
Survive."

As promised, once Randal came out of his coma and was sent home,
Hank Jr. made a return visit, this time singing him the song that helped
pull him through. Surprising Randal on his twenty-seventh birthday,
Hank Jr. spent the whole day playing guitar, hanging out with McCloy's
family and friends, and signing autographs. Hank Jr. presented him with
a very special gift, as well, a Gibson guitar designed like Hank Sr.'s, with
a plaque that read, "To Randy and Anna & Family, a country boy has
survived." Hank Jr. told Great American Country, "I, along with the

entire population of America, am so glad to see Randal home. It was touch-and-go for a while, and to know he is on his way to hunting and fishing again puts a smile on my face."

Knowing firsthand what is what like to survive a near-fatal accident, Hank Jr. has also had to live through the horror of almost losing a child. On March 15, 2006, Hank Jr.'s daughters, Hilary and Holly, who were following their father into show business, were traveling from Nashville to Louisiana to attend the funeral of their maternal grandfather, Warren White. While looking down for a second to change a song on her iPod, Hilary hit a patch of gravel and lost control of her Toyota 4Runner north of Dundee, Mississippi, flipping it over several times. Holly sustained cuts and bruises, broken wrists, and a broken leg. Hilary suffered multiple broken bones and had oxygen problems due to the bruising of her lungs. Once her breathing was under control, she underwent eight hours of emergency surgery at a Memphis hospital and then had a second surgery the next day to reconstruct her left hip and repair damage to her colon.

Hank Jr. and Becky were both at the hospital, and at a news conference, visibly shaken, Hank Jr. said, "Hilary had life-threatening injuries, and I've been upstairs with her this morning, and she is doing well, a whole lot better than she was at ten-thirty this morning." The family moved into the Peabody Hotel in Memphis and sat vigil at Hilary's bedside.

Three weeks later, on April 10, Hank Jr. was presented the Johnny Cash Visionary Award at the Country Music Awards. Backstage all he had on his mind was his daughters, commenting, "Hilary was close to death at the scene, and two days later there was another episode in the hospital where she almost passed away. The doctors came in and more or less prepared me. But she's had seven operations in three weeks, and she's turned the corner. She's coming back home soon." Echoing his own harrowing recovery from his mountain fall, Hank Jr. said, "I know one thing: me and Hilary Williams were both spared to do something."

Holly also stated, "Living through that wreck was a miracle. My sister told me one mile before it happened to put on my seat belt. I usually never would have put it on, but it saved my life. Even the fact that my arm is here is a miracle. The car was lying on top of it. We landed sideways and they thought when they pulled me out of the car that my arm wouldn't be going with me. But it was only broken. The whole experience was a real turning point for me."

When *Monday Night Football* switched from ABC to ESPN, Hank Jr. performed his song "All My Rowdy Friends Are Coming Over Tonight" in the summer of 2006 as "All My Rowdy Friends Are Coming Over Monday Night" for the first time with an all-star band that included Steven Van Zandt and Clarence Clemons from the E Street band, Joe Perry from Aerosmith, Little Richard, Bootsy Collins, and fiddler extraordinaire Charlie Daniels. Hank Jr. declared, "Bocephus ain't hard to find; ESPN is now officially one of my rowdy friends. Hold on to your hats—it's going to be an exciting season!"

That was an understatement when Hank Jr. released his CD *That's How They Do It in Dixie: The Essential Collection*, which debuted at number three on the *Billboard* Country & Western charts in July 2006. Hank Jr.'s response to the album's success, as always, was blunt and down-to-earth. "Are you shitting me? I can't believe it. I have the most loyal fans in the entire country music business. I have not had an album debut that high in many, many years. It is a wonderful feeling, let me tell you."

Spending three weeks in the top ten for Top Country Album Sales, Hank Jr. enjoyed a media blitz, with appearances on the *Late Late Show with Craig Ferguson, Charlie Jones Live to Tape* on the Wealth TV Network, GAC's *On The Streets*, ESPN's *Hot List*, *The Daily Buzz*, *Your World with Neil Cavuto*, and *The Big Idea* with Donny Deutsch. Jeff Tuerff, the vice president of marketing for his label, Curb Records, said, "The debut of the *Essential Collection* further proves that Hank Jr.'s music has mass appeal across multiple generations of consumers. A great team effort by all involved in the project!"

Never one to back down from his beliefs, Hank Jr., along with Charlie Daniels and Lee Greenwood, joined radio talk show host Sean Hannity to support the Freedom Alliance Scholarship Fund. Hank Jr. performed at benefit concerts in Jackson, New Jersey, and San Diego, helping to raise over seven million dollars. The Freedom Alliance Scholarship Fund honors the armed forces members who have lost their lives and limbs by providing their children with educational scholarships. Hank Jr. said, "I am a huge supporter of our military. I get emails on a daily basis from soldiers, and I read them all personally. I even answer many of them or send a care package of T-shirts. It is all about lifting their spirits and letting them know we care."

Twenty-five years after his song "A Country Boy Can Survive" hit number one, a remix of the same song landed in the Top 50 in January 2007. Hank Jr. exclaimed, "Well, you know that song represents a lot of America. It did twenty-five years ago and it's more profound than ever today with the state of the world. I performed this song when [Sago miner] Randal McCloy got to return home last year, and he is a true example of a miracle and a true country boy that survived."

To celebrate the song's success, Hank Jr. co-headlined the "Rowdy Frynds" arena tour with Lynyrd Skynyrd, with supporting acts Chris Janson and .38 Special. Hank Jr. assured his fans, "This is going to be a rocking party. The Skynyrd guys are my friends, and every time we get together it becomes a party." Ever since they appeared on VH-1 Classic's *Decades Rock Live*, they had wanted to work together. Johnny Van Zant said, "We've been looking for the opportunity to tour together, because his fans are our fans, and vice versa." Covering twenty dates, the tour eventually grossed over ten million dollars.

In February, Hank Jr. filed for divorce from his fourth wife, Mary Jane. Releasing a statement to the Associated Press through his publicist, Hank Jr. revealed, "Today is one of the toughest days in my life. All families experience difficulties; I hope everyone will respect our privacy during this time." The couple had shared a home in Paris, Tennessee, and the marriage had lasted sixteen years.

In late 2007, Hank Jr. was inducted into the Songwriters Hall of Fame. The following spring, on March 28, 2008, *Family Tradition: The Williams Family Legacy* opened at the Country Music Hall of Fame and Museum in Nashville. Hank Jr. kicked off the event with a question-and-answer session with the public on March 29, and Jett Williams did a similar interview on April 12. The exhibit contains over two hundred items, including the television, lamps, and liquor cabinet from Hank and Audrey's living room, Hank Sr.'s saddle, guns, dice, Nudie suits, sunglasses, and pajamas, and the suitcase that was with him in the back seat of the car the night he died. Much of the collection was donated by Marty Stuart. Originally set to close at the end of 2009, by popular demand the Family Tradition exhibit has been held over until the end of 2011.

Describing how it felt to see his life on display in a museum, Hank Jr. told the *Tennessean*, "I've been living in a museum from the time I was born. And after Daddy died, we were living at 4916 Franklin Road, and it *seemed* like a museum. Buses would stop, and people would take pictures of the house. I'd say, 'Why are these people stopping here, Mother? And the answer was, 'Because your daddy was a god.'"

Nearly discarded during a cleaning of the WSM radio station, 143 recordings of Hank's Mother's Best radio morning show were discovered and given to Hank Jr. Together Hank Jr. and Jett filed suit to stop WSM's unauthorized release of the recordings and, after an eight-year battle, won the right to reissue the shows, including over forty songs never performed outside the station. Jett said, "This treasure trove of music will introduce my daddy to a whole new generation of fans and bring memories to his existing fans. Everyone will get to know the man and his musical genius as never before. These recordings were my vehicle to get to really know the father I never met."

In November, Hank Jr. was named a BMI Icon, joining his country music peers Willie Nelson, Dolly Parton, Loretta Lynn, and Bill Anderson. Singer Blake Shelton stated, "He did the impossible twice—he became a country superstar, and he was able to step out of his dad's shadow, and both of those things weren't easy to do. The only way to do something like that is to be incredibly talented, and he deserves to win this award." Hank Jr. was honored with live performances by Lynyrd Skynyrd, Gregg Allman, and Kenny Chesney. Trent Tomlinson explained, "My live show and my sound is based around a lot of that music he used to do—'All My Rowdy Friends Are Coming Over Tonight' and that stick-it-in-your-pipe-and-smoke-it type of honky-tonk sound. It's a huge honor to be here and be part of it."

After enduring twenty-three surgeries since her accident, Hilary spent several years in a wheelchair and still has to walk with a cane. In 2009, she went back to performing in front of a live audience, the same year her sister Holly released her critically acclaimed second album, *Here with Me*. Aside from the injuries that she incurred in the wreck, Hilary Williams has also been a type 1 diabetic for twenty-two years, something that has hindered her recovery time.

Though she has faced physical challenges, Hilary's love of music helped inspire her to overcome her obstacles. "Music has always been my outlet, something that lifts my spirits and makes me feel really great," Williams said. "Even when I was lying there pretty sure that I wasn't going to sing anymore, in my heart I knew I was coming back. Monday night is a new start for me, but it's also a return to doing what I love more than anything in the world, performing in front of people."

Hank Jr. bragged to CMT, "Oh, oh, oh. Hilary's the one with the pipes. Like, that's the one. Oh, she can bust the glass in here. Unbelievable. But of course, with Holly, I like that little gravely part in the voice. I really like that. There have been some other big girl singers that have that. I don't know how many songs a week she writes. She really turns them out. She can really play. I ain't worried about her. She'll knock on any door. She'll never be poor."

The love of music is what brought Hank Jr. through his harrowing ordeal, and the same passion has been a blessing for his children. Hilary and Holly both managed to stay close to their father after their parents divorced. That was not the case with Hank III.

20

SHELTON HANK WILLIAMS III

"Lord, honey, you're a ghost." —MINNIE PEARL

HANK III WAS ONLY THREE YEARS OLD when his parents split, and Hank Jr.'s accident virtually took him out of his life for several years after their divorce. Hank III was too young to really remember his dad being around much, and by the time he fell off the mountain, as Hank III said, "Becky [Hank Jr.'s third wife] was already in place." Although Hank Jr. wrote how he wouldn't allow Becky to visit him in the hospital, she was already on his mind and in his heart.

It is ironic that Hank Jr. and Hank III both lost their fathers at the age of three. Hank III reflected, "And when he almost got killed, that cycle is still there." Hank III really doesn't have that many memories of his father when they all still lived together. "Not at all. None at all. Before the mountain fall, you have pretty much the road. Or that's after the mountain fall, I should say."

There is no doubt that Hank Jr. wasn't raised to be a father, and he was constantly told, "We're going to put you out onstage, and everybody's going to love you for it." Hank III continued, "Yeah, he [my father] was forced; I at least had the decision. So that was a big difference for the both of us. That was part of what was driving him mad, he never had much of a youth. And that goes back to him and his mom fighting; it was so deep because of the business. It was pretty intense for him. He did everything he could to kill himself, and then he made it through, and he had a whole new outlook on everything."

Hank III's first recollection of his father is of seeing him perform. "The earliest memory would have to be onstage. There was a pretty decent gap for a while where I was like three to four until I was maybe seven—there wasn't that much communication." Hank Jr. and Gwen's divorce was very bitter—"that, and then the mountain fall, and then the mind trip that all that triggered. He was just busy staying with his thing. There are early memories of hunting; besides the stage, it would have to be a hunting memory more than anything. There's just not been that much hanging out or too much of the father–son things. It was kind of hurried and rushed.

> That's part of it. It's a busy, busy life. Some people, like Ozzy, are able to take their kids out on the road and be with them. Some people aren't. That's like Loretta Lynn, the family, and all that stuff comes into play. [It's good] having a little bit of a foundation, someone to take care of the family. It's not a very good place for a kid. It could be or it can't be, but there's a lot of trauma that you have to see and deal with and be around. It's exciting, and then the excitement turns into heavy-duty stuff if you keep following that path.

Though he missed out on closeness with his father, Hank III still followed in his footsteps. Starting out as a drummer in church, he continued playing into high school. "The first time I was onstage I was, I want to say, nine or ten years old, at the Fox Theater in Atlanta, Georgia. I got my first drum kit at the age of eight. I would assume from my father. I'm not officially positive on that, but I think it was from him. And I got my first Mickey Mouse record and a Kiss record at around four or five. I have a picture to verify it."

Pondering who influenced him more, Hank III said (gesturing toward his turntable), "Well, it's hard to say I still have a Disney record on to this day. But of course, Kiss is still one of my favorites. It helped teach me how to play music, I love the energy, and also at the same time, it would send me crying to my room. Seeing Kiss on the New Year's Eve Dick Clark Special, it upset me—they were able to stay forever young. That's the beauty of the mask and the makeup. Look at Gwar, Slipknot, Kiss, Alice Cooper."

Another trait Hank III shares with Hank Jr. is not having many memories of his father when he was at home. Hank III says, "But Hank Williams very much wanted to be the father. There was a different attitude there." Out of the activities that Hank III does remember, sadly, the most vivid is of his father and the band not waiting for him. "I do have one early memory of him, when I was going to see him and I was five minutes late and they couldn't wait because I was stopping to buy a cowboy hat and they took off and left on the plane. So I remember crying over that at a pretty young age, but you know the business: 'Hurry up and go. No, we don't have a few minutes to spare.' And I remember Mom getting pretty upset on that one."

It's hard to believe that they couldn't hold the plane, since it was Hank Jr.'s private plane, not a commercial airliner. "No doubt, but that was some of the drugs working, the partying and the ladies, the attitude being, 'Ahh, we don't want to be around the kid.'"

Hank III's first time onstage was playing *Family Tradition* on the drums with his dad, he remembers, "Way back then. That's what I was doing. He was coming through town, and I was going through and saying hello, since I didn't get to really see him that much. I got up there and did my thing. I got to feel the rush of the stage, the heat from the lights, and the deafness from the music being so loud. [It was] pretty intense. Hank Jr. was drawing a pretty crazy crowd at that time too, still is to this day. But the crowds are nowhere near as controlled as they are nowadays."

Performing with his dad did not become a regular gig for Hank III. He said, "It was just one song. I was never the official drummer, but I made special guest appearances. Aside from that, I played drums in church. I played drums in the basement with my friends, I would try to create bands and have fun with it."

Hank III took drum lessons from one of his babysitters, whom he looked up to and who would always tell him,

> "Play the records, play the records—that's the best teacher you'll have." So I did that as long as I could. The only teacher I had was a man named Danny Biget. He used to play for the Atlanta Rhythm Section. And I did that for maybe five or six months. Just enough to get a couple of paradiddles. I never could grasp reading music. Still to this day, I have issues with it. Never have understood it, I've always had to just kind of wing it and get by the best that I can. It gives me motivation to keep on going to understand it.

Starting out on the drums led to a natural progression to the guitar. Hank III recalls,

> I always had a guitar around, but I always just wanted to be—it seemed like I wanted to be—a drummer. At that time, no front man, no songwriter, but yeah, there was always a guitar lying around. Even now at the Williams Family Tradition Exhibit at the Country Music Hall of Fame and Museum, they have my first acoustic that I had since I was a baby. I had a Martin and an SG, and the SG got stolen by one of my babysitters. I remember that! I always kind of had those two instruments, the main ones, around the house. It kept me busy; I always had fun with them.

His mother, Gwen, once said, "Since he was four, he's said he wants to be on the Grand Ole Opry. I've always told him if he wants to play the Opry, he's got to be good. And he's getting there." Forsaking his own dream, Hank III would one day wage his own war against the Opry's mistreatment of his grandfather's legacy.

The love of music would be Hank III's salvation, eventually helping him overcome a trauma far greater than his parents' divorce. Hank III remembered, "I want to say when my mom remarried, I'm guessing I was almost ten in Atlanta, so we probably moved when I was eight or nine. She remarried and we moved down there for a few years."

For a while, Hank III was blessed with a father figure when his mother married Steve Harrison. His stepfather worked for NASCAR, so the family moved around, to Georgia and then to North Carolina. Harrison helped build the Speedway Club in Charlotte. Hank III said,

> Being around the racing, I'll never forget it. Seein' how it all went down in the pits. My two stepbrothers and stepsister was always good to me. They would show up now and then, but that wasn't a full-time thing.
>
> When he [Harrison] was there, he tried to be a father to me. He became my stepfather when I was five or six, and by the time I was a senior in high school, their marriage was over. It was cool being around that scene. It was definitely some great memories. Hats off to my mom for at least trying to have some kind of a male figure for me. I remember that, it was a tough year for mom. She only remarried that one time, and that didn't work and then she was like, "I'm done with it."
>
> I spent all my summers growing up in Jane, Missouri, until I was able to drive. Then things like that, the farm wasn't fun to me anymore. Being around the thrills kind of was. On my dad's side of the family, there's my dad, Hilary, and Holly, and we're not that close. And then there's [Audrey's sister] Aunt Loretta, and he's always been way more tight with her than me. And they're family, but I don't really know them. When I think of family, I'm thinking of Jane, Missouri. It's still going strong to this day.

He described some of his favorite memories: "I used to love riding horses on the farm. I used to love workin' the cattle. Goin' coon huntin' with my granddad. Those are big memories, hearing the dogs runnin' in the hollers, those are always thoughts I will never forget. And Jane, even though some things were bad that happened there, those are some of the best memories. My grandmother was real dear to me. My granddad was also. I got to watch the farm be almost an empire and turn into nothin'. So it was a good and a bad feeling out there, it's been interesting. I will always hold that part of my family real close to me."

Jane, Missouri, had been a safe haven for Hank III until he was eight years old. Hank III revealed, "On the farm there was my great-uncle, who molested my mom and my uncle. My mom always told my grandmother, 'Never let Shelton go away with him … ever.' Grandmother was too naive to understand that, and sure enough I had two to three years of being abused in that kind of way." Hank III never told anyone about this nightmare and for many years suffered in silence. He said, "I never did tell my mom 'til I was probably twenty-seven or twenty-eight. She never knew."

Coming forward about his own molestation has been a difficult thing for him to do, but he says,

> I've been very open about it in many interviews; if you listen to the song "Candidate for Suicide," I say I was raped at eight years old. I've put it out there. The way I look at it, it helps those others that have to deal with that. Whether you're an average everyday person or you're some musician with a little bit of fame, those things happen to everybody. It's definitely made me the way I am—a lot harder on myself, destructive. Not really having that father figure around too much, all those things, it's tied in and has created some things within me. It seems like it should be said.

The abuse was a parent's worst nightmare. Gwen had kept a close eye on Hank III.

> My mom has always been very protective of me. She's always been really religious, and I used to scare her to death with Sid Vicious, and Kiss. I was finding the farthest thing away from country music and falling in love with it. Plastering my rooms like this [sweeping his arm around his poster-covered living room], and she was scared!

Out of that came more rebellion, between me and her. I couldn't be free. If you were wearing a Metallica T-shirt, you couldn't even walk into my house. It was pretty fuckin'—pretty weird.

I remember going to Satan seminars; I had to go to church Sunday morning, and Sunday night and Wednesday. I'm sure you can remember there were times when those Satan seminars, they played Led Zeppelin backwards, and all that stuff hit pretty hard. And I was way forced to see that. They almost sent me to Africa to a boot camp, because they were so scared of what I might become.

I was going to Christian schools, private schools, and still rebelling. Back then, probably because of my molestation, I was trying to be like Sid Vicious, and would cut myself. Put safety pins through my skin, just tryin' to be a little extreme. So she was tryin' to protect me and being overbearing. And after all these years—because we still work together. I'm tryin' to get her to run my merch, so she can work at her own pace. She can take it easy if she wants to. My mom lives about ten minutes from me here in Nashville, been working in retail forever. I'm trying to get her to take a break from that, and try to enjoy a little bit of retirement and being around her dogs. Just for her to have fun.

But still, she doesn't get to see a very happy side of me. She has to see the business, the stress. I love her, and take care of her and her financial needs, I make sure her dog is fine, just call me if you need me. All those little things, I'm there for her. But for some reason, it's always been hard for me to express my emotions to her. I think a lot of that goes back to what happened on the farm with me, and the resentment of how overbearing she was with the religious stuff—I never quite got over that. It wasn't normal!

What does that do? All it does is fuel the fire even more for me to get into the worst stuff. I do love her, we are kind of close, and I wish I could show more emotions to her. I'm workin' on it with my own therapy, to try to get past it. It was pretty devastating to her when I finally told her what happened.

It's weird, and if you want to get weird, why was my mom living on one end of the house and Hank Jr. living in the other?

Why did she try to push me into Christianity so much? She saw something standing over me that scared the fuck out of her, and she was never the same since. What was standing over me? Was it something she just saw, or was it some kind of energy? Is it that excuse, or was it because I never had a father and I was always hard on myself tryin' to grow up fast? I was fascinated by Kiss and the Sex Pistols—live fast, die young, and it's over.

If I never had been molested as a child, I would probably be a totally different person now. I might be a lot happier. Being molested got me into sex at a young age. And that opened up a whole world of tough things to deal with. Not only wouldn't I be as sick as I am, but I wouldn't have hurt as many people as I did along the way, including my own family and people that were around me. That's a tough one to deal with. When you're in AA, they tell you to go apologize to all the people, but there were people that I was too young to apologize to, and that never goes away. It's a lot of weight to pull. It happened, and I can't change it, and that's just the way it is. I just keep on truckin' through it, it's all I can do.

Like most children who suffer molestation, Hank III learned quickly to keep it to himself.

I wasn't tellin' anybody. I'm sure it was a mind game that he was puttin' on me. I just never told anybody. I was still pretty young; I was like ten or eleven. I think by twelve, he finally died. By the time I was getting' big enough to deal with it, if I wanted to fight back a little bit, he was gone. I just let it be, and finally told my mom. And she was glad I told her after he was dead, because she'd be in jail [for killing him]. That trauma is unfortunately in my bloodline, and it's been passed on. It's amazing how many people get molested in this world. But it goes to show the heavy load that is in the Williams bloodline. There's a tragic element there.

Hilary, my half-sister that got in that wreck that just about killed her, there's that recurring thing. Hank Jr. falling off the mountain, Hank Sr. dying at a young age. Me, myself, I've had some other traumatic things; it just hasn't been bone-breaking physical. I guess my trauma happened at a younger age.

In school, sports were easier for Hank III than academics, and he was awarded the varsity letter for track from Northside Christian Academy Junior High for 1986–87. He said, "Yeah, I was tryin' to be pretty athletic when I was younger. Hockey, basketball, football, soccer, and then my grades, I couldn't make them, so I was on the bench."

That's when he was diagnosed with dyslexia. "They were testing me. They knew I had problems. I went to a special class and they were taking me to see this person, so they knew something wasn't right. My mom always worked hard on her end. I still wish I could understand music after all these years. I've never been able to take a solo like I've wanted to. But it's the thrill of the moment, when you're in that moment, like the here-and-now kind of thing."

Regardless of what was happening in his personal life, Hank III was still the heir to a country music dynasty and often featured in the local newspaper. An article on Hank III stated,

At fifteen, Shelton attends Brentwood Academy in Nashville, Tennessee. When his nose is out of the books, he spends a great deal of time practicing music. But don't bet your bottom dollar it's a cover of grandpa's "Hey, Good Lookin'," or pop's "St. Dallas." "I'm into punk rock and southern rock, like the Sex Pistols, the Grave Diggers, Lynryd Skynyrd, and Van Halen."

But with "Hank" blood in his veins, he also likes the country sounds of Dwight Yoakum, Waylon, Willie, Johnny Cash and dad. … Shelton plans to make a career out of music once he's out of high school. He intends to drop his first name and go by the name of "Hank." He already performs and tours with his father during the summer and on school breaks. In fact if you look close, you will see him in his dad's latest video, "Young Country." His first love is the drums but he's also comfortable with the guitar and stepping up to the microphone.

When he wasn't playing in a band, his other passion was skate-boarding and hanging out with the other kids in a downtown park. He remembers,

What happened was, there used to be a park here in Nashville called Dragon Park. That's where all the punks, skinheads, heavy metal kids, outcasts, all hung out at. Naturally, I loved that scene. I was hangin' out there quite a bit, and Mom used to bring preachers down to try to save me and all these crazy extreme things. But all in all, the skinheads usually run the scene. They're the loud ones, they're the proud ones, they're beatin' everybody down, they got their gang.

Their apartment got trashed one night, and the rumor was that I was involved with one of the people who did trash their apartment. So I was blacklisted in town. And I knew this girl that was in the middle, she was part of the skinhead crew, who called me up and said, "Shelton, I can get you un-blacklisted if you drive two guys to Fort Campbell." So I said okay, if she could swear that I could show up and not be touched. She told me I would be fine. I show up and see about ten skins that I have never seen in my life before, and they say they need to take care of business.

There was someone that I went to school with that they claimed was running his mouth and needed to be talked to. I know what that means. I said I would drive them half the way, but since I knew him, I wasn't going to drive up to his door. I called someone to pick him up, and unfortunately they made an example out of that kid, too, and I still feel awful about it. They go and beat the kid up, and come back to me, and I take them back to Fort Campbell.

The next day I have FBI agents at my door. The kid they beat up was a federal witness. They let him know a little late. She went to jail, the other guys went to jail, for about three or four years, and they made an example out of this case. On top of that, some of the Jewish synagogues around town got graffitied with swastikas and stuff like that, so it was in the headlines. As my probation officer would say, "You were at the wrong place at the wrong time. They made a hell of an example out of you. They should have let you off when you turned eighteen, but you get to piss in a cup once a month for me until you're twenty-one."

That's about my only bad track record, really. I've been pretty fortunate over the years of not having too many problems with the law. I never officially shaved my head; I never was a skinhead. Most skinheads are rednecks with shaved heads. So they kind of looked at me a little different. They beat up everyone around me, and I'd be standin' there watchin' it go down.

In the end it was just so I could go to rock shows without getting stomped on by eight guys. That was all I was trying to do was be able to go back into the city and not have to worry about getting the teeth kicked out of my head. It was wrong place at the wrong time, and I made a bad judgment. It's as simple as that. I had to learn the hard way on that one. Everyone else did jail time except me and the kid that drove. Because they said "aiding and abetting, conspiracy," I might as well have been the one kicking the kid in the head. It was tough on my mom. I was pushin' her limits.

On probation from the time he was sixteen until he was twenty-one, and at odds with his mom, who made a move to Los Angeles, Hank moved in with the Lunsfords, who would come to play a large role in his life. A musical family with twelve kids living on a farm in Franklin, Tennessee, they helped Hank find his way. The dad, Jim Lunsford, was a fiddle player from the hills of North Carolina, and the house was a locus of jam sessions and love. Jim died not long after Hank moved in, and he was raised along with the other kids. Their mom, Francis, tried to keep a short leash on the gang, telling them bluntly that if they were going to drink or smoke, they must do it at home so as not to "drive around and kill someone." It was a fortunate situation for a young man who had a tendency to get into trouble and already had the law hanging over his head. Hank graduated from Franklin Rebel High School in 1992 and was voted "Most Individualistic" in his senior year.

Because he grew up without Hank Jr. around very much, it took Hank III awhile to fully realize the significance of his own heritage. He said, "I always knew that I had an important grandfather and father. It was the same as when you saw the movie *Your Cheatin' Heart*—there was a play that was kind of going around to the bars, and I remember one night going to see that, at a pretty young age. Jim Owens was doing it, and I remember meeting him, and how he was so gracious to the family and everything. So imagine growing up and seeing your granddad and dad on records; they were always there. You kind of know, but you don't."

Between the ages of twelve and fourteen, it finally started to sink in for Hank III how hard his father really worked. "If you look at his track record, playing for twenty thousand people a night, and me growing up seeing that, it was a double dose. Once you start living it, understanding it, trying to ride it and be part of it, then you start to see how intense the workload is."

Of course, that didn't deter him from putting a band together as soon as he could. His first real band was called Shroud. Before that, he had the Gravediggers, who didn't made it out of the garage. After Shroud there was Buzzkill and Whipping Post, and then Salida—the bands were a not-atypical progression of punk and metal from the age of twelve till about twenty.

"My vision was that I always wanted to rock out first, and grow old with my country fans. So by the time you're twenty-two, you're an old used-up rock musician, unless you're one of the chosen few like Priest, Slayer, Motorhead, AC/DC, Sabbath, so that was always my vision."

Meeting Hank III in person, you soon realize he is nothing like his public persona. Polite and soft-spoken, he struggles to maintain his outlaw image. "To me, that image was always sex, drugs, rock-and-roll, and the devil. It has been known as the devil's music. That's what rock-and-roll was to me. For some reason I was always drawn to that image, a little more.

"That's how my mom raised me. It pushed me away from the cross, and pushed me more towards the darker stuff. And what was she tryin' to do? She was tryin' to save me from all that pain and from whatever I was gettin' into. So it was a natural reaction to do that. Yeah, I'm sensitive and not necessarily that full-on evil guy."

21

BRANSON, MISSOURI

"He looks so much like Hank Sr., it's scary."
—MARY WALLACE

FINDING OUT THAT HE WAS A FATHER helped push Hank III into taking the family business seriously. He said,

Yes, that was when it turned official. Before that I was installing garage doors, I was a gofer at a recording studio, I used to work at the record shop, and those are some of the odd jobs. All right, [so I] got served, my mom is freakin' out, she's sayin', "Where the hell are you going to get this kind of money? What the hell are you going to do? It's time for you to step up."

So I went down to Music Row and got a manager, Jack Mc-Fadden—he's managed Merle Haggard, Buck Owens, Billy Ray Cyrus, so I thought I would be able to be on his level, a little bit. He said, "Shelton, I want to deal with Mike Curb because he's in Nashville more than he is in California or New York." I said okay. I met Mike Curb at the race track and he seemed like a good guy when I was younger; he knew my stepfather and all that, so that's how it came into play. [I thought], cool, if he's put out "Whiskey Bent and Hell Bound" and "Family Tradition" and "Rowdy," and all those things, he should know what the hell he's workin' with. So that seemed like a good fit to me.

I signed on the dotted line, didn't do that much research on the contract, because I believed that Jack [McFadden] had my best interest. Sure enough, he didn't. I signed the deal, and I had been screaming in bands, playin' hard rock. And now I have to learn how to sing a melody, and I don't want to go to the bars. Now I'm just all of a sudden supposed to just show up in front of a bunch of pissed-off big rednecks and be great.

And then when the legal stuff got involved, everything just kind of got flip-flopped on me, and I had to get into country to be able to rock. When you're makin' twenty to fifty dollars a week, and a judge tells you that playing music isn't a real job, and you owe fifty thousand dollars in back pay, insurance, and doctors' visits, and all these other things, it's a pretty big load to take on being an "independent punk rocker."

Hank III was only twenty at the time, and the mother of his son waited until the child was two and a half years old before filing a lawsuit against him.

Facing that much debt at such a young age, Hank III turned to his family roots to remedy the situation. He figured,

I think I'll go to Branson, where half the audience is asleep, they're older folks, I'll do a Hank Williams tribute show for a month or two, and then after that, I'm going to be carving my own niche. So that's why I went to Branson, and there's a connection there. My mom used to be in the *Sheppard of the Hills* play in Branson, and that's how she met, or one of the ways she met, Hank Jr. But I do have family ties to that area. But that's why I went. Because I had to cut my teeth somewhere, and I had to do two shows a day, six days a week.

He appeared at the White River Theater, and the show's advertisements read, "Hank Williams III pays tribute to his legendary grandfather, Hank Williams Sr. 'If you weren't fortunate enough to see Hank

Williams perform, you've been given a second chance. Don't miss Hank Williams III." —Mel Tillis." To show that Hank Jr. approved of his son performing Hank Sr.'s music, he was also quoted as saying, "His standing ovations prove that Hank done it this-a-way."

It was a great experience for Hank III, who got to hang around Mel Tillis, Charley Pride, Roy Clark, and Boxcar Willie, doing lots of radio shows, singing every day, learning to perform his grandfather's songs just like his father did. It taught them both how to sing.

Back then I had "the moan," as they would call it. It's like a crack; if you listen to Hank Williams sing, he had that thing. And I used to fuckin' nail that easy. I used to yodel easy, and get in that twangy sound. The curse of screaming, and doin' all that, I've lost the yodel, I've lost 'the moan'—that's fine because it's caused me to create my own voice a little bit out there. On a good day, I can get a little bit of that lonesome sound going on.

But if you really listen from 1998 to 2002, the country voice was pretty spot-on, for a while. And then everything else started catching up with it. I've had Elvis's people that wrote number-one songs for him, that worked with him; I was telling them my dream. And they said, "You'll never be able to do that. Your voice will not handle it, you're not going to have the energy for it, and hats off to you for wanting to try it, but it's not gonna work." So far I've done pretty good hangin' in there with it, but I know what they were talkin' about. Right now the biggest fight that I have is maintaining my voice.

That's the hardest thing, but after a lot of screaming, I still have no cysts on my vocal cords; the Vanderbilt Voice Center says that my vocal cords are in great shape. Right now the biggest thing I have to do is quit smokin'. That's the make-or-break situation for you. You can lose your twang, and this ain't no diss, because I love Tom Waits's sound, or you can sound gravelly and low and sing like Johnny Cash for the rest of your life. That's what you have to face, so we will see.

Look at my dad. Back in the day he could sing way high, but after the mountain fall, it's a lower, deeper thing. So I have that problem, and unfortunately I can't be like Judas Priest's lead singer [Rob] Halford, who never lost his voice! He sounds just as good as he did when he started. And fuckin'—that's awesome! Some people are gifted like that, and I have to fight for it a little more. Screaming, after a number of years, definitely takes its toll.

After a couple of months in Branson, Hank III took his tribute to his grandfather overseas. "I went to Japan and Europe. Not for very long, maybe two weeks. The guy that took me over there was pretty historical. He's the 'Road Mangler,' Phil Kaufman, who stole Graham Parson's body and burned it in the desert. He was my tour manager. I was sittin' on the plane, and he threw me his book. Pretty cool, I definitely regret that I was kind of a sissy over there, complaining about things around him. But it's hindsight. I said I'd never go back until I had a rock record."

In Europe he was literally booked as "Hank Williams." He looks back now on most of the shows as being successful, as singing his grandfather's music came naturally. Some of the audiences were filled with older fans who just wanted to hear Hank Williams. Hank III took some flak for selling out, but taking care of his son was more important to him than his pride.

The audiences loved it, and Dave Casper wrote in the Gainesville, Georgia, *Eagle Eye:* "Hank Williams III, a ringer for granddad. The kid, twenty-two, crooned old Hank songs with melodic perfection in such great inflections, he would have fooled any but the most keen eared purists among his granddad's fans. The real eerie part though was how much Hank III looked like the country genius who departed this world on New Year's Day 1953. Slim, and fine featured, the grandson could have been Hank reincarnated."

Academy of Country Music magazine quoted Merle Kilgore saying, "As you can plainly see, there is a common thread running throughout the Williams family; that common bond is the burning desire to succeed and excel in every aspect of life. If history proves itself with this family, country music will welcome Hank III to a long career in the industry."

Hank III's stint in Branson also brought him plenty of press back home in Nashville. After he appeared downtown one night with Merle Haggard, a local newspaper stated, "Merle introducing Hank III to Nashville: Merle Haggard and Shelton Hank Williams III, the twenty-something son of Hank Jr., both recently showed up unannounced at Wolfie's in downtown Nashville. The Hag graciously signed autographs, as well as performed. Shelton was reportedly dressed like his grandfather, and sang one of the late Hall of Famer's songs. Williams, who bills himself as Hank III, returned a few nights later to thrill a crowd at Barbara's Nightclub. Word has it that Hank III inherited his granddad's looks and pipes." There was no question that Hank III naturally followed in his father and grandfather's footsteps. What makes him remarkable is how he has chosen to do it.

22

RISIN' OUTLAW

"I knew I wouldn't be a good bank robber, 'cause I couldn't keep my cool." —HANK III

HANK III SIGNED WITH CURB RECORDS IN 1999, and his debut solo album, *Risin' Outlaw*, spawned acidic tunes like "Trashville" and "Dick in Dixie." Definitely not your run-of-the-mill country. This was Hank III's country, and when he attempted to name his next record *This Ain't Country*, Curb refused to release it and stopped him from issuing it on another label, the situation resulting in Hank III's "Fuck Curb" campaign. Attitude goes a long way in the Williams family, and Hank III sold T-shirts with "Fuck Curb" emblazoned on them at all his shows. After he won in court, he came to an agreement with Curb Records and dropped his campaign.

To keep busy during his legal battles with his record label, Hank III switched to bass guitar and played in the band Superjoint Ritual with Pantera's former lead singer, Phil Anselmo. Working with Anselmo was a dream come true for Hank III. He said, "Oh, it was awesome, just the energy of the show. He was a hero—I was workin' for one of my heroes. So it was a great opportunity. I'll never forget it, I gave it my all. I approached every show like it was the last. It was full-on being part of that. It went by pretty quick.

"Hats off to him for showing me all the behind-the-scenes at Ozzfest [the annual summer rock tour that was created by Sharon Osbourne to feature her husband, Ozzy]. The rock bands that I met out there. Philip is definitely one of the most interesting guys I've ever been around. There will never be another Philip Anselmo. It's just kind of strange when you get to meet your heroes like that. It was a big deal for me, and in the country world and the rock world, I try to gather a little bit of their wisdom. What they have to say about it."

Joe Fazzio, the drummer from Superjoint Ritual, toured with Hank III and played on his second album for Curb, *Lovesick, Broke and Driftin',* which was released in 2002. One of the reviews declared that Hank III was "one of the few living saviors of country music."

Two years later, Curb again refused to release his next collection of songs, called *Thrown Out of the Bar,* and Hank III went back to court, this time winning the right to release the album, retitled *Straight to Hell.* It was issued in two formats on Curb's new rock label, Bruc. One was a censored version for sale at Wal-Mart, and the uncensored version was the first country album on a major label to have a Parental Advisory warning. One of the album's songs, "Pills I Took," was written by Those Poor Bastards, a Wisconsin band that Hank III has embraced. Music lover and author Stephen King endorsed the new album by saying, "I no longer drink, but I love songs about boozing, and these are beauts. The Hank III album is called *Straight to Hell,* and I imagine the Nashville establishment wishes young Mr. Williams would go there, posthaste. Me, I hope he sticks around. This is the real country: hollow of eye, pale of face, and bursting with the rhythm of the damned."

A big music fan himself, when Hank III goes out to see someone perform, his taste in music can be very diverse. He said, "It depends, anyone from High on Fire to Mastadon, to bluegrass music sometimes. If it's someone from the past that I grew up listening to, it'll get me out of the house."

One of his favorite performers is David Allan Coe:

[He] has definitely been there for me like a grandfather with wisdom and everything, and helped protect me. Then you've got Jimmy Martin—his love and what he did for the music and everything

190

was just amazing. It's really hard to pick just one as far as helping me try to get it; it was David. And just seeing what happened to him in the business, having all those hit songs and have nothin' to show for it. It's interesting.

Jimmie Rodgers always had a great voice. Webb Pierce, George Jones, Waylon, Willie, Johnny Paycheck, there's just tons of them. They feel good to me when I'm listening to them. My dad was really, *really* tight with Johnny Cash, and they had a million stories together. He [Hank Jr.] used to light [Johnny's] cigarettes before he went out onstage.

As for listening to the new country, Hank III said,

Alan Jackson was probably the last time I was really listening. Aside from that, Wayne Hancock, and Dale Watson, it just seems that the sound that I like isn't as produced or polished. On that big scale, Dwight Yoakum feels kind of natural to me. When I'm going through the list of songs, it seems like it's the older artists. I'm pretty out of the loop on what country music is nowadays. I hear what some people have to say about it, and I get people come up to me and thank me for what I do, 'cause there's not many out there that try to keep it real like that. If I listened to the radio a little more I'd have a better answer for you, but I'm still stuck with the ones that were.

It would be interesting to hear what Hank Sr. would have to say about today's country music, including his own grandson's. Hank III laughed at that idea and said, "I would think he would say that it's immature. Just because of his Shakespearean talent, he was such a good writer. I would think he would say 'You've got some growin' up you need to do and some work.' He might have respected the energy that I've put towards it. But he was pretty cocky. I think his advice would be to work on the songwriting a bit more."

When Minnie Pearl first saw Hank III, she said, "Lord, honey, you're a ghost." Of the connection he said, "Yeah, it's there. History repeats itself, and it's in the bloodline. But I'm a big fan of Hank Williams and his music. Every once in a while I'll try to get in his mode. But I still believe that each man is a little different. It's in my blood, but he came and went and there never will be another one like him.

"But reincarnation, it's hard to say. It's come up in some of my meetings, past life and stuff. I've had dreams that I've been sittin' at a bar talkin' to him. I've never had a dream that I was him, I've always been myself, but it gets pretty deep. All I can remember is that I was just excited to be able to talk to him."

Hank III has a hard time choosing a favorite song of his grandfather's.

I've always said there is too many, not one; the emotion in each song is different, what he did was way different. It is my favorite sound. I can identify with it, and feel it—it really caters to the moods. If you're sad and upset, that kind of music can soothe you. Hank Williams and Hasil Adkins are two of my biggest people out there that can help those emotions when they get real strong like that.

The last time I took my cousins to the Country Music Hall of Fame and Museum, they said, "Yeah, Elvis and Hank Williams were two of the most miserable people on earth." But they had that gift. I think he might have been a little miserable, but not all the time. That's just how some people see it.

You can see by some of the footage out there that he was an easygoing, happy soul a lot of the time. Then again, the tougher side would show up. It's a never-ending battle, I know that. A lot of things that I look at on the religious side is if someone might be very comfortable with what they're doing. Someone like Ozzy, his lyrics completely speak to me. Ozzy might be the Prince of Darkness, but he's got some light lyrics. He talks about the things that everybody goes through.

I just know in the country world, as Marty Stuart says, "It's a line and you have to decide what team you're on." And that's my hardest problem, which we've said a lot. It makes me wonder how to deal with it. Do you look at it from an artist's perspective, or a religious perspective? That's my biggest cross to bear.

I always thought I knew my path. And then it got a lot more complicated. But as far as Bon Scott being pretty forward, about his lyrics and everything, AC/DC doesn't seem like a devil rock band. Them, Motorhead, and people like that give me hope as far as doing my thing and not having to worry too much about it. They're playin' music because it feels good and they enjoy it. Not all their songs are on a grim topic. It's feel-good-and-have-fun stuff. I'm definitely trying to tap into that more. I've got some healing to do, and at least I'm aware of my problems. Changing it is the tough part. Whether its addiction or shaking people's hands, I'm a lot better than I was, I can say that.

I've written enough to have my own catalog. I'm lucky enough to have a gift. I'm hanging in there with it, doing what I can. My motto is to be as gracious with the fans as I can, trying to be there for them, do the show and say hello to as many people as I can. That is one of things that have taken us to the level we're on, without much marketing behind us. It's a love-and-hate situation. Sometimes it's great, sometimes it's awful. It's a long show, a lot of drunks, a lot of people saying, "Hold on, I can't operate my cell phone." It takes a lot of patience. That's one thing I've always had is a lot of patience … for most things.

Recalling the night he played in Knoxville for four hours straight and then stood out in the rain to sign autographs, Hank III said,

The day I stop doing that, they'll say, "Oh, that fuckin' asshole, he's sold out. He won't talk to me anymore." I've seen that happen with some of my heroes, so I'll keep trying to do it for as long as I can and keep the good faith in it.

It goes back to having those heroes. You don't want to disappoint. Everybody has their bad day. Just like my granddad, what started freaking him out when a lady would say, "Hank, touch my baby so it will be gifted." That didn't sit well with him. I've always said it, I'm no better or no worse, I'm just here and thankful to be doing what I do. I've never used that as a way to fight with somebody, that power status. I'm gonna keep on keepin' on, that's what I say.

At thirty-seven years old, Hank III just seems to be getting started. He explained, "Yeah, there is that whole aspect, too. What happens if Hank Jr. dies tomorrow? Where will that put me?" Of course a number-one hit would be the ultimate goal for Hank III, but chart-topping success has remained elusive, which brings up the question of how much Curb Records really supported Hank III.

They knew I wasn't going to play their game the way I was supposed to. That's what it boils down to. And I've had my close friends around town that have said, "Shelton, you need that number-one song." To keep you alive, keep you here, keep you more powerful, I'm not sure what.

And it's not just been Curb trying to push me on that angle, but Mike Curb has said himself, "I don't know how to market you. You're too independent-thinking," and I argue back that I have given him more than one way to market me. I've given you two, now three, and it could be a political thing being in the Bible Belt. What I say, what I do, they don't want that coming out on their label. They can't respect what I do or what I've said in the past. When you look at it from that way, it makes a little more sense.

I guess I've rubbed some people the wrong way—maybe it's a Curb thing, maybe it's a Hank Jr. thing. But maybe it's a "right song at the right time" thing. Unfortunately, I don't know if I'll ever have that, because for now, I write songs for myself. And maybe someday, it just seems if you want that right song at the right time, you have to work with the right producer and the right songwriter. That's the way this town works.

Although he attempts to write songs with other artists, including Kostas, who does a lot of work in Nashville, Hank III suffers from ADD and dyslexia, making writing for him a chore. Spelling words correctly is even harder.

But looking at his prolific collection of work, it's hard to believe that writing is a struggle for Hank III. He said his songs are

> starting to add up. Look at the song list—like Fugazi would say, "You better know every damn song I've got," because if that fan asks for it, you had better be ready. It's kind of the way I treat my band. We don't really have a set list, but we'll start with "Straight to Hell," and we'll do a bunch of the same ones, but you had better be ready, because there might be one that we haven't played in five years.
>
> The set list is definitely big. It shows I can play for four hours and ninety percent of that show is my own material.

When Hank III takes the stage, he attacks it with the same velocity as his father and grandfather have done before him. His live shows are an experience of incredible endurance, for his band and the audience.

Hank III agreed, "It's gathering up, and it will just be getting' more and more when I get that big creative thumb off my back. Curb basically took what I gave them for the new album, no problems, the artwork went smooth, no rejections on songs, and it was recorded right here in my living room. It was a lot smoother process than *Damn Right Rebel Proud* was."

So superstardom isn't something Hank III is consciously avoiding? He claims,

> I do come from that interesting family, but I've taken the longer approach, trying to hang in there, and I've made it past my age of death, which was twenty-seven and twenty-nine. Those were the numbers that always scared me. I made it through that and then started reevaluating some things. Nowadays, that huge fame— what's fame, a great marketing plan? It's hard to say what it actually is, when you have some awesome talent there, and some awesome people are into it. And then you don't have that much talent and millions of people love you, it makes you question it.

Do the numbers—I've got *Risin' Outlaw, Lovesick, Broke and Driftin', Damn Right Rebel Proud, Straight to Hell,* and *Rebel Within,* out in almost ten to eleven years. How many albums did Hank Jr. put out in ten or eleven years? I'll bet it's up to twenty [albums]. So they have been holding me back as a creative artist, doing what I do, shutting down great opportunities, and all these things that I work towards. So who knows what will happen once I get out there and have some creative freedom, and really get to be a musician the way that I want to be.

It's like a new beginning that will be great on one hand, and on the other hand it's going to be awful as far as control, stress, taxes—and I don't have that great of a business team behind me. So that makes it a little more complicated. I've got people pulling out their hair, asking, "Why can't this dude do his fucking job?" It's a never-ending game, but I keep hoping for the Merle Kilgore, or the awesome badass tour manager that will be out there with me. Or the merch guy, besides Merle Kilgore, you had Eddie Pleasant running merch or Larry Doolittle. Let's see, I've had about forty merch people, about 120 tour managers, and keeping that rotation, it's tough.

Starting his own record label would make perfect sense for Hank III. He agreed,

I'm only looking for distribution. That's it. That's what Henry Rollins would advise me. That's all you need. You've given enough away so a lot of people know who you are. You've laid down the foundation. I think that a lot of people think, "Yeah, you're Hank Williams, but you've carved your own niche." And some people respect that in the music business and you should be able to go out there and do your thing. I look forward to making my country records, makin' my stoner-rock records, makin' my sci-fi soundtracks, and having creative freedom and not having to go through five lawyers to put out one damn song.

Let's just say I pick up a guitar and I strum it and I wrote this song and it's called "I Want to Be Free." Who owns that song? Curb Records does, and that goes back to my creative flow being nonexistent. But there's all kinds of things I'm looking forward to and having fun with. I still go down in that basement and play those drums. I do a lot of different sounds, and I can't wait for it to be heard.

It's interesting, if you look at it like an independent thinker like Hank Jr. who's a number-one-hit-sellin' guy, there's complications there. I'm glad it's not just me being that dude that people just can't get along with, I'm glad it's a five-time Entertainer of the Year havin' legit problems, or Tim McGraw, or LeAnn Rimes. Like one lawyer put it, "It's hard to believe that they [Curb Records] just don't like good business." The trick is, don't be too rich and don't be too poor. That makes it a lot easier, and hats off to the people who understand the business—Henry Rollins, Danzig, Sharon Osbourne, all those people who have the natural ability to be inquisitive and question things.

What did the "Fuck Curb" campaign do? "It finally got me to the right lawyers that helped me get my publishing back." Something Hank Sr. would have definitely done, and something Audrey certainly would have been proud of.

23

FOURTH GENERATION

"Hank Williams is like a Cadillac. He'll always be the standard of comparison." —JOHNNY CASH

WHILE STRUGGLING WITH HIS OWN DEMONS, Hank III has had to learn to be a father to his only son, something he couldn't relate to. Hank Sr. and Hank Jr. were never there for their sons, but this time around, Hank III has the opportunity to break that cycle. He said, "It's huge that we can now be in each other's lives. I am very thankful for it. Right now his nickname is C4, that's what I call him. He was raised by his mother, and his name is Coleman Finchum, and he just turned nineteen in May of 2010.

"I finally got to be reunited with him after all these years, just a couple of years ago." While Hank III was shopping for clothes, the woman behind the counter said, "You probably don't recognize me, but I'm the mother of your child." Hank III explained,

> I said it was nice to talk to her without having to go through a lawyer for once. And she said, "I think it's about time you know your son. He's been going through some hard things, but then again, I think you would be real proud of him. Here's my number."
>
> And I've always said in interviews that one day my son would track me down and beat my ass, I'm sure. He didn't wait; he called me that night and said he was glad he finally got to talk to me, and

he was stoked to have the chance to finally be around me. Then I met him for lunch and we hung out a little bit, and then I started hearing the horror stories. I started hearing what he had to deal with, and what's happening here and now, and stepfathers putting their hands on him, and before I knew it, I had to [protect him]; he was in a violent, unhealthy situation.

He ended up living here, and Mom ended up hating me, once again. And I had to tell her, this isn't about you, this is about Coleman. This is about him, and try to look at it that way. I'm not out trying to get mad at you, but we have to listen to what he is saying.

I had to go to court and I had to do all these things, and the judge was like, "Isn't this kid getting ready to be an adult?" Yeah, but he's having a lot of problems. Now Mom is threatening to call the police if he's over here. It's just kind of re-looping itself. I've done whatever I can to make him happy. He knows I'm not the best father, but I'm honest with him. I never planned to be a parent. I always wanted to be a musician and be out there doing my thing. At first it was like a buddy-buddy thing, and then when he started living here, a couple times I had to put down the foot and call him out a little bit. But things are good, he's real creative, he's real smart. He wants to be a writer, and that's what he's going to college for. There is no telling what he's going to do, but he has a natural gift. He knows that I love him. He finally met Hank Jr., and there is just a couple more, and that will be everybody. I can't tell you how many times he has been called a liar saying that he knew me. He even had a psychiatrist tell him that once.

Becoming a father himself has been a healing experience for Hank III. He agreed, "It's got its pluses and minuses. It is definitely healing, because I thought I would never get to know him. I seriously thought I would never have the opportunity that I have. So, it's great to see him get excited, it's awesome to be able to take him out on some of the hunting trips. To see his energy and be part of his life."

Coleman has inherited the love of writing, but has Hank III passed on any physical likeness?

> So, so, you would have to judge for yourself. Maybe a little bit. But I don't think you would call it out. It's not that—I can see a little bit of young Hank Jr. in his face, but it's hard to say. He's got dreadlocks right now, and he's tall and skinny. I'll give him that.
>
> Hank Jr. wrote a line, "I hope my son never picks up a guitar." If you look at it from his angle, it's different. If you look at it from Billy Ray Cyrus's angle, it's different. He could have been talkin' about himself, and putting himself in my shoes. I know I'm behind Coleman in whatever he wants to do. Whether it's singin', not singin'. He knows he doesn't want to be stressed, he doesn't want to work nine to five, and he doesn't want a job that's gonna make him miserable. He wants to go to college and become a writer, and I will support him in what he wants.

Not wishing to repeat with his own son the type of relationship he's had with his own father, it's been difficult for Hank III to watch Hank Jr. record and perform with Kid Rock. Where Hank Jr. and Hank III have never been close, Hank Jr. has publicly called Kid Rock his "rebel son."

Pushing the limits of country, Kid Rock includes partially naked women dancing onstage as part of his live show. Hank III expounded,

> That's always been a rap/hip-hop thing, the "pimp" thing, that's Detroit. And that's his thing. I've never dissed Kid Rock as a musician, I've been around him as strictly Bobby Ritchie, where he's come in and said, "What's up?" I got to see a little bit of the attitude from him, but I never did make it a little bit of a problem until he told me how to treat my father. That's when I started pushin' the button on him, a little bit more. And for some reason, my dad and him embraced it, and I'm not the only one who noticed it. David Allan Coe, all kinds of folks have asked, "What's the deal?"

It's hard to say, I don't know what the attraction is. It's definitely—even the Detroit folks would say, "I'm sick of seeing every fucking band that comes to town bring him onstage." It was tough for me to see him dancing on the piano that Jerry Lee Lewis is playin' on. He's crossed genres, and come and seen me play on Broadway before.

As Hilary would say, "Kid Rock really loves you. I don't know why you have to be like that to him." I told her, "I'm not being that way to him—did you know that he tried telling me how to be to my own father, which I said was none of his business? You don't know what I've been through with him, and it's great that y'all have a good relationship." She said, "Oh! Really?" It is what it is.

When I went and saw Holly get married, I sat at the back, and Kid Rock sat with the family. I just don't want to be around it. Now they [Hank Jr. and Kid Rock] share the same management. So what am I going to do? Show up at Holly's wedding and be an asshole, and make a scene? No, that's her great, holy day and I'm going to show up and be respectful, and sit in the back. I was there for Hilary and Holly.

Me and Hilary have always been a little more closer. Just in general. Holly and I just haven't been around that much, and whenever I do see her, it's always a great big hug and a smile. Hilary has been a little more spiritual, and has brought me to my knees with all that's happened to her. There's something there.

The feelings are mutual. Hilary wrote in her book *Sign of Life*, "Shelton is one of the most distinctive performers on the planet ... And despite his rebel image, Shelton is polite. He's also the spitting image of my grandfather."

Hank II said,

The last time I saw Hilary, I'd been up for two days, over in Europe doing a huge tour, and I get home, and things aren't great at home. So okay, Metallica and Lamb of God and a bunch of guys are in town. I show up when the show's over, and I never

202

did get to write Hilary when she was hurt and in the hospital. I always meant to, but I was holdin' a little grudge. I'll be damned if I didn't start cryin' in front of all my heavy metal dudes! It was real deep, and she was cryin', too. It's weird how those things line up sometimes. That was close to two and half to three years of guilt on my end. Of not gettin' to write her, and not going to see her, and just not being a good family member to her, in her worst time ever. And she knows that I am way sorry about it. You can't really be forgiven for something like that. It was a tough one for me. I guess it says a lot that I was still able to show emotion in front of all the tough guys. They can still see that maybe that's what makes me different.

That was last summer [2009], and she's still walkin' with a cane. She's had twenty-some operations, it's heavy. The pain that she has endured, and survived and everything, she's a miracle. It's not right for me to say what she experienced, but I will say it was a good thing. What's life? Some people say it's nothing, some people say it's bad, some people say it's good—at least she had a good experience. You can definitely say I'm sorry for not being the brother I should have been, when she was hurt. And now we have time to make up for it, and she's excited about meeting Coleman. We say hello every now and then. I know the family recognized it. I wasn't there, and I can understand how that would be.

And Becky [Hilary's mother] has always been very nice to me. Even when she was married and divorced, she's always been a very gracious lady to me. The girls obviously maintained a closer relationship with Hank Jr. while growing up, but it took years for Hank Jr. to turn into a stay-at-home dad.

Agreeing, Hank III said, "A little bit, but now he has actually been able to be a father to Sam and Katie. That's the actual reality. He's had enough time that he's not workin' that much, he's at home more. He's drivin' them to school, pickin' them up, and still with Hilary and Holly, there was the divorce, and all those things. They were definitely closer, no ifs, ands, or buts on that, but they kind of missed out on what Sam and Katie are getting right now.

It was surprising after so many years of marriage that he and Mary had divorced. Hank III had been completely unaware of that development. He said, "What do I know? Everybody's got addiction problems. I've got them, Hank Sr. had them, my dad had them. But he's been doing pretty damn good. And Mary's had a tough battle with it. More than anything, that might be the reason why. I know they've had their ups and downs and really tried to make it work. I've definitely had a bigger problem with Mary than I have with all the other wives, for some reason. It's just one of those things."

Tormented by wondering how his father really feels about him, Hank III continued, "I've always had that issue with him, or the wondering, what's the problem? Sorry I pissed you off, or sorry I was born, a thorn in your side, or what that deal is. I'm just not sure how it is."

Still struggling financially while his father enjoys the comforts of success, Hank III likened his situation to the pair of extremely beaten boots that reside in his personal display at the Family Tradition exhibit at the Country Music Hall of Fame and Museum. He said, "As one writer in Spain would say, 'Your boots you had that were all duct-taped up, seems like it's like your life. You barely hold it together, but you hold it together somehow.'

"I've never seen any of the Hank Williams money. It makes me who I am, and keeps me down-to-earth. That's the way I look at it. If I wasn't a musician, I'd be a farmer. I'd be workin' the land or something. That's where I feel peaceful, workin' outside. That could be the Indian thing in me."

Mixing his metal with country has always been quite the balancing act for Hank III.

As my therapist would say, "I'm stubborn." They let me do my thing at the Blue Grass Inn, but Robert's, you can't really cuss. They don't let a mosh pit happen. At the Blue Grass Inn, they know what I'm doing. Even at Tootsie's, they would beat the crowd up and not understand what's happenin' in there, and they would be throwin' out most of the folks.

I've been in Denver, Colorado, where it's two hundred people and one security guard. I hope everybody takes care of each other. Then you get twenty security guards, and the last show I did in Nashville, you can't hold a lighter in the air, you can't hold a T-shirt in the air, you can't take a picture, you're gonna pace in front of me like a pit bull ready to fight. I thought people came to a show to have a good time. It ain't right. The last two shows I've played there was one security guard, it's a small club and everybody's having a good time. They're there to enjoy it. It's a fine line, and I've been having more problems with security lately. It's just time, I'm doin' the time.

Jimmy Martin would say, "If you're going to do country music, you gotta love it, you've gotta eat it, you've got to breathe it, you've just really got to be part of it." I guess that's why I try to work outside as much as possible. I have that darker image out there, but in reality I like drivin' an old truck and havin' my animals. Being around the country vibe. It feels good to me.

Let's say I'm going to build a fence, usually I'll do it myself. In comparison to Hank Jr., who is used to having people around to do things for him. He was born into that. More than once he's gotten mad and talked about his money, and I don't know where that comes from. I've never been someone to say, "I've got this, and you don't, so fuck you."

I've said it in a song, and I've said it in articles, and I've always respected Hank Jr. as a musician. I love a lot of his work, his live show, and all the instruments he plays, and what he's done, but as a father, he ain't been the best.

Look at his awards show. Did you see the *Bocephus Tribute Show*? [It featured] Kid Rock, Shooter Jennings, Hilary Williams, Holly, everybody's there … Except me. No invitation, no nothin'.

If you look at Shooter Jennings's career, him and his dad had a wonderful relationship, and they were all tight. The way he has approached the music business, he's been takin' the easy way a lot more so than the hard way. Because Shooter wanted to be a rocker, his band Star Gun was his big vision, his dad died, he grew the beard, put on the glasses, and let Mama start runnin' the show. He's got marketing behind him, number-one songs. Whenever people refer to us, "It's you and Shooter, man!" I say, "Now, hold on a minute, you go look at his crowd, and then come look at mine. There's a big difference there, and I've fought a lot harder than that kid has for what I got." I guess it depends on your outlook—if you've been fucked by your own family, then who you gonna trust?

Regarding his firstborn son, Hank Jr. was quoted as saying,

Yeah, he's got it. Oh, Hank III, he's got it. He's a lot like the grandfather and the father. People don't realize Hank Sr. got out there and played the fiddle, and then he played the bass and then he played the lap [steel guitar], which Hank Jr. has been known to play everything up there. He can play anything. You gotta have it in your heart. You better mean what you're singing or you need to get out of this business. That's where I'm really lucky, because they know I mean what I'm singing or I ain't gonna sing it. Musically, he's got it. If you ever see him live, there's no doubt about it. He's gonna do what he wants to do. His grandfather did it, his father did it, and he's gonna do it. End of story. [Laughs.] That's what's gonna happen, folks.

24

MARRIED TO
THE ROAD

*"I want you to know that I thought about Hank when
I walked out on that Opry stage for the first time. All
I could think about then was, 'This is the same stage
Hank Williams was on, and now I'm here.'"*

—ELVIS PRESLEY

FOR THE PAST SEVERAL YEARS, Hank III has lived in a haunted house
just outside the Nashville city limits. The land it sits on was once dotted by several houses that stood during the Civil War. Often there is an old man that appears in his kitchen, and one night the kitchen window opened by itself. Hank III laughs it off. "I don't take it too seriously. I have to live here." He did reveal, though, that one time he had to take a band member to a hotel in the middle of the night, due to something he had seen. Afterward he refused to stay overnight there again.

The modest one-floor ranch is more of a country music museum than a house. Inside, every inch of wall space is covered by posters, pictures, ticket stubs, bandanas, jackets, Christmas lights, and vintage country memorabilia. Sitting in the foyer is a motorcycle sporting a dead alien lying prone across the seat. Hank III's last two albums were produced on a Korg D-1600 digital recorder right in the living room, where he tracks each band member individually. When he's not busy with music, Hank III expresses himself with his own style of "hellbilly" artwork, and loves helping to rescue stray dogs, adopting three of his own.

Over the years, Hank III has forged a relationship with the renowned artist Joe Coleman, who painted an elaborate portrait of Hank Williams Sr. that hangs in Hank III's kitchen. Coleman is a painter/performer/collector of oddities, and his work has been exhibited in museums and galleries around the world. Some fans who own his pieces include Iggy Pop, Leonardo DiCaprio, and Johnny Depp. Hank III looks up to Coleman. "He's my hero, my mentor, the guy that I would say, 'If my psychologist was Joe Coleman, everything would be okay.' I've been around Joe since I was fifteen, bein' a fan of his stuff. I finally got the relationship, got to hang out with him, now he and his wife are 'Uncle Joe and Aunt Whitney'—you know, I'm almost like family."

Although he considers himself married to the road, Hank III has spent over a decade with his live-in girlfriend, Melissa Miller. They've been friends since high school, but he confesses that none of it is easy. Performing and then talking to all his fans afterward has taken its toll. "But as far as my excuse on that is that so many people say, 'Man, you're the only musician that I can shake his hand, and I appreciate it.' It might be cheesy, or whatever, but that's the way that I look at it. Willie Nelson held that motto for a long time; Hank Sr. did, as long as he could. But it's something I have to deal with, and see how I'm going to approach it.

"Right now I'm still actin' like, right now I can still play three hours and just keep doin' what I do. It's gettin' tougher."

Not only has Hank III fought for his own identity in the music business, but he has also, as mentioned previously, continued to wage a war to get his grandfather reinstated into the Grand Ole Opry. His song "The Grand Ole Opry (Ain't So Grand)," which appears on his album *Damn Right, Rebel Proud*, is just the tip of the iceberg.

Don Helms was one of the last people Hank Sr. talked to about returning to the Grand Ole Opry. Hank III says,

They told him that they were going to reinstate him if he cleaned up his act. And that never happened, and they're still riding his name to this day. Reinstating Hank Williams into the Grand Ole Opry would be "showing respect where respect is due." You would think Hank Jr. would have more political power, to make sure that respect is being shown in the right way, than I do. I don't know what that loophole is, but there is something kind of strange there. Who knows if it was because a black man taught him music, or that he wasn't joined up with the right team, or the right church, or the right whatever. What political figure did he piss off back then?

It's tough. I've had people tell me, "Why don't you move to a bigger city where your kind of thinking would be a little more accepted?" I was born and raised here, and I don't like change that much. And things are getting—it's not like the old days in the Bible Belt. Things are loosening up a bit. I'm trying to stick it out, just like Jimmy Martin did. He was an outsider in the bluegrass world.

But things are a little more in-deep for me, since I've been messin' with both sides of the table. It's been tougher. I do what I can to show my respects. Because I've been loose with words like *shit*, *fuck*, and *goddamn*, I was never embraced that well by the Hank Williams people in Georgiana for Hank Williams Days. People around here, it's been a little tougher. There's been more respect paid to Chet Atkins than there has been to Hank Williams.

Hank Williams has been an institution in Nashville, and the Country Music Hall of Fame has done an incredible job of preserving that history. It's odd that the Grand Ole Opry hasn't started its own Hall of Fame. Instead of reinstating Hank, they could just make him their first inductee. Hank III is open to that idea. He said,

They definitely have plenty of money, plenty of power, and plenty of opportunities to do whatever they want, I would think. And it's just not Hank; he's just a scapegoat right now. What is one of their sayings—"We bank in Hank." It's just showing respects. The Rock and Roll Hall of Fame has showed respects to him, the Country Music Hall of Fame has. These people built the Grand Ole Opry.

Look at Jimmie Rodgers, Hank Williams, Porter Wagoner. And the fact that they always came back every Saturday night, got paid scale, which wasn't that much. Hank always came back on the biggest night of the week, no matter where he was. Of course you assume he is still a member of the Grand Ole Opry. I can't tell you how many people who sign the petition, young to old, that just don't understand it. It's more of a campaign for history.

You ask anyone who has played the Opry how it feels to stand on that stage and they always say, "Oh, to stand on the same stage that Hank Williams or Roy Acuff played on" … Four times out of five they're dropping Hank's name on it.

Hank is so much a part of the city that the Grand Ole Opry has even used a Hank Williams impersonator to greet people at the door. That's where it really drew the line with me. I at least got to say it onstage and on TV, I will never step back in this place until respect is shown.

Who knows why Hank Jr. hasn't gotten behind that idea. Maybe he feels he doesn't need to. Hank III said,

I don't know if it's true or not, but I've sent him a few things on it, and I was playin' down on Broadway and he was playin' at the Opry, on a Friday night. And I sent him a letter saying that I hope with your power and your status that you will do some things to help the campaign or change some people's minds. What I actually said was, "I hope you find somewhere else better to play than the Grand Ole Opry, until they show respects to your father." And Hank Jr.'s reply was, "Well, I'm done with the Opry."

If that's going to be true or not, who knows. He hasn't taken that much, and that's business deals and such, who knows what that loophole is. At one time I heard that Hank Jr. was going to buy the Grand Ole Opry! There is something there that I am definitely not tuned in to, being the underdog. Maybe Hank Jr. feels like Hank doesn't need it. Hank Williams Sr. is who he is, and if the Grand Ole Opry doesn't recognize that in the proper way, it just shows how totally disrespectful or disconnected they are.

At least the Museum of Country Music has shown their respect and acknowledges his status in the business. Every other jazz, country, rock, blues—it doesn't matter, if it's a music museum, they're showing respect. But where the Mother Church of Country Music doesn't, it's just strange.

Continuing to make musical history, on June 16, 2009, the Williams family unveiled albums from all three generations, including *127 Rose Avenue* from Hank Jr., Holly Williams's *Here with Me*, and a posthumous release from Hank Sr., *The Unreleased Recordings: Gospel Keepsakes*.

Championing the economic strife of the working class, Hank Jr.'s latest single, "Red, White and Pink-Slip Blues," stayed on *Billboard*'s Hot Country Songs chart for weeks, and the video for the song ran on regular rotation on CMT.

Like Hank III, Hank Jr. decided to leave Curb Records. He issued this statement after the release of *127 Rose Avenue*: "You want to know the bottom line? This is my last album, and he's [Mike Curb] history … We will move onward and upward, you just wait. We'll have a lot to talk about. I've had some recording ideas that they didn't care for. Well, there's a lot of other labels that do care about it. … We're going to get off this old, dead sinking ship. … They were going to [use] a picture of me from seven years ago when I was twenty-five pounds heavier. That was going to be the cover. It was 'Ho-hum,' basically. Well, we didn't ho-hum this one."

25

REBEL WITHIN

*"I don't like being told what to do, and I don't need to
be told what my record should sound like."* —HANK III

I DRINK HERE AND THERE—I used to drink a little bit. I've always had
a motto: If somebody buys me a shot, I'll do it. I'm pretty much like
that a good bit, and I've only been dosed once out of my whole career.
That's not too bad. I've always been more of a drugger than a drinker.
I don't know; I've never really had the tongue for it. I can social-drink,
things like that, but I've never had to have the need to always have a
beer or anything like that," says Hank, whose image and family name
might imply a hard-drinking man.

> The drugs … I've been thankful and lucky. I would have to say I'm
> about the best-behaved drug user out there. Because I have my
> work ethic, and a lot of it is for the work more than the buzz. When
> I was younger, it wasn't really the situation as much. But my brain
> is definitely an acid casualty. I did a lot of that, which probably
> changed my ways of perception. I never shot heroin—I've never
> put a needle in my arm, never smoked crack. I've been pretty lucky
> to be around some of the people I've been around; I've watched a
> lot of my friends die, and was able to stay strong through it.

In August of 2009, Hank III proudly released *Assjack*, his debut
showcasing his metal band of the same name. The easiest comparison is
Pantera, if Pantera were from Nashville and had a GG Allin fetish. The

energy they generate onstage is nothing short of amazing. Performing both country and his hyper-amped metal in one show is very grueling and takes hours of preparation. Hank III has a difficult time deciding which section of the show is harder. He explained,

> It's about the same. Sometimes the mosh pit is more violent during the country [part of the] show. And it depends on what kind of voice I have that day or what kind of energy is in the room. If I have a great voice and the energy from the crowd is awesome, the country set feels amazing.
>
> A lot more people are bonded, and that's just the way it is, there are more people watching the country than there is the rock. And now, if I'm sick and not feeling good and the voice is all ragged out and I'm really having to push, I can't wait until I get to the rock, because I'll sound more natural and I'll do my thing. It's kind of the best of both worlds, and it's such a release on both angles, it's not like I favor one more than the other.
>
> In country I feel a little more uptight—if you watch me, I'm stiff, because I'm thinking about trying to sing in key. And I got this hat on my head, and these cowboy boots, I'm just kind of stiff. If I have an awful voice, I feel like I'm cheatin' my fans; the country fans are there, and they're let down. I'm not able to deliver the way that I want to. So that goes back to that love/hate situation I was talkin' about. It just never ends.

Hank III has written dozens of songs that could have been chart toppers, but what does it take? Is it simply the timing? He pondered,

> It's timing, and a little more maturity, possibly. I have to come in and tell a little bit wiser story. I guess I would say that it's more immature, now it's party, drink, have fun, raise hell, and that's the ongoing theme, and that's my crowd. My crowd wants to hear those kind of feel-good songs.
>
> After a while, my own brain starts thinking, "All right, I need to put out that 'Outlaw's Prayer,' or something like that where Johnny

Paycheck would get real deep on." David Allan Coe has always been very precise with his lyrics and telling a really deep story. A little more maturity, as I'm gettin' old, and tryin' to get some wisdom in there. I've always wanted to paint multiple pictures with the words and moods.

Clearly, Hank III's diversity has been a blessing and a curse. Covering such a broad spectrum has at times seemed to work against him. He agreed, "Probably. When you see us in San Diego, you have the older folks, the Mexicans, and the rocker-billy kids, the punk rockers, the skinheads, the average everyday jocks. My friend at Kawasaki would take his CEO there and say, 'Look at this audience! It's all over the fuckin' place. It shows that this kid is breakin' down barriers.'"

On May 25, 2010, Hank III released *Rebel Within*, his last recording for Curb. It features eleven songs, "Gettin' Drunk and Fallin' Down," "Rebel Within," "Lookin' for a Mountain," "Gone but Not Forgotten," "Drinkin' Ain't Hard to Do," "Moonshiner's Life," "#5," "Karmageddon," "Lost in Oklahoma," "Tore Up and Loud," and "Drinkin' over Mama." His sound rings back to the pickers from Hank Sr.'s day, especially in "Tore Up and Loud," where Hank III's voice sounds like it's coming out of a 1940s radio. As soon as the album was released, HBO choose to use "Karmageddon" in an episode of its hit vampire television series *True Blood*.

Hank explained how he felt about the album.

I'm hangin' in there. A new beginning is just around the corner. I'm tryin' to get the team in place. That's the hardest thing I have to do right now. There's no telling what will be the single. You won't hear us on radio except for Mojo Nixon on Sirius will play us. That's the only dude out there that will play me a little bit.

There's a couple of slow ones, a couple of fast ones, a couple of hell-raisin' ones. They have one that's out of the box, the one me, Warren Denny, and Tomi Lunsford worked on. It's a different sound than what's been on any of my other records. It's almost like a campfire kind of song. We'll see how that one strikes some people.

There's a flip side, look at Slayer. That is the most satanic words out there and Tom [Araya] has always got a smile on his face, he's very soft-spoken. They're family, and they just seem happy. And if you look at them and look at me, I might seem a little more unhappy. But I'm dealin' with it, and I guess it's ridin' that line. It's a tough one, especially where I come from—it's not accepted as much. [Slayer's happiness] is just what I've noticed, seein' the wives and the kids on the road, smiles, it just seems that they're easygoing guys.

Being raised to fear God, I never understood that concept. I don't fear God as much as I fear hell. Of course the devil is a lot scarier, because that's the way he was painted to be. That's what you're supposed to think. Look at Hank Williams, how much Jesus, how much God, and the good he sang about—he was still really torn. As far as what Hank Williams was singin', most of his songs were sad songs, which were hits. His religious songs were both scary and sad, and [some were] happy; there's a fine line there. It's a hard line to deal with. When you're singin' about it and talkin' about it, the scariest words that Hank Williams ever said? That there is no light, and that's pretty fuckin' scary.

26

KARMAGEDDON

"Write songs for yourself; don't write 'em for anybody else." —JOHNNY CASH

APPEARING IN MAY OF 2010 on the *Marty Stuart Show*, which airs on RFD TV in Nashville, Hank III once again stepped into his grandfather's shoes. It was a bittersweet experience for him. He confessed, "They asked me to do it, but they're not askin' me for me. They're asking me for Hank. All right, you know, I'll show up. I know how to pay respects, and respects are due."

Hank III described donning one of his grandfather's trademark suits for that performance.

> The Hank Williams suit that I wore on Marty's show, it was weird, because the top half fit fuckin' perfect! The bottom half, I always knew I was a little taller than him, but I was able to wear it pretty comfortably and get away with it. It was a highlight and a letdown.
>
> To be in that circle, Marty would say, "You know, brother, I consider you one of my own. I've always said that since the day that I have known you as Shelton." I've been around Marty since I was ten years old or something. But still, Chris Scruggs has got to go on that show and do his thing. BR549 has gotten on that show and do their thing, and on and on and on. Well, yeah, I've got my bad songs, but I've always written some standard songs that I could sing in front of Grandma and Granddad. But at least hearing Marty

say that on his own time, and getting to talk to him for a couple of hours—because I don't get to talk to that many musicians around here that have some of the stories that he does, and a collector like he is. It was cool.

Even though Hank III was told,

"You've got to cover this up [part of the album artwork], and you got a sticker of a devil girl puttin' her tail into another devil girl's mouth, we have to cover that up." Okay, but on the flip side, on a rodeo you can show someone getting' stomped half to death, and that ain't gonna freak Grandma out, but okay, I'll cover up a little art for you.

It's that Bible Belt thing, and that's part of the woes I have to deal with. I have always thought it was natural for me to sing about the dark when my granddad sang about the light. That's the way I've always looked at it. As time and life goes on, I guess it's getting a little more complicated. Or trying to balance that out and keep going with it. Those are some of the struggles that I have to deal with, and Hank had to deal with. There's information that he had the exact same problems as me, but he was singing about God a lot more than I am. And you would think, if he was singing that much about the Christian way, that his demons wouldn't be as bad.

But when he was in Mississippi seeing a nun, he was really worried about his soul. And there isn't that much written about that. It was a definite struggle he was going through, worried about being saved. I have that struggle with light and dark, and good and bad. I see one thing, and karma kind of catches up to you after a while. Some people are guilt-free, and some people aren't.

Grateful for what he has achieved in the music business, Hank III was quick to point out that much of the credit goes to his girlfriend, Melissa. He said,

We've had our ups and downs and she's helped me keep going. She's taken care of me when I've been sick, when I've been happy.

… We're hopin' that we're going to be together for a while. I want it to be known that I know how tough it's been for her. She was stickin' with me when it was way hard.

She's been waiting to get married after all these years, and a lot of women would not be waitin' that long at all. If we make it or we don't make it, I still want it to be known. We're fightin' for what we have. We keep workin' towards it, we might make it official one day. I just want her to be happy—hopefully that involves me still being around. A lot of food has been cooked for the band, a lot of good vibes have been brought into the picture. When I have twelve guys at my house, she deals with it. She's a natural nurturer. It's just like the Wild West when you've been ridin' for days, and you come home and somebody is there to wash you off, give you some food, and make you feel wanted; she's had to do that more than once. We had our first big Christmas this last year where everyone was at the house. Coleman, his girlfriend, my mom, Melissa's family, and that's never happened, so it was a pretty big deal.

Carrying on the tradition of supporting our troops, a special appreciation presentation was made to Hank III, who performed in Houston, Texas, on March 13, 2010, benefiting Homes For Our Troops, an organization that provides specially adapted homes for severely wounded veterans.

On April 12, 2010, Columbia University announced that the Pulitzer Prize Board was awarding a posthumous Special Citation to Hank Williams Sr. for his lifetime achievement as a musician. In six short years, Hank Sr. recorded over 170 songs with 11 number-one hits. The citation lauded Williams for "his craftsmanship as a songwriter who expressed universal feelings with poignant simplicity and played a pivotal role in transforming country music into a major musical and cultural force in American life." His music reflected "the hopes and struggles of everyday Americans, and his compositional skill and fusion of genres, experts say, became the measure by which country music is judged."

The citation was an honor Don Helms would have been proud to see his friend receive. Helms's opinion of Hank's songwriting was very concise: "That's the direction of Hank's writing. He got into people's souls, and he was singing to them about what they already knew."

EPILOGUE

FAMILY TRADITION

"Who else has been covered by everyone from Bob Dylan to Tony Bennett to Coldplay to Buddy Guy? He deserves this honor on every level, and the family is really happy about this. His genius will always live on, and it's nice to know that people are still remembering him with accolades more than fifty years after his death." —HOLLY WILLIAMS

HOUSED IN A SPECTACULAR 37-million-dollar building designed to resemble a radio tower with a sweeping piano keyboard, the Country Music Hall of Fame and Museum originally opened its doors in 1967 at 222 Fifth Avenue South, just a few blocks from downtown Nashville. Their motto is "Honor Thy Music," and the outer stone walls are engraved with quotes from the country music icons that helped build the place. Hank Williams Sr.'s immortal comment declares, "You ask what makes our kind of music successful I'll tell you, it can be explained in one word, sincerity."

The exhibit Family Tradition: The Williams Family Legacy has been held over by popular demand, attracting thousands of visitors since its opening on March 28, 2008. The five-thousand-square-foot exhibit is co-presented by SunTrust and Ford Motor Company. On loan from his son, Hank Sr.'s main guitar, his treasured 1944 Martin D-28 with an ebony fretboard and diamond-shaped inlays, is on display in public for the first time. Among the two hundred items shown are furniture from Hank and Audrey's living room, including her desk and typewriter, Hank Sr.'s Bible, cufflinks, dice, sunglasses, and silk pajamas. The modest leather suitcase that was in the back seat of the car on the night he died sits simply in a glass case.

The bulk of memorabilia is on loan from Hank Jr., Lycrecia, Hank III, Jett Williams, and collector Marty Stuart. Throughout the display are television screens playing exclusive video conversations with Hank Jr., Hank III, and Hilary and Holly Williams. In his interview, Hank III endorses the Williams family fire by confidently stating, "I deliver like no other show."

Up until just a few years ago, Hank III didn't have anything of his grandfather's. He explained,

> Right now, I have a tie, and the only reason why I have that is because I bitched on national TV that I don't have anything of my grandfather's. About four years ago, Hank Jr. gave me one of Hank Sr.'s guns. And then two weeks ago, I was doing the *Marty Stuart Show* on RFD TV. So yes, [Marty] gave me a gun, and a fishin' lure, a ring, a letter that was written by some doctors, and a check that Hank Williams wrote. Because I told him I didn't have anything with his handwriting on it. And in time, I hope to come across a few other things.

Looking over the personal items that were lovingly preserved and protected all these years reminds you that the Williams family is like any other. They've had their triumphs and their tragedies. Undeniably, Hank Williams Sr. passed on an unfathomable ability to write the simplest of songs that transcend the hardest parts of life.

Museum director Kyle Young stated,

> Independently of each other, [Williams family members] each agreed to sit for lengthy oral history interviews that have allowed us to tell a new story in their voices. Now, 55 years after Hank

Williams' death, Lycrecia Hoover joins her brother, his children and Jett Williams to help them collectively address their legacy for the first time. They have opened their hearts and their archives to facilitate a fascinating story told from their perspectives and with their personal heirlooms.

These are ordinary lives made extraordinary by an alignment of talent and bedrock values, and by the quests for personal and professional identity that continue to move each generation through the earthly joy and sorrow of the times they live in," he said. "We fully expect that Family Tradition will be recognized as a story that will preserve country music history and bring it home to thousands of visitors in search of community, family entertainment, intellectual diversity and cultural competence.

After the Family Tradition exhibit opened, Hank Jr. told the Country Music Hall of Fame, "What would I want people to take away from all this? That picture of Audrey Williams and her children, Hank and Lycrecia, sliding down in the snow. Forget the fame; forget the songs; there's a family having fun. Remember that."

In a separate interview, Lycrecia added,

I'm hopin' that with all the stuff they've got up there, that people'll have a little better view of what Daddy was really like—that he wasn't just being loony or miserable all the time, that he did enjoy life. I'm trying to get people to understand that we had a normal household. The kids got out and went to school every morning, came home every afternoon. Daddy might be doing a radio show at lunchtime—but morning and night, we ate together; Mother would cook breakfast for us. When they came off the road and Daddy was home, he'd get down on the floor and roll around and play with us. Hank Williams was a great guy to me.

Jett Williams said, "Today Hank Jr. and I co-own the estate, so we do business." For fifteen years now we've agreed and disagreed on every point. We do not do social, but we still make public appearances together. I also think that by having the Williams family exhibit at the Country Music Hall of Fame, it kind of sums it up that we're all under the same roof. We get along to get along."

Both Holly and Hank III performed at the Country Music Hall of Fame and Museum in the Ford Theater in 2009. When Hank III played his grandfather's song "I'll Never Get Out of This World Alive," he tipped his hat to the museum for "treating Hank Williams—in all his ups and downs—with the utmost respect."

That respect is evidenced throughout the exhibit. One of the most heralded poets of modern music, Bob Dylan, is quoted as saying, "The sound of Hank Williams' voice went through me like an electric rod. … When I hear Hank sing, all movement ceases. The slightest whisper seems sacrilege."

Country compatriots also had intense admiration for Hank. Willie Nelson said, "Countless poets, authors and composers have reported the feeling of awe that when their best work came it seemed as if some force beyond their control was controlling what they wrote. I don't know if Shakespeare said as much, but I'm sure he felt it. Closer to home, one of my favorite writers, Hank Williams, used to say, 'I pick up a pen and God moves it.'"

Johnny Cash nailed what Hank Williams has meant to country music. He said, "Hank Williams is like a Cadillac. He'll always be the standard of comparison."

Hank Sr.'s only son has also risen to the standard of comparison, influencing artists like Alan Jackson, Tim McGraw, Kenny Chesney, Brooks & Dunn, and Clint Black. He is still the voice of Monday Night Football and appears live only when he's not hunting or spending time with his family.

Hank III continues to perform, promoting his latest album and never letting up on his crusade to reinstate his grandfather into the Grand Ole Opry. In true rebel fashion, he decided to name his new record label Do It Yer Fuck'n Self. *Mojo* magazine featured a Tom Waits interview of Hank III, with Waits saying, "I had heard he does a country set that bore an eerily physical and vocal resemblance to his grandfather, Hank Williams Sr. It is not an impersonation, but it does contain the blue spark of the family jewels. So, I got to be transported, and how well I was. Kidnapped. Willingly." He continued, "Hank III has that high and lonesome voice with a crack in it. He has the righteous fury of the deeply wounded and there's blood in his eyes."

Hank III told Waits, "I could have taken the easy road but the hard road is more me. I've always had that independent streak in me. I went to Franklin Rebel High School and that's what my granddad did, he marched to his own beat and that's what my dad did … no video, no airplay and we made it in *Billboard*'s Top 10, man. And shaking those hands and saying hello is what did it."

Inheriting musical genius certainly doesn't hurt. Wayne "the Train" Hancock said about Hank III, "You know the man's gonna make some crazy music. Anybody that don't get it best be movin' on." Hank III's mentor and close friend David Allan Coe said, "I like Hank Sr. and I like Hank Jr. But I like Hank III better than both of them."

Over the years, all three men have inspired lyricists to reference them in over seven hundred songs, including some written by Hank Jr. and Hank III. In "Family Tradition," Hank Jr. asks his father why he has to "live out the songs that you wrote." Hank III honors his grandfather in "Country Heroes," David Allan Coe wrote about Hank Williams's ghost in "The Ride," and Alan Jackson paints an eerie encounter at Hank Sr.'s grave in "Midnight in Montgomery."

Author and Hank Williams historian Steve A. Maze likes to call what the fans do "hankin' around," and the name Hank has been turned into a verb and a noun describing style in some of the newer country songs. Brooks & Dunn sing in "Play Something Country," "Hank it up a little, let's rock this bar," and Jason Aldean belts out, "Bend those strings until the Hank comes out," in "Crazy Town"; in "My Kinda Party" Aldean sings, "he's 'chillin' to some Skynryd and some old Hank."

Hank Williams, the man whom some believed to be illiterate, has now become one of the most influential artists in music history. The woman behind him helped propel two men to superstardom, while promoting and managing many others along the way. Was Audrey really who they say she was, or was she an underrated savvy businesswoman? Lycrecia once said, "My mother also had a real business sense about her; she was way ahead of her time."

Hank and Audrey did have an incendiary relationship, but their flames fueled every hit song Hank ever wrote, defining country music forever. Hank Williams Sr. created the legacy that Hank Jr. had to live up to and that Hank III had to come to terms with.

No matter what happens, as ol' Hank used to say at the end of his shows, "If the good Lord's willin' and the creeks don't rise, I'll see you soon. I'll be home soon, Little Bocephus." And as Hank III always says, "You gotta just keep on keepin' on." After all, it's a family tradition.

ACKNOWLEDGMENTS

THE FIRST TIME I MET MY EDITOR, Mike Edison, he was at the BookExpo in New York City in 2007, waiting in line to get a copy of my book *Let There Be Rock: The Story of AC/DC*. Over the next two years, we corresponded and finally agreed on a project that we were both excited about. My deepest gratitude to Mike for believing in me and *Family Tradition*. Mike is a very gifted writer, and I would not have been able to write this book without him. His passion for music, his guidance, and his divine patience will forever be appreciated.

Sincere thanks to the amazing and extremely talented Hank Williams III. Without his cooperation, honesty, and support, this book wouldn't have been possible. Hank invited me to visit him in Nashville, and he and his lovely lady Melissa opened their home to me for two days. Mind you, that invitation also included picking me up at the airport, taking my bag up to my room, and driving me to and from my hotel to his home for interviews. Hank Williams III epitomizes what a true southern gentleman is all about. I was instantly taken by his shy and humble demeanor. Getting to know him has been an honor and a privilege.

Special love and thanks to my daughter, Teal, and son, Jamey. They make me so proud, and I thank God for them every day. They truly are my heart and soul.

To my sisters Lori and Kathy, my aunt Ruby, my cousin Sandy, and all the fantastic women in my life: Jennifer, Terry, Dawn, Tamara, Dawnette, Ronnie, and Toni. Thank you all for always being there for me. You ladies rock!

To all the men in my life: John, Joe, Eric, Mark, Kerry, Brian, Jack, Jim, Andrew, Chad, Bob, and James. Thank you all for your help and unwavering support, and especially to James, for creating the index in record time.

To Andra Dalto, for her help in connecting me with Hank III and for her dedicated support and assistance with this project.

To author Steve A. Maze for lending immediate guidance on what books to research, including his own *Hank Williams and His Drifting Cowboys*. Steve's collection of the stories behind all the musicians who played with Hank Sr. was fascinating and extremely helpful.

To Joe Matera, an accomplished musician from Down Under, who is also a renowned music journalist. Thank you for the articles on Hank Sr. and for all your support and encouragement.

To Don Coleman, a musician and AC/DC tribute singer from Canada. Don is a selfless performer who has built his career donating his time and talents to help raise thousands of dollars for charities. He has been a great friend and comrade, and in honor of my book he wrote a song called "Three Hanks," available on iTunes.

To Mario Rimati, and to everyone who was instrumental in sponsoring my trip to Udine, Italy, in May 2010 to do a book signing and see AC/DC play in front of 47,000 screaming fans! My entire trip was a dream come true.

To BandX, (www.bandx.rs), an AC/DC tribute band from Belgrade, who brought me to Serbia to celebrate the release of their debut CD, *Wild Ride*, in November 2010. Love and light to Billy, Dragan, Darko, Darko, Igor, and all their families and friends. BandX rastura!

To Bernadette Malavarca and Angela Wesley Hardin for their help and total dedication to detail.

And to Mickey Rochon, a loyal fan of Hank Williams III who gave me the idea to write this book. That idea started me on this journey, and I wouldn't be here without you. To a mister from another sister, thank you, Mickey.

RECOMMENDED LISTENING DISCOGRAPHY

Hank Williams Sr. / Luke the Drifter

Singles

"Calling You," Sterling, 1947

"Never Again (Will I Knock on Your Door)," Sterling, 1947

"Six More Miles (To the Graveyard), MGM, 1947

"Wealth Won't Save Your Soul," MGM, 1947

"Move It on Over," MGM, 1947

"(Last Night) I Heard You Cryin' in Your Sleep," MGM, 1947

"I Don't Care (If Tomorrow Never Comes)," MGM, 1947

"I'm Satisfied with You," MGM, 1947

"Fly Trouble," MGM, 1947

"On the Banks of the Old Pontchartrain," MGM, 1947

"Pan American," MGM, 1947

"Rootie Tootie," MGM, 1947

"I'm a Long Gone Daddy," MGM, 1947

"I Can't Get You Off My Mind," MGM, 1947

"My Love for You (Has Turned to Hate)," MGM, 1947

"I'm a Long Gone Daddy," MGM, 1948

"I Saw the Light," MGM, 1947

"I'll Be a Bachelor 'til I Die," MGM, 1948

"My Sweet Love Ain't Around," MGM, 1948

"The Blues Come Around," MGM, 1948

"Mansion on the Hill," MGM, 1948

"Lovesick Blues," MGM, 1949

"Mind Your Own Business," MGM, 1949

"Wedding Bells," MGM, 1949

"You're Gonna Change (Or I'm Gonna Leave)," MGM, 1949

"Lost Highway," MGM, 1950

"My Buckets Got a Hole in It," MGM, 1950

"There'll Be No Teardrops Tonight," MGM, 1950

"Lost on the River," MGM, 1950

"I Heard My Mother Prayin' for Me," MGM, 1950

"Dear Brother," MGM, 1950

"Jesus Remembered Me," MGM, 1950

"May You Never Be Alone," MGM, 1950

"Sunshine," MGM, 1950

"I've Just Told Mama Goodbye," MGM, 1950

"I'm So Lonesome I Could Cry," MGM, 1950

"A House Without Love," MGM, 1950

"I Just Don't Like This Kind of Livin'," MGM, 1950

"Why Should We Try Anymore?" MGM, 1950

"My Son Calls Another Man Daddy," MGM, 1950

"Long Gone Lonesome Blues," MGM, 1950

"Why Don't You Love Me (Like You Used to Do)?" MGM, 1950

"Too Many Parties and Too Many Pals," MGM, 1950

"Beyond the Sunset," MGM, 1950

"The Funeral," MGM, 1950

"Everything's OK," MGM, 1950

"They'll Never Take Her Love from Me," MGM, 1950

"Honky Tonk Blues," MGM, 1950

"Moanin' the Blues," MGM, 1950

"Nobody's Lonesome for Me," MGM, 1950

"Help Me Understand," MGM, 1950

"No, No Joe," MGM, 1950

"Dear John," MGM, 1951

"Cold, Cold Heart," MGM, 1951

"Just Waitin'," MGM, 1951

"Men with Broken Hearts," MGM, 1951

"Hey, Good Lookin'," MGM, 1951

"My Heart Would Know," MGM, 1951

"I Can't Help It (If I'm Still In Love with You)," MGM, 1951

"Howlin' at the Moon," MGM, 1951

"I've Been Down That Road Before," MGM, 1951

"I Dreamed About Mama Last Night," MGM, 1951

"Pictures from Life's Other Side," MGM, 1951

"Ramblin' Man," MGM, 1951

"I'd Still Want You," MGM, 1951

"Baby, We're Really in Love," MGM, 1951

"Crazy Heart," MGM, 1951

"(I Heard That) Lonesome Whistle," MGM, 1951

"Half as Much," MGM, 1952

"Honky Tonkin'," MGM, 1952

"Let's Turn Back the Years," MGM, 1952

"I'm Sorry for You, My Friend," MGM, 1952

"Settin' the Woods on Fire," MGM, 1952

"Window Shopping," MGM, 1952

"Jambalaya," MGM, 1952

"I'll Never Get Out of This World Alive," MGM, 1952

"I Won't Be Home No More," MGM, 1952

"You Win Again," MGM, 1952

"Why Don't You Make Up Your Mind?" MGM, 1952

"Be Careful of Stones That You Throw," MGM, 1952

"I Could Never Be Ashamed of You," MGM, 1952

"Kaw-Liga," MGM, 1952

"Your Cheatin' Heart," MGM, 1953

"Take These Chains from My Heart," MGM, 1953

Mother's Best Flour Radio Shows on WSM 2008

Albums

Hank Williams Sings, 1952

Moanin' the Blues, MGM, 1952

Memorial Album, MGM, 1953

Hank Williams as Luke the Drifter, MGM, 1953

Hank Williams Jr.

Albums

Hank Williams Jr. Sings the Songs of Hank Williams, MGM, 1964

Your Cheatin' Heart: The Hank Williams Story Soundtrack, MGM, 1965

Father and Son, MGM, 1965

Ballads of the Hills and Plains, MGM, 1965

Country Shadows, MGM, 1966

Hank Williams/Hank Williams Jr. Again, MGM, 1966

My Own Way, MGM, 1967

Time to Sing, MGM, 1967

Luke the Drifter Jr., MGM, 1969

Songs My Father Left Me, MGM, 1969

Luke the Drifter Jr. Volume 2, MGM, 1969

Live at Cabo Hall, MGM, 1969

Hank Williams Jr. Singing My Songs (Johnny Cash), MGM, 1970

Removing the Shadow, MGM, 1970

All for the Love of Sunshine, MGM, 1971

I've Got a Right to Cry, MGM, 1971

Eleven Roses, MGM, 1972

Send Me Lovin' and a Whole Lotta Lovin', MGM, 1972

The Legend of Hank Williams in Song and Story, MGM, 1973

After You, Pride's Not Hard to Swallow, MGM, 1973

The Last Love Song, MGM, 1974

Living Proof, MGM, 1974

Hank Williams Jr. and Friends, MGM, 1975

Insights into Hank Williams in Song and Story, MGM, 1975

Bocephus, MGM, 1975

One Night Stands, Curb/Elektra, 1977

The New South, Curb/Elektra, 1977

Family Tradition, Curb/Elektra, 1978

Whiskey Bent and Hell Bound, Curb/Elektra, 1979

Habits Old and New, Curb/Elektra, 1980

Rowdy, Curb/Elektra, 1981

The Pressure Is On, Curb, 1981

High Notes, Curb, 1982

Strong Stuff, Curb, 1983

Man of Steel, Curb, 1983

Major Moves, Curb, 1984

Five-O, Curb, 1985

Montana, Curb, 1986

Hank Live, Curb, 1987

Born to Boogie, Curb, 1987

Wild Streak, Curb, 1988

Lone Wolf, Curb, 1990

America, the Way I See It, Curb, 1990

Pure Hank, Curb, 1991

Maverick, Curb, 1992

Out of Left Field, Curb, 1993

Hog Wild, Curb, 1995

A.K.A. Wham Bam Sam, Curb, 1996

Three Hanks: Men with Broken Hearts, Curb, 1996

Stormy, Curb, 1999

The Almeria Club, Curb, 2002

I'm One of You, Curb, 2003

That's How They Do It in Dixie: The Essential Collection, Curb, 2006

127 Rose Avenue, Curb, 2009

Hank Williams III

Albums

Risin' Outlaw, Curb, 1999

Lovesick, Broke and Driftin', Curb, 2002

Straight to Hell, Curb, 2006

Damn Right, Rebel Proud, Curb, 2008

Assjack, Curb, 2009

Rebel Within, Curb, 2010

BIBLIOGRAPHY

Books

Cook, Lorianne, and Charlie Chase, with Mickey Herskowitz. *Crook and Chase: Our Lives, the Music, and the Stars*. Morrow, 1995.

Escott, Colin, with George Merritt and William MacEwen. *Hank Williams: The Biography*. Little, Brown, 2004.

Hemphill, Paul. *Lovesick Blues: The Life of Hank Williams*. Viking, 2005.

Haislop, Neil, Tad Lathrop, and Harry Sumrall. *Giants of Country Music*. Billboard Books, 1995.

Knickelbine, Mark. *Classic Country Music Trivia Quiz*. Quiz Master Books, 2008.

Maze, Steve A. *Hank Williams and His Drifting Cowboys*. 2004.

Rockwell, Harry. *Beneath the Applause*. 1973.

Williams, Hank, Jr., with Michael Bane. *Living Proof*. Putnam, 1979.

Williams, Hilary, with M. B. Roberts. *Sign of Life: A Story of Family, Tragedy, Music, and Healing*. Da Capo Press, 2010.

Williams, Jett, with Pamela Thomas. *Ain't Nothin' as Sweet as My Baby*. Berkley, 1990.

Williams, Lycrecia, with Dale Vinicur. *Still in Love with You: Story of Hank and Audrey Williams*. Rutledge Hill Press, 1989.

Magazines/Articles

Bowe, Brian J. "Satan Is Real: Hank III." *Creem* magazine. (July 2006).

Buchalter, Gail. "Hank Williams Jr. Fell Down a Mountain and Lived: Now He's Climbing High."

Buchalter, Gail. "On the C & W Charts." *People* magazine. (October 22, 1979).

Cahill, Greg. "Hellbilly Hank: Country Singer Wrestles with a Family Legacy." *Metroactive*.

Dellar, Fred. "The King of America." *Mojo* magazine. (December 1998).

Egan, Peter. "Hank's Last Drive." *Road and Track*. (April 2008).

Erlewine, Stephen Thomas. "The Almeria Club Records." *All Music Guide*.

Hawkins, Martin. *Record Mirror*. (May 1, 1971).

Hayden, Courtney. "Reinstating Hank Williams to the Grand Ole Opry: Every Underdog Has Its Day." *Birmingham Weekly*. (December 16, 2008).

Henry, Jerry. "Mary Wallace: Hank Williams Historian." *The Planet Weekly*. (April 6, 2009).

Hodges, Gerald. "Former Drifting Cowboys on Stage Again." (2002).

Kerby, Jeff. "Broken Bottles, Hard Luck, and Duct Tape: Kerby's Exclusive Interview with Hank III. (September 2007): www.KNAC.com.

Lilly, John. "Hank's Lost Charleston Show." (2002).

Maze, Steve A. "Yesterday's Memories: Hankin' Around." By Steve A. Maze. (2006).

Mazor, Barry. "Hank Williams Family Legacy." *The Wall Street Journal*. (May 8, 2008).

McCall, Michael. "Son of a Gun: Take III." *Los Angeles Times*.

Morthland, John. "*Hank Williams Jr. and Friends*, Review." *Rolling Stone*. (April 8, 1976).

Nashville City Paper. "New Exhibit Explores History of Williams' Family." (March 28, 2008).

"Passages." *People* magazine. (July 16, 1990).

Register Herald. "Hank Williams Film in Pre-Production." (February 22, 2009).

Rollins, Lisa L. "Hank Williams Sr. Daughter Gives Rare Interview." (November 12, 2008).

Rumble, John. "The Son, the Suit and Hank Williams Sr.: Hank Jr. Loans Famous Costume to the Country Music Hall of Fame." *CMT News*. (January 31, 2001).

Russell, Rusty. "Hank Williams: Lessons from the Lost Highway." *Guitar Player*. (November 1996).

Scaggs, Austin. "Hank Williams III Takes On Grand Ole Opry." *Rolling Stone*. (October 30, 2008).

"20 Questions with Hank Williams Jr.: He Talks 'Family Tradition,' Freedom and Fishing with Lee Ann Womack." *CMT News*. (June 14, 2006).

Valentine, Brenda. "Hank Williams Jr.: A Man of All Seasons." *WTO* magazine.

Waits, Tom. "Hank Williams III." *Mojo* magazine. (July 2010).

Walker, John. "Hank III Tells Us How It Is." (October 27, 2008).

Watts, Cindy. "Jett Williams Finds Her Place." *Tennessean*. (January 18, 2009).

Williams, Jonathan. "Hank III Still Raisin' Hell." *Prick* magazine. (March 2006).

Worcester Telegram and Gazette. "Hank Williams Mentor Buried in Obscure Grave." (August 10, 2006).

Wynn, Ron. "Singer from Legendary Bloodline Comes Back from Horrific Accident." *The City Paper.* (July 5, 2009).

Websites

Alabama Talk Line. March 23, 2009. http://pub3.bravenet.com/forum/243824250.

Answers.com. December 3, 2009. www.answers.com.

Audrey's Dream. March 19, 2009. www.audreysdream.org.

Blender. February 23, 2010. www.blender.com.

Bullz-eye. February 23, 2010. www.bullz-eye.com.

Cajun Crawfish Pie. December 3, 2009. www.cajuncrawfishpie.com.

CMT. May 21, 2009. www.cmt.com.

Country Music Hall of Fame and Museum. September 2, 2010. www.countrymusichalloffame.com.

Dave's Diary. December 3, 2009. www.nucountry.com.au.

Dave's on Tour. February 23, 2010. www.davesontour.com.

The Drifting Cowboys Website. March 19 and 23, 2009. http://www.angelfire.com/ny3/thedriftingcowboys.

Dorseyland. January 25, 2010. www.dorseyland.blogsome.com.

Encyclopedia of Alabama. March 25, 2009. http://encyclopediaofalabama.org

Events-in-Music.com. March 25, 2009. http://www.events-in-music.com.

Great American Country. January 18, 2010. www.gactv.com.

Guild. February 23, 2010. www.guildguitars.com.

Hank Williams. February 16, 2009. www.hankwilliams.com.

Hank Williams Jr. May 13 and 21, 2009. www.hankjr.com.

Hank Williams Sr. February 16 and 24, 2009. home.online.no/~smpeders/ind-hank.htm.

Hank Williams Sr. Biography. March 25, 2009. www.musicianguide.com.

Hank Williams Sr.'s Daughter Gives Rare Interview. March 25, 2009. http://country-musicians.suite101.com.

Hank Williams Sr.—Grave of a Famous Person. March 25, 2009. www.waymarking.com.

Hank Williams: The Complete Website. February 24 and 25. http://www.angel
    fire.com/country/hanksr/.

Hank III. May 27, 2009, and February 23, 2010. www.hank3.com.

Hankville. May 13 and November 30, 2009. www.hankville.com.

The International Traditional Country Music Fan Club. March 23, 2009. www.
    itcmfc.com.

Judd Films. June 29, 2009. www.juddfilms.com.

Live Daily. May 29, 2009. www.livedaily.com.

LP Discography. January 21, 2010. www.lpdiscography.cz.

Metroactive. December 3, 2009. www.metroactive.com.

Reinstate Hank. May 27 and June 29, 2009. www.reinstatehank.org

Rock and Roll Hall of Fame and Museum. February 16 and 25, 2009. www.
    rockhall.com.

Rockabilly Central. December 3, 2009. www.rockabilly.net.

Tune In Music City. January 27, 2010. www.blogs.tennessean.com.

Wikipedia. February 16 and May 13, 2009. www.wikipedia.org.

Yesterday's Memories. February 26, 2010. http://www.ymemories.com/news.
    php

INDEX

Christian Science, 26, 115
Christmas, 32, 42, 56, 64, 80, 100, 101,
  130, 207, 219
Cincinnati, Ohio, 35, 41, 52
Circuit Court of Montgomery,
  Alabama, 46
City Auditorium, 109
Civil War, The, 128, 207
Clark, Dick, 171
Clark, Elsie, 41
Clark, Roy, 185
Clement, Helen, 39
Clement, Zeke, 39
Clemons, Clarence, 165
Cline, Patsy, 21, 49, 108
Clooney, Rosemary, 70
"Clovis, New Mexico" (song), 136
CMT, 119, 168, 211
Cobo Hall, 119, 128
Coe, David Allan, 2, 190, 201, 215, 225
Cohn, Nudka (Nudie), 54
Coke, 161
Coldplay, 221
"Cold, Cold Heart" (song), 64, 65, 68,
  69, 75, 81, 84, 91, 101, 103, 159
Coleman, Joe, 208
Coleman, Whitney, 208
Collins, Bootsy, 165
Collins, Jud, 25
Colter, Jessi, 148
Columbia Records, 51, 68, 74, 75
Columbia, South Carolina, 120
Columbia University, 219
Community Hospital, 142
Como, Perry, 69, 84, 117
Congregational Church, 157
Continental Divide, 137
Cook, J. H., 116
"Cool Water" (song), 38
Cooper, Alice 171
Copas, Cowboy, 34, 45, 52, 56, 108
"Country Boy Can Survive, A" (song),
  153, 162, 163, 166
"Country Heroes" (song), 2, 225

Country Music Association, The, 122,
  154, 155
Country Music Awards, 164
Country Music Hall of Fame and
  Museum, 2, 3, 84, 161, 162, 167,
  172, 192, 204, 209, 210, 221, 223,
  224
Country Music Hall of Fame Walkway
  of Stars, 4
Country Music on Broadway (movie),
  121
Country Radio Seminar, 162
Coursey, Farris, 63, 90
Cowboy Junkies, The, 70
Cramer, Floyd, 90
Crandall, Eddie, 118
"Crazed Country Rebel" (song), 2
"Crazy Heart" (song), 74
Crazy Tennesseans, The, 14
"Crazy Town" (song), 225
Crempton Bowl, The, 100
Criswell, Chris, 38
"Cross on the Highway" (song), 162
Crook and Chase, 70, 154
Cuba, 95
Cullman, Alabama, 132, 146, 153
Curb, Mike, 183, 194, 211
Curb Records, 165, 189, 194, 197, 211
Cyrus, Billy Ray, 183, 201

Daily Buzz, The (TV show), 165
Dallas, Texas, 45, 77, 97, 98
Damn Band, 2
Damn Right—Rebel Proud (album), 2,
  195, 196, 208
Daniels, Charlie, 129, 136, 148, 165,
  166
Danzig, 197
Darvon, 132
Davis, Jimmie, 81
Davis, Oscar, 45, 50, 55, 63, 73, 94, 94
Day, Jimmy, 90
Dayton, Ohio, 55
"Dear Brother" (song), 44